APPROACHES
TO ETHNOGRAPHY

Approaches to Ethnography

Analysis and Representation in Participant Observation

EDITED BY Colin Jerolmack
AND Shamus Khan

OXFORD
UNIVERSITY PRESS

Oxford University Press is a department of the University of Oxford. It furthers the University's objective of excellence in research, scholarship, and education by publishing worldwide. Oxford is a registered trade mark of Oxford University Press in the UK and certain other countries.

Published in the United States of America by Oxford University Press
198 Madison Avenue, New York, NY 10016, United States of America.

© Oxford University Press 2018

All rights reserved. No part of this publication may be reproduced, stored in a retrieval system, or transmitted, in any form or by any means, without the prior permission in writing of Oxford University Press, or as expressly permitted by law, by license, or under terms agreed with the appropriate reproduction rights organization. Inquiries concerning reproduction outside the scope of the above should be sent to the Rights Department, Oxford University Press, at the address above.

You must not circulate this work in any other form
and you must impose this same condition on any acquirer.

Library of Congress Cataloging-in-Publication Data
Names: Jerolmack, Colin, editor. | Khan, Shamus, editor.
Title: Approaches to ethnography : analysis and representation in participant observation / edited by Colin Jerolmack & Shamus Khan.
Description: New York, NY : Oxford University Press, 2018. | Includes bibliographical references..
Identifiers: LCCN 2017010036 | ISBN 9780190236045 (hardcover) | ISBN 9780190236052 (pbk.) | ISBN 9780190236069 (updf) | ISBN 9780190236076 (epub)
Subjects: LCSH: Anthropology—Methodology. | Participant observation.
Classification: LCC GN33 .A55 2018 | DDC 301.01—dc23
LC record available at https://lccn.loc.gov/2017010036

1 3 5 7 9 8 6 4 2

Paperback printed by WebCom, Inc., Canada
Hardback printed by Bridgeport National Bindery, Inc., United States of America

CONTENTS

List of Contributors | vii
Introduction: An Analytic Approach to Ethnography | xi
Colin Jerolmack and Shamus Khan

1. Microsociology: Beneath the Surface | 1
   Jooyoung Lee

2. Capturing Organizations as Actors | 31
   Katherine Chen

3. Macro Analysis: Power in the Field | 61
   Leslie Salzinger and Teresa Gowan

4. People and Places | 95
   Douglas Harper

5. Mechanisms | 129
   Iddo Tavory and Stefan Timmermans

6. Embodiment: A Dispositional Approach to Racial and Cultural Analysis | 155
   Black Hawk Hancock

7. Situations | 185
   Monica McDermott

8. Reflexivity: Introspection, Positionality, and the Self as Research Instrument—Toward a Model of Abductive Reflexivity | 211
   Forrest Stuart

INDEX | 239

LIST OF CONTRIBUTORS

Katherine Chen is an Associate Professor in the Department of Sociology at the City College of New York and the Graduate Center, CUNY. She specializes in the study of organizations, with a focus on democratic and relationship-building practices; her other research interests include work and occupations, economic sociology, social movements, urban community, and cultural sociology.

Teresa Gowan is an Associate Professor of Sociology at the University of Minnesota and the author of the ethnography *Hobos, Hustlers, and Backsliders: Homeless in San Francisco*. Recent work includes comparative studies of self-making and poverty governance in the drug treatment industry and a study of a French alternative economy.

Black Hawk Hancock is an Associate Professor of Sociology at DePaul University. His past ethnographic research explored the revival of swing dancing, and his current ethnographic research focuses on the Mexican workers who form the backbone of the contemporary restaurant industry in Chicago.

Douglas Harper has written, photographed, and filmed several ethnographies. His first, *Good Company, A Tramp Life*, has been translated and published in Italian and French, and has recently been issued as a third edition. He has taught visual ethnography at the University of Bologna and the University of Amsterdam, and has had tenured positions in several universities in the U.S. His current work is on the visual identities of cities, including the uses of public areas, public art, and semiotic organization of space.

Colin Jerolmack is an Associate Professor of Sociology and Environmental Studies at New York University and the author of *The Global Pigeon*. His current ethnographic research project focuses on how shale gas extraction (fracking) impacts rural community life.

Shamus Khan is professor and chair of sociology at Columbia University, where he researches culture, inequality, education, and elites and teaches courses on research methods and theory. He is the author of *Privilege: The Making of an Adolescent Elite at St. Paul's School*, an ethnographic study of an elite boarding school, and co-editor of *The Practice of Research: How Social Scientists Answer their Questions* (with Dana Fisher). In addition, he has published his research in both academic and popular outlets such as the American Journal of Sociology, Annual Review of Sociology, The New York Times, and The New Yorker. Khan received his PhD in sociology from the University of Wisconsin-Madison

Jooyoung Lee is an Associate Professor of Sociology and Bissell-Heyd Fellow in the Munk School of Global Affairs at the University of Toronto. He is the author of *Blowin' Up: Rap Dreams in South Central* (University of Chicago Press, 2016), Senior Fellow in the Yale University Urban Ethnography Project, and a member of the Homicide Research Consortium, a multidisciplinary group of scholars studying the causes and consequences of homicide.

Monica McDermott is an Associate Professor of Sociology at the University of Illinois, Urbana-Champaign. Her research focuses on the ways in which race and class interact in the contemporary United States.

Leslie Salzinger is Associate Professor of Gender and Women's Studies and an affiliated member of the Sociology Department at the University of California, Berkeley. She is the author of *Genders in Production: Making Workers in Mexico's Global Factories*. Her current work in progress, *Model Markets: Peso Dollar Exchange as a Site of Neoliberal Incorporation*, analyzes foreign exchange markets as crucial gendered and raced sites for Mexico's shift from "developing nation" to "emerging market."

Forrest Stuart is an Assistant Professor in the Department of Sociology at the University of Chicago. Broadly speaking, his work examines the causes, contours, and consequences of urban poverty, violence, and resilience.

Iddo Tavory is an Associate Professor in the Department of Sociology at New York University. His overarching interest is in the interactional patterns through which people come to construct and understand their lives across situations.

Stefan Timmermans is Professor and Chair of the Department of Sociology at the University of California, Los Angeles. He is also a professor at the UCLA Institute for Society and Genetics.

INTRODUCTION: AN ANALYTIC APPROACH TO ETHNOGRAPHY

COLIN JEROLMACK AND SHAMUS KHAN

Ethnography is a method of social science inquiry in which the researcher embeds herself in the ongoing interactions of a particular social setting or set of relations in order to understand and explain members' lived experience. As a matter of course, ethnographers follow, observe, interview, and participate in the routines of the people they study. This allows them to capture meanings, behaviors, intentions, and interactions that are often glossed by methods that are more distant (e.g., surveys) or contrived (e.g., experiments). Unlike other methods that presume what people do on the basis of what people tell the researcher, ethnography seeks direct observation of social action. Perhaps the most basic justification for ethnography is that "being there" to observe people acting and interacting in the course of their everyday lives can yield more valid data about real-world social behavior than self-reports (Jerolmack and Khan 2014). This strength can also be a weakness; the ethnographer must grapple with how things she cannot directly see (e.g., social structure) influence her field site.

Once someone chooses to focus on a particular issue and to study it through participant observation, beginning an ethnography can be straightforward—you show up somewhere and spend time there. When Colin Jerolmack (2013) became interested in the working-class male subculture of rooftop pigeon breeding in Brooklyn, he simply dropped by a pigeon supply store that he found in the phone book and began talking to pigeon breeders, who invited him onto their rooftops. However, even when gaining access is easy (and routinely, it is not), the ethnographer becomes quickly overwhelmed by the field—there is simply too much data, too many potential directions the research can take. Every moment is a potential observation, and it is quickly succeeded by new moments. Despite the neatly packaged holistic accounts of "primitive" groups that make up the canon of anthropology, the truth is that even the most punctilious ethnographer studying the most bounded field site cannot record and analyze everything. To make fieldwork manageable in a way that is methodologically defensible (i.e., not arbitrary), the ethnographer must decide what aspect of social life will be privileged in data collection and analysis—e.g., the micro foundations of interaction, the logic or dynamics of institutions and organizations, or the workings of macro social forces like power. That is, she must select what we call an approach to ethnography.

In sociology and, to a lesser degree, anthropology, it has become almost axiomatic that there are two contrasting systematic approaches to ethnographic data collection and analysis: induction and deduction. However, the premise of *Approaches to Ethnography* is that, regardless of whether ethnographers build theory from observations (induction) or use observations to test theory (deduction), they usually approach the field armed with one or more particular analytic lenses that lead them to focus on—and make possible the illumination of—a distinct thread of the social fabric. Rather than provide step-by-step instructions for practical problems such as selecting a research site and recording data, this volume emphasizes the analytic choices ethnographers make both before and after site selection and research, which shape the kinds of questions that get asked and answered through participant observation. Our aim is to introduce students and practitioners to the basic modes of analysis that typify ethnography and to demonstrate how these different ethnographic styles illuminate different dimensions of the social world.

All of the chapters are written by practiced ethnographers who delineate one of the approaches and reflect on how that approach patterns the way they select and enter a field site, record observations, and build explanations. Taken together, the chapters reveal that the analytic lenses that ethnographers adopt shape the kinds of questions formulated and claims made in ways that are at least partly independent of whether they adopt an inductive or deductive stance toward theory.

While the approaches to ethnography that this volume enumerates are by no means definitive, exhaustive, or mutually exclusive, neither are they merely provisional. Our identification of these analytic lenses, and the way in which we relate them to one another in the book, are a distillation of our own scholarship and teaching of how to read, perform, and write ethnography. We believe that the result is an important way of thinking about, teaching, and doing ethnography, one that augments the traditional pedagogical emphases on theory construction and the mechanics of fieldwork while providing a novel heuristic for understanding the various ways that ethnographers explain situated social action.

Induction and Deduction

Iddo Tavory and Stefan Timmermans (2009, 2014)—two of this volume's authors—have surveyed the vast literature on how to select and analyze an ethnographic case and conclude that two alternative approaches hold tremendous sway: grounded theory and the extended case method. Grounded theory is a quintessentially inductive approach, in which analytic categories and formal propositions "emerge" from deep engagement with observational data (Glaser and Strauss 1967). Conversely, the extended case method is for the most part deductive—instead of "discovering grounded theory," we begin with a set of theoretically informed expectations and enter the field seeking to test whether they can explain what it is we observe (Burawoy 1998).

As Tavory and Timmermans (2014: 10) point out, grounded theory is "mainstream qualitative data analysis" in sociology and has also spread across "nursing and medical research, computer and information sciences, education, law management, and anthropology"; its "heuristic principles have been incorporated into the most widely used qualitative data analysis software programs." In its most orthodox version, grounded theory commands the researcher "literally to ignore the literature of theory and fact of the area under study, in order to ensure that the emergence of categories will not be contaminated by concepts more suited to different areas" (Glaser and Strauss 1967: 37). In practice, adherents of the spirit (if not all the dictums) of grounded theory emphasize the rigorous coding of interview and observational data so that the analytic categories that they construct—and which become the foundation of theoretical explanations—are firmly anchored in members' meanings and lived experiences and not imposed from some "outside" understanding. For many, the presumption that underlies this commitment can be traced back to W. I. and Dorothy Thomas's (1928: 572) old dictum, "If men define situations as real, they are real in their consequences." That is, since people act toward situations and others on the basis of the meanings they ascribe to them, we must erect our explanations of social action on the foundation of subjects' own interpretations.

Grounded theory's emphasis on social context and "ethno-narratives" (Tavory and Timmermans 2009: 244) dovetails with anthropologist Clifford Geertz's classic notion of ethnography as "thick description." For Geertz (1973: 26), "the essential task of theory building" is "not to codify abstract regularities" or "generalize across cases" but rather to generalize within cases. A thick description depicts sufficient social context for the analyst (and reader) to decipher how members establish, read, and communicate meanings with each other. Geertz famously showed how difficult this ostensibly unambitious analytic project is by delineating how much cultural competence is required to decipher the meaning of someone winking in a particular context—the wink could be an involuntary eye twitch, conspiratorial, flirtatious, or parody, and yet in most instances cultural "insiders" have little trouble interpreting a wink. The object of ethnography is to make explicit "the stratified hierarchy of meaningful structures" that makes such interpretation possible (Geertz 1973: 7).

Grounded theory and thick description suggest that the starting point (and, for thick description, also the ending point) for any ethnographer should be grasping the actor's point of view and the shared meanings that make social action possible and intelligible. Yet these inductive approaches offer precious little practical guidance on how to handle the many analytic choices the ethnographer must make in the course of site selection and data collection. For instance, Shamus Khan (2011) was interested in how privilege operates at elite educational institutions. So he obtained permission to spend a year working at a private boarding school, where he had intimate access to both staff and students. Khan had many choices for how to direct his work. He could have chosen to do an "organizational ethnography," focusing his data collection on the practices and discourses of staffers charged with admitting and cultivating "the best and the brightest" (e.g., Stevens 2007). Or he could have adopted a conversation-analytic perspective, drilling down on the discursive "ethno-methods" that students deploy in everyday talk to construct and make sense of privilege (e.g., Maynard 2003). As it happens, Shamus instead focused on embodiment, i.e., "how privilege becomes inscribed upon the bodies of students" and manifests as a corporeal disposition (Khan 2011: 16). All three of these approaches could be carried out inductively (i.e., theorizing from the data). Yet each one molds data collection and analysis in a distinct way. For instance, they require selecting different units of analysis—the organization, a conversation, or physical bodies—which then delineate different units of observation for the ethnography—a set of formal rules, turn-taking, or clothing. And these choices then influence the dimensions of social life that require explanation (and those that are necessarily bracketed).

In contrast to the inductive approach, deductive ethnography, perhaps best represented by the extended case method, potentially offers more guidance on how to approach the field and data collection. Michael Burawoy is, perhaps, the most prominent champion of this method; his insights grew out of the Manchester school of anthropology. The starting point for an ethnographer deploying the extended case method is not members' meanings but rather preexisting theory, which guides case selection and analysis. Burawoy (1998) commands the ethnographer to select a field site that poses a puzzle vis-à-vis a particular social theory. The theory tells the ethnographer "in advance what kind of empirical observations should be seen in the world" (Tavory and Timmermans 2014: 18) if that theory were true. Discrepancies between hypotheses and observed realities become the foundation upon which the ethnographer (re)constructs theoretical principles. Moreover, because social theories are for the most part explanations about how social structures shape situated action, for Burawoy the primary task of ethnography is to reveal how external political, economic, and social forces impinge upon the local setting under study. Those who adopt this approach often perform multi-sited ethnography, with each setting serving as a theoretically strategic research site and empirical variations across cases postulated as a result of differences in macro social structures.

Just as the notion of a "pure" grounded theory, in which the researcher enters the field with no analytical priors, is an "epistemological fairy tale" (Wacquant 2002: 1481), it would be a caricature to portray the extended case method as disinterested in building theory from observations. Even the most deductive-minded ethnographer looks for surprises in the field that cannot be explained by existing theories. Burawoy (1998: 16) himself encourages an iterative relationship between theory and data, mandating that we "seek not confirmations but refutations" of our "favorite theory" in the field that force us to deepen existing theories or invent new ones.

The extended case method seemingly provides clearer instructions than the inductive method on how the ethnographer should handle the analytic choices she encounters in selecting her site and collecting data. Some of these decisions are suggested by the theory one enters the field with, which articulates what processes or "variables" should be observed and posits relations between them. For instance, Burawoy (1979) brought Marxist labor theories onto the shop floor that he studied, which delineated the boundaries of the empirical field (Tavory and Timmermans 2009) and allowed him to focus all of his observations and analyses on the discrete question of why workers consent to their exploitation. However, there is a way in which this deductive method may be harder for the first-time ethnographer to use as a guide for organizing field observations— it directs the researcher to look for something she often cannot tangibly see in the field (e.g., social structure, power). As Burawoy (1998: 15) notes, although observed phenomena are theorized as "effects of other social processes," these macro forces are difficult to directly observe and "for the most part lie outside the realm of investigation." The traces of them become more "visible" when one adopts a particular theory that posits their causal connection to situated action. Moreover, among ethnographies that begin with a theoretical puzzle, one still finds tremendous variation in how their authors approach data collection and analysis. For example, both Desmond (2007) and Vaughan (1996) looked at how bureaucracies shape members' perceptions of risk; both were motivated by theories that failed to explain their case. Their shared unit of analysis was the organization. For Desmond, who asked why US Forest Service firefighters risked their lives for so little recompense, the foil was theories of masculinity and thrill-seeking. For Vaughan, who asked why NASA engineers green-lighted the ill-fated *Challenger* space shuttle launch despite knowing of design flaws, the foil was conceptions of managerial misconduct. Notwithstanding their shared commitment to theory reconstruction and a focus on government agencies, Desmond and Vaughan deployed different analytic lenses to solve their particular puzzle—Desmond (like Khan) made unconscious bodily disposition (habitus) his unit of observation, whereas Vaughan focused her observations on discursive organizational culture. The selection of these foci reflects the researchers' particular analytic sensibility and guided their selection of observational units in ways unrelated to whether theory came first or last (or somewhere in between).

Approaches to Ethnography

It is curious that the hackneyed "inductive versus deductive" narrative persists as the master frame for delineating the possibilities of approaching and carrying out ethnographic research and analysis. After all, many ethnographers do not locate their own work within this rigid typology, and even those who rhetorically position their analysis as inductive or deductive routinely tack recursively between data and theory in practice. Moreover, we have already seen how ethnographers typically approach the field with distinct "socially cultivated ways of seeing" (Tavory and Timmermans 2014: 40) that pattern how they go about making, and making sense of, observations in ways that may be only loosely connected to induction or deduction. Thinking about ethnography in terms of approaches is useful because it provides the would-be fieldworker with a schematic compass. Like Blumer's (1954: 7) idea of "sensitizing concepts," these analytic lenses do not "provide prescriptions on what to see," as theories do, but rather aid us in parsing the buzzing confusion of the field by "suggest[ing] directions along which to look" during one's fieldwork and analysis. It bears repeating—the fieldworker cannot observe and analyze everything, so one must make a choice about what to look at and how to look at it. Given this, ethnographers should have a working knowledge of the ideal-typical approaches and understand what the trade-offs and consequences are for adopting a particular way of seeing. Delineating these approaches also helps us evaluate ethnographic texts because it provides the reader with a heuristic tool for identifying the (often unelaborated) presumptions and interpretive frames that undergird authors' descriptions and analyses.

Using examples from their own research, all of the authors in this volume provide an account of how their particular approach works in practice and address issues that are central not just to ethnography but to the social sciences more generally—e.g., the logic of sampling and comparison (e.g., across sites, situations, people, or time); how they chose what to observe for their analysis; how each approach answers the "so what" question and constructs generalizable claims; and what the particular strengths and weaknesses are of a particular approach to ethnography. We have divided the chapters on approaches into four parts in order to juxtapose some key contrasts in analytic focus, though, as we will continue to argue, some of these approaches are most often combined and interwoven in order to gather the most robust data possible. The first part covers microsociology, organizations, and macrosociological/comparative ethnography; the second part juxtaposes people and places to mechanisms/processes; the third part addresses dispositions and situations; and the last part is concerned with reflexivity.

The first three chapters look at how ethnographers generate explanations at different levels of analysis, from micro interactions to organizations to macro social forces. The microsociology approach, represented here by Jooyoung Lee, is grounded in the analytic presumption that face-to-face interaction is far more than a site where actors reproduce stable features of society by invoking ready-made symbols and conforming to preestablished recipes of action. In this view, meaning and social order are made, modified, and transformed through mundane social encounters as well.

Lee strikingly reveals this by utilizing video recordings to analyze streetcorner "rap battles." Rather than looking at how sociological "variables" like race, gender, power, and status might shape the structure and significance of these improvised group "freestyle" sessions, Lee employs a microsociological approach to illuminate how shared meanings and formulas of action arise endogenously—i.e., within the context of the interaction—from active social negotiation among the rappers in response to the immediate demand to keep the "cipher" going. For Lee, the unit of analysis is the interaction, and observational units include patterns of speech, bodily negotiations, and other social mannerisms that constitute a "freestyle" rap session.

By contrast, adherents of the organizations approach deal with meso-level phenomena and are attuned to how the formal, structured, and (often) hierarchical groups that actors are routinely embedded in (e.g., the workplace) mediate the meaning and content of situated social action. Fieldworkers in this vein tend to have as their unit of analysis the organization itself. However, they are likely to make observations on a range of phenomena, from the ways that organizations define the goals of collective behavior and influence the cognitive frames that actors use to interpret and respond to situations, to how routine interactions both maintain and transform organizational forms. Katherine Chen's chapter draws upon her research on the Burning Man festival. Like Lee, she observes the actions of people involved in an ostensibly creative and spontaneous social scene. But her analytic focus is very different, as are the claims she makes on the basis of her data. Rather than focusing on how meaning and order emerge from situated interactions over the ten-day festival, Chen focuses on how festival organizers work year-round to shape participants' experience of Burning Man, recruit and socialize members, and navigate legal issues. Her unit of analysis is the organization; her observations trace the many instantiations of its organizational logic, from business documents like meeting minutes and conversations that reveal how people respond to Burning Man's structure to the "controlled chaos" of fire starting. By analyzing the organization behind Burning Man, Chen is able to show how its shadow operations ensure a safe and (somewhat) orderly gathering that nonetheless appears to most participants to be organic and anarchic.

Finally, the macro analytic approach adopted by Leslie Salzinger and Teresa Gowan draws ethnographic attention to how structural forces and institutions impinge upon particular settings and social groups. This sensibility is akin to the central thrust of what C. Wright Mills (1959: 8) called the "sociological imagination," in which the analyst explains actors' personal situations or "troubles" by situating them in relation to exogenous "public issues." In this approach, observed practices are understood as clues to the discursive (material and cultural) structures that produced them—and which they produce in turn. In order to illuminate the structuring capacity of these macro forces, the authors first focus their observations on processes of subjectification. Salzinger highlights contrasts in how workers understand and enact gender across four different shop floors to reveal how local meanings and subjectivities are produced "from above"—i.e., by managerial styles and transnational networks geared toward profit maximization. Similarly, Gowan demonstrates how three discourses on homelessness rooted in criminal justice, the shelter system, and the radical advocacy movement constitute both antithetical policy streams and distinctive homeless iconographies, profoundly constraining life on the street. Salzinger and Gowan then pivot to "studying up," analyzing the formation of elites and institutions that shape the lives of the less powerful. Salzinger here focuses on the emergence of transnational currency traders in the market, and Gowan on the development of mandatory drug treatment as neoliberal governance. In examining the constitution of powerful selves and the (re)constitution of fields, they show how the "macro" itself is made.

Micro-level approaches are most often thought of as a form of grounded theory that engages in inductive analysis (in order to generate generalizable claims), and macro-level approaches are most often thought of as deploying an extended case method with deductive reasoning. There is more than a grain of truth to this categorization. However, it is often the case that such a dichotomy does not neatly map onto the actual practice of ethnography. As we shall see, the level of analysis does not require a corresponding epistemological logic for the production of social knowledge. The choice of a particular lens (micro/organizational/macro) may be combined with either a deductive or an inductive logic to produce a rich and rigorous text. Further still, these lenses may be combined with one another: e.g., in generating a meso-level account of the inner workings of power in an organization, the ethnographer may touch on small-scale interactions and conversations between members of that organization and zoom out to the larger political and economic context in which such organizational processes are embedded. Even though the ideal-typical approaches that we highlight in this book are commonly blurred in actual practice, we maintain that this heuristic is more useful than the inductive-deductive typology for clarifying the analytic choices that ethnographers make and for constructing one's ethnographic object of analysis in a logical and empirically rigorous way. Rather than ask if they are taking an inductive or deductive approach, ethnographers might instead ask what the key units of analysis and observation are and then articulate a clear account of how a particular observation allows for claims that bolster their analysis.

The second part of the book juxtaposes an approach centered on people and places with one that emphasizes processes and mechanisms. By analytically distinguishing these two approaches, we show how some ethnographers prioritize people's distinctive biographies and places' unique histories, while others are more interested in illuminating abstract social mechanisms. "Character-driven" ethnographies, Douglas Harper shows, provide a complex and extensive portrait of participants and allow them to tell their own story. While Harper recognizes the ethnographer's "mandate" to generalize, his research on peculiar characters like a train-hopping tramp and a jack-of-all-trades repairman shows that people's aspirations, motivations, and decision-making cannot be adequately described or explained by reducing actors to social types or "outcomes" of structural forces. By documenting how actors narrate their lives over time, Harper shows how his participants are themselves aware of the social forces shaping their particular circumstances and how they alter these circumstances. Thus, Harper's imperative to "give voice" is not simply an act of compassion or a narrative device; his in-depth character sketches enable him to highlight the contingent and idiosyncratic—rather than the predetermined and patterned—dimensions of social life. The focus is on getting the person right and, in so doing, challenging general accounts of social relations. Relatedly, he shows how places embody singular traditions and meanings that shape local culture and social identities in particular ways. For instance, Harper shows how the uniquely egg-rich pasta dough that is central to the culinary heritage of Bologna, Italy, resulted from the need to add eggs to the soft wheat that is native to the region in order to create pasta that does not break apart in spaghetti presses. In this way, cuisine, culture, and identity are emplaced.

By contrast, those ethnographers who are interested in processes and mechanisms have a different relationship to showing the lives of their subjects. Adherents of this approach are rarely concerned with depicting the idiosyncratic dimensions of a place or with giving voice to particular people. Instead, inspired by the work of Georg Simmel, this approach typically starts from the premise that situated interactions should be analyzed as instantiations of what Georg Simmel ([1911] 1971) called "social forms." The ethnographer's task is to illuminate these generic social patterns rather than describe the particular people and places through whom they operate. Iddo Tavory and Stefan Timmermans spell out how such an approach enables ethnographers to elucidate causal mechanisms and specify how they can generalize from their case: Tavory's close analysis of mundane interactions among Orthodox Jews in Hollywood serves as the basis for a more broad-ranging explanation of how patterns of social identification sustain religious life. Similarly, Timmermans's punctilious rendering of doctor–patient discussions about genetic testing aims not to enable the reader to walk in the doctor's or patient's shoes but rather to construct a generalizable thesis about how actors develop a shared understanding of medical uncertainty. In both cases, the people "stand in" to help illustrate the workings of generic social mechanisms. In contrast to Harper, the aim is not to get the particulars of the story right but rather to enumerate a general set of social patterns; these patterns may not hold in all specific situations, but they reveal an essential social process and the ways that the process works (e.g., the mechanism behind it).

The third part of this book contrasts dispositions with situations. The dispositional approach—which in recent years has increasingly been called "embodiment"—focuses on how durable, and often unconscious, habits of thought and action structure situated interaction. Scholars who use this analytic lens draw inspiration from Pierre Bourdieu's (1977) idea that the body is a "memory pad" to show how prior social experiences imprint themselves upon the bodies of actors and produce patterned ways of acting and being—dispositions. While the unit of observation is almost always the bodies and interactions of people, the unit of analysis can be far less micro. Black Hawk Hancock takes the reader into the swing scene in Chicago—where white dancers today celebrate the Lindy Hop, which was first danced in African American neighborhoods in the 1920s. Hancock shows how cultural expressions are appropriated, spatially separated, and racialized. Yet his arguments do not rest solely on passive observations of who dances what; instead, Hancock subjects himself to the relations under study. He shows how dancers develop dispositions that embody racial histories, in part by learning this craft himself. Embodying the relations under study, Hancock argues, enables one to become a practitioner of a

Introduction: An Analytic Approach to Ethnography

particular cultural form and, with competence, comprehend the details and subtleties that remain invisible to those who have not acquired that practical knowledge. And it is this invisible "habitus," stamped on the body, that structures action and inscribes racial domination. Here, the unit of analysis is the body, and the observations center on how individual bodies become vessels for reproducing larger social structures.

By contrast, those who take a situational approach are less interested in the embodied dispositions of actors than in how the context of a situation influences what it is that people do. A strict situationist approach suggests that it is not something "inside" actors that determines how they act; rather, the situation—how it is defined, understood, and experienced—determines the possibilities for action. Thus, situationists aim to understand how actors define the kind of situation they are in and specify how social action is a response to the "demand characteristics" of the situation (Faulkner and Becker 2009). By "sampling" on hundreds of cross-racial encounters among strangers that Monica McDermott witnessed during her fieldwork in public spaces, she shows the power of this approach to enumerate how particular factors distinct to the setting shape the way that people think about and interact with members of another race. Features of the situation, McDermott explains, also play a role in determining whether or not race becomes relevant at all in interaction—regardless of the habits of thought and action pertaining to race that actors may bring to the encounter. Perhaps even more poignantly, by observing how the same people interact with different races across situations, McDermott can begin to empirically document the occurrence of prejudice—regardless of whether or not the offending parties view their own actions as prejudiced. While situationists observe how people act, their emphasis is on how the social situation generates behavior rather than on personal characteristics or the influence of macro structures.

The final part of the book leaves contrasts behind and focuses on positionality, introspection, or what is often called "reflexivity."

A basic condition for a successful ethnography is becoming part of the lives, organizations, situations, or processes under study. But the necessary consequence of this integration is that ethnographers become part of—and therefore influence—the very things they study. To address how such positioning shapes observation, ethnographers regularly reflect upon and make clear their role within their field site. The aim is both to interrogate the generation of data and to enumerate for the reader the conditions of observation. Rather than view their embeddedness in the field strictly as "contamination," however, introspective ethnographers are attuned to the ways that the novel situations created by their presence can reveal deeper insight into social reality. Forrest Stuart demonstrates this by reflecting on his experience researching police–resident relations in Los Angeles' Skid Row. When Stuart first began his fieldwork, he found that some people avoided him and many found him suspicious. At first, he thought it had to do with his conspicuous note-taking (most of what people were doing was illegal, like selling loose cigarettes). However, after being slammed against a fence by police officers looking for a white suspect, he discovered the true reason: though his father is black and his mother is Mexican, he was read on Skid Row as white because of his skin tone, clothing, and bodily comportment. Through this experience, Stuart learned that being read as white was a disadvantage on Skid Row because police believed that white people entered the area only to obtain illicit goods such as drugs. Soon his subjects were offering tips for "'blackening [him] up,' as they jokingly referred to it," so that he would not bring additional police scrutiny to the block. Thus, it was Stuart's own experiences that generated the insight that Skid Row's predominantly black inhabitants shunned and chased off whites because they feared their presence would attract the police.

The aim of each chapter in this volume is to guide readers through the analytic implications of the choices they make. Each approach privileges and illuminates a distinct aspect of social life. When observing social relations, the single scientist cannot explain everything; to try to do so weakens rather than strengthens the analysis. Yet ethnographers have focused so much on the differences between induction and deduction that they have failed to be explicit about the other analytic choices they make. This volume aspires to make clearer what it means to choose to focus on, say, situations instead of embodiment; to show readers how one would actually convey a convincing account of social life through that lens with data; and to reflect on the advantages and disadvantages of using particular analytic lenses.

These analytic choices may not determine observational units, but they certainly guide them. As such, the field becomes a more clearly delineated space where observations concentrated on a particular realm of social life (e.g., the situation, or structure) allow the researcher to interpret data and develop claims from within a distinct analytic tradition. Analytic lenses also provide the ethnographer with strategies and guidelines for sampling. While quantitative social science methods seek to sample across demographic difference to "represent" a population, ethnographers who are interested in units of analysis that do not align with such an understanding—i.e., that individuals are the unit of analysis—will develop different sampling strategies for their observations. For example, we may be interested in how the same situations influence different people; this would mean observing the same kind of situation again and again, while sampling on how different actors experience it. Conversely, the observer could be interested in how the same person experiences different situations. As such, the sampling would not be on the individual, but instead across situations and over time. In turn, an ethnographer interested in how macro forces structure situated action might choose to sample across several ethnographic field sites that vary along a key dimension (e.g., gender). Thus, ethnographers can sample across a variety of dimensions—kinds of situations, kinds of interactions, kinds of places, etc. Although they may observe only a relatively small number of people, they can potentially build robust claims by sampling across thousands of observations. The analytic lens that one deploys plays a large part in determining which sampling strategy makes the most sense. Working within a particular approach to ethnography allows the ethnographer to construct empirically defensible claims; readers attuned to the approaches identified in this volume are well positioned to evaluate the plausibility and generalizability of those claims.

As ideal types, each of the approaches are shown to be useful for decoding and designing ethnography. As mentioned, in the real practice of ethnography, scholars commonly deploy more than one analytic style to better understand their object of study. And so scholars who choose to focus on mechanisms will, at times, "show the people" if members' narrated meanings turn out to be a crucial cog in the ethnographer's causal story. Yet as practitioners plan their ethnographies and as readers evaluate them, making clear the necessary set of analytic choices is a first-order priority. Moreover, it is important to understand the logic by which different approaches can be stitched together—e.g., there is a "natural" affinity between micro and situational approaches (e.g., Katz 1999) and between macro and dispositional approaches (e.g., Bourgois and Schonberg 2009), but dispositional and situational explanations of social life are less likely to coexist in one text because they are grounded in contrasting analytic sensibilities. This volume helps us understand the range of analytic sensibilities found in ethnography and how they fit together. Not only does providing such analytic clarity shift ethnographers away from tired debates about the advantages of induction or deduction, it also provides a foundation for methodological advances by outlining a set of best practices for making critical observations—from the micro to the macro—and for capturing and conveying a process, situation, disposition, or narrative.

References

Blumer, Herbert. 1954. "What is Wrong with Social Theory?" *American Sociological Review* 18: 3–10.

Bourdieu, Pierre. 1977. *Outline of a Theory of Practice*. Cambridge: Cambridge University Press.
Bourgois, Philippe and Jeff Schonberg. 2009. *Righteous Dopefiend*. Berkeley: University of California Press.
Burawoy, Michael. 1979. *Manufacturing Consent*. Chicago: University of Chicago Press.
Burawoy, Michael. 2003. "Revisits: An Outline of a Theory of Reflexive Ethnography." *American Sociological Review*, 68(5): 645–679.
Desmond, Matthew. 2007. *On the Fireline*. Chicago: University of Chicago Press.
Faulkner, Robert R. and Howard S. Becker. 2009. *"Do You Know . . . ?" The Jazz Repertoire in Action*. Chicago: University of Chicago Press.
Geertz, Clifford. 1973. *The Interpretation of Cultures*. New York: Basic Books.
Glaser, Barney and Anselm Strauss. 1967. *The Discovery of Grounded Theory*. New York: Aldine Publishing Co.
Jerolmack, Colin. 2013. *The Global Pigeon*. Chicago: University of Chicago Press.
Jerolmack, Colin and Shamus Khan. 2014. "Talk is Cheap: Ethnography and the Attitudinal Fallacy." *Sociological Methods & Research* 43(2): 178–209.
Katz, Jack. 1999. *How Emotions Work*. Chicago: University of Chicago Press.
Khan, Shamus Rahman. 2011. *Privilege: The Making of an Adolescent Elite at St. Paul's School*. Princeton: Princeton University Press.
Maynard, Douglas. 2003. *Bad News, Good News: Conversational Order in Everyday Talk*. Chicago: University of Chicago Press.
Mills, C. Wright. 1958. *The Sociological Imagination*. New York: Oxford University Press.
Simmel, Georg. [1911] 1971. *On Individuality and Social Forms*. Chicago: University of Chicago Press.
Stevens, Mitchell. 2007. *Creating a Class*. Cambridge: Harvard University Press.
Tavory, Iddo and Stefan Timmermans. 2009. "Two Cases of Ethnography: Grounded Theory and the Extended Case Method." *Ethnography* 10(3): 243–263.
Tavory, Iddo and Stefan Timmermans. 2014. *Abductive Analysis: Theorizing Qualitative Research*. Chicago: University of Chicago Press.

Thomas, W. I. and D. S. Thomas. 1928. *The Child in America*. New York: Knopf.
Vaughan, Diane. 1996. *The Challenger Launch Decision*. Chicago: University of Chicago Press.
Wacquant, Loïc. 2002. "Scrutinizing the Street: Poverty, Morality, and the Pitfalls of Urban Ethnography." *American Journal of Sociology* 107(6): 1468–1532.

APPROACHES
TO ETHNOGRAPHY

Chapter 1

Microsociology

Beneath the Surface

JOOYOUNG LEE

Freestyling, or improvised rhyming, is one of Hip Hop's most time-honored skills. This was especially true at Project Blowed, a Hip Hop open mic workshop in South Central LA.[1] On Thursday nights, rappers got together and freestyled on the street corner outside of the open mic. Regulars, or "Blowedians," were drawn to freestyling for many reasons. It was a fun and challenging pastime—a way for rappers to showcase their skills in front of a live peer audience. They also enjoyed freestyling because it distinguished them from mainstream artists. Aspect One, a New York native who had moved to LA as a kid, was out on the block one night and said, "I hate all that jiggy

---

1. Rappers at Project Blowed come from a long tradition of freestyling in the area. Before Project Blowed opened in the mid-1990s, underground rappers would get together and practice their rhyming at a nearby health food store called the Good Life Café. When the Good Life closed in 1995, rappers from that scene moved to a nearby community center called KAOS Network. They started a new open mic called Project Blowed and arranged to hold it every Thursday night. For more about the Good Life Café, see Morgan (2009).

dumb shit they play on the radio. At the Blowed, it's like, 'Who got bars?' We care if you can spit."[2]

He wasn't the only rapper who felt that way. Early on, I met another rapper named Open Mike who was critical of watered-down, commercial Hip Hop. In his mid-twenties at the time, Open Mike's peers knew him as one of the most talented emcees in the scene. He could "style" on his opponents, switching between different cadences and blending different rhyme schemes.

A few months into my fieldwork, we met up one Saturday afternoon outside KAOS Network, the community center in which Project Blowed was housed. Open Mike told me that he grew up listening to indie rock and was a Bboy (breakdancer) in Chicago before moving to LA. Later in high school, he got hooked on rhyming. Each day, he'd spend hours working on his craft. Sometimes he did this alone. Other times, he'd rhyme with others in ciphers, which are freestyle sessions where people take turns rhyming with each other. The cipher was a proving ground, where rappers competed for status and respect. Open Mike said:

> Freestyle rappin' is a very egotistical sport. So half the time out there you got everybody saying that they're the greatest person to ever hold a microphone, ever. And there's only certain ways that you can say that, and not make it sound like you're not talking about everybody standing around you right there.

Other rappers told me similar things. They talked about wanting to be the "king of the block" at Project Blowed. People kept tabs on

---

2. "Bars" refer to lines in a song. But when rappers use the term in everyday conversation, they are more often using it to talk about a person's skill level. Underground rappers at Project Blowed and in other scenes will say things like, "He got bars," "She got bars," or simply "Bars!" after someone says something clever in their rhymes. Similarly, rappers will also say that someone can "spit" or is an "ill-spitter" when they talk about people who are skilled rhymers.

each other's performances. Blowedians knew who had skills and who didn't. These reputations were sticky and followed people around, shaping a person's standing in the local scene. My analysis could have ended here. The cipher at Project Blowed was, in many ways, a twist on a familiar story in sociology: young black men campaign for respect through alternative means when faced with constrained options in schools, the labor market, and other mainstream social institutions.[3]

But the closer I looked, the more I began to see interesting stuff happening *within* the cipher. I adopted a microsociological lens and found that the cipher wasn't only a proving ground; it was an interaction deserving its own analysis. Beneath the surface of campaigning for status and respect, rappers were also working together to keep the cipher going smoothly. They were attuned to each other, coordinating turns and defusing tensions and misunderstandings.

My findings highlighted a central premise in microsociology: social organization is not a given in any situation. People work together to create and sustain it. This realization was eye-opening and challenged my previous understandings. It inspired me to look closer at processes that were unfolding as people rhymed together. This lens showed me how rappers were using their bodies, movements, and emotions to keep the cipher going amid emergent challenges. It showed me that there is much for sociologists to study in a close analysis of how people do stuff together. But before I get into all that, I should tell you a little more about microsociology and how this perspective fits into ethnographic fieldwork.

---

3. Elijah Anderson (1999) writes about this in his study of black communities. Young black men who feel constraints in schools and the labor market invest in the "code of the street," informal rules about interpersonal behavior—particularly violence. Instead of gaining respect and status through schools and other mainstream social institutions, they invest in public displays of toughness. Robin Kelley (1998) also writes about this in his historical analysis of Hip Hop culture. He describes how young people come to see Hip Hop as "play labor," a means for getting ahead in the world when good jobs don't seem available or in abundant supply.

Zooming into Interaction

Although there are many ways that one might define microsociology, I will adopt a simple definition here: microsociology is the study of how people interact with each other.[4] This perspective draws from many different yet complementary traditions (i.e., symbolic interaction, ethnomethodology, phenomenology, conversation analysis). What these traditions share is a perspective that the social world can be broken down into observable and comparable interactions. Large-scale social structures, culture, the economy, and other macro phenomena that sociologists study are at their core recurring, face-to-face encounters among different people.[5] This is not just an epistemological position; it also sets up a practical research strategy. The microsociologist's goal is to look for recurrent interactions that, when linked together, make up a larger structure. At the level of interaction, microsociology shows that social organization is a fluid, ongoing accomplishment.[6]

As such, microsociology is a perspective that zooms in on subtle and often imperceptible patterns in interaction. It inspires the researcher to look for variations in taken-for-granted processes that are often missed by other research methods. This is inspired by the data. When we look closely at *how* interactions unfold in real time, we realize that people behave in complex ways that defy commonsense understandings. We also see that interactions cannot be adequately explained by reference to social forces that are external to

---

4. I was introduced to microsociology at UCLA. I had taken courses in ethnography and a course with Melvin Pollner in ethnomethodology, phenomenology, and observational sociology, which was affectionately known by students as "EPOS." The course introduced me to a number of traditions, all of which continue to shape my thinking and work. But in addition to giving me a broad overview of the vast field of microsociology, this course got me thinking more critically about the methods sociologists use to understand interactions.

5. Fine and Fields (2008) refer to this approach as a stance of "sociological miniaturism" and argue that we can observe large-scale processes in interaction.

6. Melvin Pollner (1982) writes extensively about this. He shows that people use mundane reasoning to construct a shared definition of the situation with others.

the situation like "culture" or "structure," terms that gloss the actual techniques that people use to make social life mutually meaningful. This perspective thrusts researchers into the minutiae of everyday social interaction.

This perspective also "decenters" the individual, placing an emphasis on the dynamics of situations. Erving Goffman once described his view of the social world: "[T]he proper study of interaction is not the individual and his psychology, but rather the syntactical relations among the acts of different persons mutually present to one another . . . Not, then, men and their moments. Rather moments and their men" (1967: 2–3). Antiquated gendered language aside, Goffman's perspective points us in a useful direction. From afar, a person's attitudes, their demographic profile, and psychological dispositions give us different ways of explaining individual behavior. But on their own, these measures are often poor predictors of how people will act in different situations. More problematically, they neglect the messy and sometimes unpredictable ways that people *interact* with each other. Microsociology allows us to get at this level of analysis; it provides us with an orientation and methods that zoom into the collaborative work people do to make interactions mutually sensible and flow without a hitch.

Evolving Methods of Studying Interaction

If interactions are what we want to understand, how to best study them? What methods of data collection give us the best ways of depicting "what happened"? These questions have inspired different approaches to studying interaction.

Nearly half a century ago, conversation analysis (CA)—which grew out of Harold Garfinkel's ethnomethodology—developed cutting-edge studies of how people talk to each other. This research was motivated by key orienting questions: How is mutually intelligible social interaction possible? What are the methods people use to achieve this? CA scholars used tape recordings of everyday conversations to open new insights into the nature and social organization of talk. Early CA work uncovers the contours of pauses, turn-taking, and how people repair misunderstandings with one another.[7] Scholars working in this tradition are principally concerned with showing how social actors create and sustain shared meanings and social organization in the flow of interaction.

More recently, CA scholars have studied talk in different institutional contexts.[8] CA scholars pioneered work on how journalists interview politicians and other public figures (Clayman and Heritage 2002), doctor–patient interactions (Heritage and Maynard 2006), and courtroom plea bargaining (Maynard 1984). To this day, CA remains a powerful—if underutilized —method and has opened a broader discussion of the methodological riches and challenges of analyzing nitty-gritty aspects of interaction.

Fieldworkers, however, have been slow to adopt CA (or its anthropological cousin, discourse analysis) into their ethnographic toolkits. Part of this reticence might be because of formal CA's narrow focus on talk as the primary object of inquiry. Ethnographers, even those of a microsociological persuasion, are rarely interested in talk for its own sake. Instead, ethnographers are broadly interested in depicting a social world. Talk is important insofar as it opens broader insights into the people and community life under investigation.[9]

---

7. The field of CA is vast. I cannot do it justice in this chapter, but interested parties may want to check out some of the classic studies in this field. For more on the theory and method behind CA, see Sacks, Schegloff, and Jefferson's (1974) work on the systematic study of turn-taking in conversation and Schegloff's (1992) work on conversational "repair."

8. John Heritage (2005) distinguishes "basic" CA from "institutional" CA. The former treats conversation as an institution—as a thing in itself to be explained. The latter uses the methodological tools developed in CA to highlight how people interact in hospitals, news interviews, and other social situations.

9. May (2001) zooms in on how African American patrons at a local bar talk about race, work, and other issues that are central to their lives and worldview. He shows

But CA's value is much greater than just the focus on talk as an object of inquiry. CA encourages a particular orientation to data and analysis. It encourages researchers to study how the structure of interaction shapes the meaning people make of it. When researchers do this, they are often surprised at what they find. Taken-for-granted processes are often more varied and complex than previously thought. For instance, Mitchell Duneier (1999) uses CA to complement his rich ethnographic study of homeless sidewalk vendors in Greenwich Village, New York. In a chapter analyzing how the (mostly) black men attempt to "entangle" white women passersby in conversations they seek to avoid, Duneier's close attention to speech reveals that it was not what the men *said* that was deemed offensive or threatening (e.g., "Good morning" or "Hi, beautiful)—it was *how* they said it. For instance, they broke the normal rules of interaction by continuing to talk to the women even when they clearly signaled that they wanted to end the conversation. It was the men's commandeering of the flow of the interaction, and their flagrant disregard for the norms of public encounters, that made these interactions so uncomfortable for women. Yet Duneier's analysis moves beyond just a catalog of what these men said and how passersby responded. His ethnographic fieldwork *contextualizes* these interactions: it was the differences in race, class, and gender between the interactants, Duneier argues, that made these rather mundane conversational breaches so unsettling for the women who experienced them.

Ethnographers can learn a lot from Duneier's study, as it shows how one might adopt CA to understand how sociological abstractions like race and power are actually constituted through personal, social, and existential dilemmas that people negotiate in everyday face-to-face interaction. The power of this approach lies in its how talk can provide ethnographers with a window into people's lives and their broader social worlds.

appreciation for how the fleeting details of interactions shape—and are in turn shaped by—broader social contexts.

Studying Bodies and Emotions

Additionally, microsociologists zoom in on the ways people use their bodies and emotions.[10] Ethnographers like R. Tyson Smith (2014) have opened rich insights into this growing field. Smith culls observations and interviews with indie wrestlers to reveal the intimate, collaborative work they do to pull off death-defying moves that *could* lead to serious injury. Behind the scenes, wrestlers rely on subtle bodily tells and moves to coordinate their actions in wrestling matches. They also work together to create scenes on the mats that convey seemingly authentic expressions of pain and agony. When done well, these performances convey "kayfabe," the illusion of realness. Although Smith's work is ostensibly about wrestling, it points to a much broader, comparative microsociology of how people use their bodies in collaboration.

As it turns out, bodily collaboration is a recurrent theme in other ethnographies about dancing,[11] play in different contexts,[12] the ways people coordinate sexual encounters with strangers,[13] and

---

10. Jack Katz (1999) writes about the emotional aspects of the social world. Using different case studies, Katz illuminates the ways emotions shape everyday social interactions in a variety of contexts.

11. Joseph Schloss (2009) has written a compelling ethnographic study of Bboys and Bgirls (breakdancers). His study uncovers the various rituals that dancers use to initiate battles and the collaborative dimensions of battling, which is a form of ritualistic dance-fighting. Black Hawk Hancock has also written about this in his study of Lindy Hop and the broader world of swing dancing (see chapter 6, this volume).

12. For more work on the sociology of "play," check out Michael DeLand's (2013) work on disputes in pickup basketball games and Colin Jerolmack's (2013) work on human–animal interactions that challenge the presumption of intersubjectivity as a necessary ingredient of play.

13. Laud Humphreys's (1975) controversial study of casual sexual encounters among men in public bathrooms points to the many ways people coordinate their activities with touching and subtle eye contact.

the social organization of violence.[14] To create a composite picture of "what happened," these studies corral different data (i.e., field notes, interviews), underscoring how much of routine social life consists of embodied and emotional activity.

Fortunately, ethnographers interested in these topics now have new tools at their disposal. The rise of inexpensive video recording devices represents a boon to fieldworkers who want to go deeper into how people use their bodies to convey meanings and structure interactions. Previous work in video analysis provides useful lessons. Writing about archaeological digs, Charles Goodwin (2003) shows how people use their bodies to communicate with each other. Team members use different gestures like pointing to create "activity frameworks" that anchor people's perceptual awareness in a situation. Team members also communicate with one another through drawings and traces that they leave in the dirt with their fingers (2003: 18). Goodwin shows that people use their body, the local environment, and other practices to create shared understandings.

Others have used the camera to convey the power of emotions in interaction. For instance, Jack Katz (1999) uses raw video data to analyze how people align their emotional responses. Despite what people might think, Katz shows that laughter is not a spontaneous psychological reaction even in situations that are ostensibly funny. Laughter is something that people *accomplish* together. There is a process to laughter through which people construct the same thing as a funny, shared experience. First, people have to calibrate their perceptions of "what is going on here," making sure that everyone has a shared understanding of what is funny in the situation. From there, Katz shows how people can lose themselves in humor that bubbles up once everyone "gets it."

Together, these studies go beneath the typical layers of interactional analysis. They hold valuable lessons for ethnographers

---

14. A number of ethnographers have written widely about the interactional structure of violent crime. For more on this, see Contreras (2013), Jackson-Jacobs (2013), Anderson (1999), and Garot (2010).

who are interested in shining a light on the varied domains of social interaction. In addition to talk, they showcase how people use their bodies and emotions to create meanings together. And perhaps most important, they show us that interaction is not predetermined by "culture" or "structure." People interact in creative and sometimes quite surprising ways. When you look close enough at the small stuff that people are doing, you begin to uncover the multilayered, creative, and collaborative work people do together to make interaction flow.

Touching and Turn-Taking

Now back to Hip Hop. The rappers I met would always tell me that it was important for people to share the stage in the cipher. They'd say that it was bad form to "hog the mic," or keep rapping when others wanted a turn. Managing this problem sounded easy enough.

But as I talked to more people, I began to realize that turn-taking wasn't always so straightforward. For starters, there weren't any formal rules about how long a person should take while rhyming. Should a person just rhyme until they felt they were done? Should they rhyme sixteen bars (lines), which is the equivalent of a verse in a written song? Or should turn-taking be determined by the next person in the queue jumping into their rhyme? None of this was clear to me, and as I asked around, I realized that it wasn't always so clear to rappers, either. This clued me into something important that we should hold dear as ethnographers: we cannot always rely on people's accounts of interactions. While accounts are important and key us into how people make sense of what happened, they are often poor substitutes for our own observations—particularly of interactional processes.[15]

---

15. Jerolmack and Khan (2014) show how people's accounts of behaviors are often poor proxies for the way people actually behave.

This inspired me to look closer at what was happening. When I did, I noticed that rappers would use different verbal cues to set up their transition into the cipher.[16] They'd briefly interrupt the current person rhyming by saying things like "Yo," "Uh huh," and "Yeah." From there, the person rhyming would typically finish their last thought and let the new rapper have a turn. For example, in one memorable cipher, I wrote field notes about how Nocando verbally announced his intention to have a turn in the cipher. He interrupted Flawliss's turn and told the audience, "And here's how Nocando do it":

Wildchild, Flawliss, Nocando, and Big Flossy are at the center of a large cipher. There is a crowd of about twenty people huddled around them and OG Larry, a former gang member who often brings his guitar to the corner and strums while people rhyme over his music. Tonight OG Larry is out on the block and has attracted the attention of an active cipher within moments of strumming his guitar. He strums a slow guitar riff that gives rappers a melody to rhyme over. Wildchild starts off and rhymes in double time. His verse sounds really fast, and I have difficulty making out what he's saying in his rhymes. He speeds through a verse and then Flawliss jumps in, rhyming at about the same speed. His rhyming is also quite fast, which makes it hard for me to hear what he's actually saying in his rhymes. Then Nocando jumps into the cipher. But instead of rhyming in double time,

---

16. To make sense of this, I turned to a classic article by Sacks, Schegloff, and Jefferson, who show that speakers often change during a conversation and that one party normally speaks at a time (1974: 700–701). Although there are moments of conversational overlap, these are typically brief. And when they disrupt the flow of a conversation, people do different things to "repair" a misunderstanding. Similarly, Sacks et al. show how people select the next speaker with direct questions and specific complaints about a person—both of which invite certain people to respond (1974: 716–720).

he transitions slowly into his turn, announcing, "And here's how Nocando do it." His verse is much slower than that of the previous two rappers.

I also shot a video of this interaction. I hadn't had my camera for very long, but many rappers were eager to get their videos on YouTube, which was becoming a launching pad for rappers looking to build a wider fan base and get discovered. I was eager to help and figured that videotaping ciphers would be one small thing I could do to give back.

The video added more layers to my analysis. It showed me that Nocando's verbal declaration was embedded in a sequence of interactional moves. Flawliss was rhyming when Nocando started walking from the outside of the circle (frame1.1). Nocando then tapped Flawliss on the shoulder with a rolled-up flyer, signaling that he wanted to get inside the cipher (frame1.2). Flawliss then moved a little out of his way to give him room to edge his way into the cipher (frame 1.3). He did all of this *before* announcing, "And here's how Nocando do it." And then Nocando launched into his verse (frame 1.4).

1	Flawliss:	Better better, rip that better,
2		Bust that, bust that, Flaw, flaw, flaw, driff, driff,
3		I forgot that letter,
4		Fuck that shit, I divide that shit,
5		I just slide the shit,
6		And when I clide and shit, my mind is sick,
7		I'm back and double double time that shit, Woah!
8		Better slow that, hold back, slow that slow that, slow that,
9		Give it back and double fo', better two betta fold that,
10		All I do is bust shit til your shoulders clap,
11		When I hold that back, hold that back,
12		Show that back,
13		Ay that punchline, yo that's black . . .

14	Nocando:	[*Nocando walks from outside the cipher, taps Flawliss, and then moves to the center of the circle*]
14		... And here's how Nocando do it.
15		It's halftime on this crew music,
16		Too stupid, freestyle moves fluid,
17		It's got viscosity, on top of me,
18		These emcees wanna uphold a dope emcee,
19		But I'll kill them and start a colony,
20		Ominous, bombin' em,
21		I'm on Battlestar Galactica
22		Bombin' Andromeda with yo mama cuz,
23		She likes the way I often fuck,
24		I keep crashin' like an asteroid,
25		Grown man, Nocan from a battleboy
26		With missiles that I can't deploy.

This excerpt reveals the complex nature of turn-taking in the cipher. Nocando did much more than verbally announce his intention to rhyme. He used a combination of physical touching and movement through space to set up his transition. Technically, he could have started rhyming from the outer rim of the cipher. But people prefer not to do this because it is hard for them to be heard by others in the cipher. Those who do this get ignored, or they are chastised for "fucking up the vibe." To be heard, rappers tend to position themselves in the middle of the action—in the "attention zone." By observing these practices, rappers were also reproducing a set of local practices that others learned as part of their socialization at Project Blowed. They were, in effect, reproducing the idea that the center of the cipher—the attention zone—was where people should locate their bodies if they wanted to be heard.

The excerpt also shows that turn-taking requires collaboration. The person currently rhyming has to stop rhyming for the transition to work. They have to cede their spot in the attention zone and

FRAME 1.1   **FRAME 1.2**

FRAME 1.3   **FRAME 1.4**

let the next person have their chance. This entire sequence might have played out differently if Flawliss had not felt the tap, stopped rhyming, or angled his body so that Nocando could enter the cipher. Flawliss helped make this transition work because he gave Nocando the stage.

Microsociology enhanced my analysis of the cipher. Beneath the surface layer, I began to see all the stuff people were doing to make the cipher work. In addition to using verbal cues, rappers were using nonverbal gestures to tell other people that they wanted to rhyme.

More specifically, rappers used the power of strategic touching and their movement through space to communicate their intention to rhyme.

Uncovering Hidden Creativity in the Cipher

Freestyling is awesome to see and hear live. When rappers do it well, they seem to come up with witty, tongue-twisting, and thought-provoking rhymes on the fly. A talented freestyle rapper seems possessed by a flash of creative genius. Unsurprisingly, many rappers reinforce popular images of freestyling. They tell you that everything that comes out of their mouth is "off the top," unscripted, and emerging in the moment. This narrative fits the popular images of freestyling as pure improvisational magic.

But as I looked closer at the action, I soon realized that this was a half-truth. The microsociological lens inspired me to dig deeper. My video data from many different ciphers revealed that rappers were repeating some of the same words, rhyme schemes, and sequences in different freestyle sessions. This keyed me into how rappers recycle old rhymes and rehash them in new word combinations. At first, some rappers were mum about this, since it challenged their claims of "coming off the top" or wholly improvising in the moment. But after rappers got to know me better, many admitted to using "pre meds" [pre-meditated] or "go to" rhymes to stay afloat in the middle of freestyling. These "canned resources" would give them baseline rhymes that they could deploy in the moment to keep from "falling off," or not being able to sustain a smooth and continuous rhyme flow.[17] Everybody was doing this, but few talked about it out of fear that it would diminish people's perceptions of their skills.

---

17. I write about this in more detail in the context of face work in the rap cipher (Lee 2009, 2016).

This opened up new lines of inquiry. As I dug deeper, I started to see other ways that rappers were improvising in the moment. Specifically, I noticed how rappers were building off each other in the cipher. They borrowed words, phrases, and other schemes from other rhymers, particularly the person who preceded them in the evolving queue. Adept rappers were taking something that immediately transpired and using it as a jumping-off point in their own rhymes. These weren't the most captivating or thrilling moments in their freestyles, but they were ironically closer to the ideal of pure, spontaneous freestyling.

I first noticed this while watching Flawliss freestyling with Dizaster. It was Thursday night and the corner outside Project Blowed was bumping. As usual, different "ciphers" dotted the corner. A large crowd gathered around CP's tricked-out Honda Civic. He was parked in the yellow loading zone, and the "Lambo" doors were swung open, beats bursting out of the speakers in his trunk.

I squeezed my way through the crowd and found a space near the middle of the cipher. Once there, I turned on my video camera. Flawliss, Dizaster, CP, and a few other rappers were there. CP kicked off the cipher and was followed by Dizaster and then Flawliss. Flawliss was piggybacking on a concept that he heard in Dizaster's rhyme:

1	CP:	yo, um, listen, yo, yo,
2		I'm sumthin' like a boss,
3		these niggas is nothin' to *me*,
4		they ain't fuckin' with *me*,
5		why they tell me that,
6		straight fuckin' with *me*,
7		ya'll niggas never wanna see
8		that little blood in the street,

9		put a cuff on your knees,
10		ya'll niggas ain't touchin' a g,
11		ya'll niggas is under a g,
12		I'm over the 5,
13		listen man I am over the guy,
14		over the clouds over the sky,
15		I am over your ride,
16		post up with a rifle or a shotgun,
17		pop son, pop, pop, drop son,
18		you don't want it with the glock son,
19		you don't wanna have the paramedics
20		call the fuckin' cops son...
21	Dizaster:	...who the emcees at,
22		they don't wanna battle,
23		I'm strong enough to rip your body away from its fuckin' shadow,
24		I spit it like pussies with hysterectomies,
25		I'm heavyweight like this nigga standing next to me,
26		your styles is fat,
27		when we rap, verbal combat,
28		niggas is quick to react,
29		*reflexin' in a session*,
30		they best to use discretion,
31		slice the adam's apple with a scalpel for testin',
32		will leave him in a chapel for testin',
33		been convalescing,
34		been that way *since I was an adolescent*,
35		*19 might seem* ahead of my time,
36		but when they flow like you ...

37	Flawliss:	. . . Yo, yo, yo,
38		*since I was an adolescent,*
39		young boy move,
40		I had mad addresses but the young boy knew,
41		one day you come back like DJ Screw,
42		handle my death put 16 in your chest,
43		I ain't never been a battler, played the streets,
44		but the flow is deep I ain't Memphis Bleek,
45		but I meant to speak
46		but the lynch is deep,
47		ya'll niggas suck like fuckin' leeches to me . . .

In bar 34, Dizaster rhymed, ". . . been that way *since I was an adolescent.*" Flawliss continued the same strand of thought, using this phrase to transition into his turn at bar 37: ". . . Yo, yo, yo, *since I was an adolescent.*" People were borrowing words, phrases, and other kinds of utterances from each other. The cipher was like a big brainstorming session; people shared ideas and built off each other, often in creative—but rarely acknowledged—ways.

I decided to watch the footage again. This time, I paused and rewound the video, coding people's emotional responses. Upon rewatching, I noticed that CP was building on the emotional responses of audience members, incorporating their cheers and utterances into his unfolding freestyle rhyme. For example, in one part, an audience member made the sounds of a gun ("pop, pop"), which CP spontaneously incorporated into his unfolding freestyle ("pop son, pop, pop, drop son"). I incorporated these into the same evolving transcript (emotional responses are in square brackets):

1	CP:	yo, um, listen, yo, yo
2		I'm sumthin' like a boss,
3		these niggas is nothin' to me, [*what?!*]
4		they ain't fuckin' with *me,*
5		why they tell me that,

6		straight fuckin' with *me*, [*woah!*]
7		ya'll niggas never wanna see
8		that little blood in the street, [*ahh!*]
9		put a cuff on your knees,
10		ya'll niggas ain't touchin' a G, [*oh, shit*]
11		ya'll niggas is under a g,
12		I'm over the 5,
13		listen man I am over the guy,
14		over the clouds over the sky,
15		I am over your ride,
16		post up with a rifle or a shotgun, [*pop pop*]
17		pop son, pop, pop, drop son, [*pop pop, eww, wooh*]
18		you don't want it with the glock son,
19		you don't wanna have the paramedics
20		call the fuckin' cops son . . .
21	Disaster:	. . . who the emcees at,
22		they don't wanna battle,
23		I'm strong enough to rip your body away from its fuckin' shadow,
24		I spit it like pussies with hysterectomies,
25		I'm heavyweight like this nigga standing next to me,
26		your styles is fat,
27		when we rap, verbal combat,
28		niggas is quick to react,
29		*reflexin' in a session*,
30		they best to use discretion,
31		slice the adam's apple with a scalpel for testin',
32		will leave him in a chapel for testin', [*wooh!*]
33		been convalescing,
34		been that way *since I was an adolescent*,
35		*19 might seem* ahead of my time,
36		but when they flow like you . . .

The casual listener and audience member might be drawn to more impactful rhymes in a freestyling sequence. They might be blown away by something that sounds polished. Chances are, they are responding to a canned resource—a rhyme that a person has encountered thousands of times before. Rappers are good at disguising their use of canned resources and can drop them into new sequences often without being detected.

But there is a more subtle kind of creativity in the cipher. Rappers create something from the unfolding action and put their own spin on it. From small phrases and utterances made by another rapper, to more fleeting emotional responses, rappers are always taking stock of what's happening around them. The most skilled are then able to take these moments, incorporate them, and build them into a seamless freestyle rap.

The microsociological lens showed me that there was much more going on than meets the researcher's eyes and ears. Researchers might be tempted to take what people say at face value. But this approach has limits. People have a stake in representing themselves in particular ways, and the ethnographer should be wary of this. In addition to gaining a clearer perspective on how people interact with each other, the microsociological perspective gives us the power to depict the subtle, fleeting, and often invisible ways people are creatively responding to local cues and demands in the situation.

Breaking Frame

And then there were the battles, which are lyrical duels in Hip Hop culture. Whenever I asked rappers, they'd always tell me that somebody would start a battle when they felt "disrespected" within the cipher. Alpha MC, a local rapper known for his deep baritone voice, once told me, "It's just about respect, man. Like, if we out there rhymin' and vibin' and we cool, then there's no problem. But if you start disrespectin', then we gonna have a battle." Many other rappers would say similar things in casual conversation, describing the battle as a peaceful way for parties to resolve these moments of disrespect. The person who felt disrespected would "call out" the other person, challenging them to a lyrical duel in front of their peers. Then, both parties would take turns dissing the other person in front of a live audience, who cheered them on.

But what did rappers consider signs of disrespect? The microsociological lens inspired me to unpack this idea. Disrespect, after all, encapsulates a range of behaviors that a person interprets as offensive or untoward. Even though I could imagine what this might look and even feel like in the context of the cipher, I was compelled to see it with my own eyes and write about it accordingly.

I found three main interactional processes that rappers were interpreting as signs of disrespect. By far, most people described battles as a way to resolve moments where they felt cut off in the middle of their freestyle. For example, CP said, "Most times you call somebody out because they cuttin' you off. Like, there ain't no rules about it, but if you ain't done and somebody comes in [to the cipher] too fast or they too loud, then you might call them out."

Rappers also called people out who were "throwing subliminals" (indirect disses at them). Flawliss would often talk about this, as he was often the target of subliminal attacks. Once, while reflecting on a battle he had recently been in, he sighed, "A lot of times you got your emcees who think they finna [going to] go out and serve everybody. So they might say some shit that sorta sound like it's about you. Like, if I'm in a cipher and somebody starts talkin' about how they always servin' fat rappers, then I know they talkin' about me. And that's what gets that shit poppin'."

Lastly, rappers called out people they thought just needed humbling. Once, Sahtyre told me that he sometimes called people out if he thought they were getting too cocky and confident about their skills. He smirked while telling me about a time when he did this: "Like, sometimes it ain't even about them cuttin' you off or nothing. Like, you could just not like the guy or maybe they look like they need some humbling, like they start thinking they're servin' everybody and you just there to remind them that they still wack as fuck."

Whatever the case, battling at Project Blowed was *supposed* to be playful. Rappers would lose the respect of their peers for breaking frame or trying to escalate battles into something more than just play. By escalating a battle into something more than a playful dissing contest, rappers were effectively admitting that they could not match wits with another rapper. Threats of violence were frowned upon at Project Blowed, which was a scene that prized lyrical skills above all else.

But even though people weren't supposed to escalate battles, it sometimes happened. Battles are fraught with tension, and emcees sometimes got upset and offended, which led some people to call another person out to battle. Once this happened, I realized there were key ways that rappers kept these tense moments from actually becoming fights or violent situations. That is to say, there were subtle kinds of cooperation *within* moments of emerging conflict. The microsociological lens made it possible for me to see and appreciate these fleeting moments.

I first learned about this while watching Big Flossy and E.Crimsin battling. The two had been going at it for the past couple weeks, and this time the battle escalated into a near fight. At one point, both parties had stopped rapping. This is the first indication that people are no longer just playing. The switch from rhyming to threatening language or yelling represents a frame break. Big Flossy was visibly upset and asked E.Crimsin if he was going to let him rap. E.Crimsin wouldn't back down, though, and continued dissing Big Flossy, who yelled back and insulted E.Crimsin.

From there, Big Flossy and E.Crimsin started drifting closer together and lightly pushing each other. This is another moment of escalation. Moments like this, where parties make physical contact, are ripe for shoving and more aggressive physical contact. As both parties get closer and use more force, they increase what Randall Collins (2008) describes as "confrontational tension," catapulting the situation closer to violence. This was a pivotal moment.

Microsociology: Beneath the Surface

But this disagreement never erupted into a real fight. Instead of doing things that could have further provoked Big Flossy, E.Crimsin smiled and got out of the way, showing a last-ditch moment of deference that defused the situation:

Flossy: [*speaking directly to E.Crimsin, who is rapping*] Hold up! Let me rap! (frame 1.5). Let me rap! (frame 1.6). Let me rap, though! [*Both become entangled here in light pushing*] (frame 1.7). Let me rap! [*E.Crimsin smiles and backs away*] (frame 1.8).

FRAME 1.5

FRAME 1.6

FRAME 1.7

FRAME 1.8

The two last frames are especially important. Here, both Big Flossy and E.Crimsin have broken from the "play frame" and have moved closer together. They stopped rhyming and were entering into each other's personal space. As they got closer, both extended their arms and lightly pushed each other (frame 1.7). If either party ramped up the intensity of their pushing, there would be a good chance of further escalation, resulting in more aggressive shoving or even fighting.

This is how many street scuffles start: people look for a reason to turn yelling and blustering into real violence. To start a fight, people have to move into striking or grappling distance. They have to be close to each other, eliminating physical distance from the other person. Of course, people might only be posturing with no intention of fighting.[18] And they can also disentangle themselves from the other person by backing and turning away or showing that they do not want to fight. But it becomes harder for one or both parties to walk away as both get closer and as their bodies get increasingly entangled. As they inch closer, people become further committed to a line of future action; the person who backs down from a near challenge risks losing face.

As Curtis Jackson-Jacobs (2013) shows us, fighting often requires that people mutually agree to a fight. Combatants have to see fighting as a solution to challenges of "interpersonal sovereignty." This provides the spark that launches parties into mutual combat. But before it got there, E.Crimsin defused the situation by deferring to Big Flossy, giving him space. Beyond the words and the shared history of the participants, the video segment shows how people negotiate nonviolence with each other.[19] By backing down,

---

18. Randall Collins (2008) writes extensively about the interactional and emotional pathways to violence. Contrary to what most people think, Collins shows us that only a select few are good—let alone competent—at violence. Many perform as if they want to become violent because it helps them save face when challenged. Others might also bluster, without any real intention of engaging in violence.

19. Collins (2008) writes about the many challenges that people face in overcoming "confrontational tension." In different violent situations, actors have to find emotional pathways around this confrontational tension, which makes most people reluctant or afraid to get into violent situations.

smiling, and deferring to Big Flossy, E.Crimsin provided both parties with a way out. He didn't press the issue with Big Flossy, and he showed through his body language and emotional affect that he didn't want to escalate their conflict until it became a full-on fight.

The microsociological lens showed me the limits of the conventional view of rap battles (and ciphers, for that matter) as ego-driven, competitive interactions. Though rappers talked about the battle as pure conflict, close observation reveals that, ironically, battling required cooperation in which people mutually agreed to keep the encounter playful. Even at the height of apparent conflict (e.g., dissing), rappers routinely engaged in collaborative repair work to help other emcees save face so that rap battles did not become fist fights. These insights, which challenge and enhance our understanding of Hip Hop culture, were made possible only through a microsociological approach to rapping.

Some Challenges

The microsociological perspective offers many useful insights for the ethnographer, but it is also limited without an appreciation for the larger cultural context in which the observations occur. Our interpretations of micro-level interactions rely on information and perspectives that can be gained only through deep, immersive fieldwork with people who are in the communities we write about. While microsociology can go a long way toward depicting variations in the way interactions unfold, on its own it may be limited in its ability to answer larger questions about why these interactions matter to people or how these interactions shape the ways people see each other and themselves. For ethnographers who write about identity, culture, or community, micro-level interactions represent one piece in a larger puzzle that we must uncover through rigorous fieldwork methods.

For instance, while conducting fieldwork at Project Blowed, I made a number of videos where a rapper would momentarily fall off while freestyling in the cipher. Although there was no standard definition, rappers would talk about someone falling off when that person couldn't keep freestyling until the next person was ready to jump in and have a turn. Ciphers are sort of like games of "hot potato." Each person who rhymes in the cipher is expected to pull their weight and keep the interaction afloat.

When this happened, I kept noticing that rappers were quickly jumping in and rhyming when another person started falling off. After collecting a number of these examples, I became convinced that rappers were helping each other save face. Their actions reminded me of Erving Goffman's (1967) theories of "protective face work," which holds that friends, family, and other social intimates help each other save face during potentially embarrassing situations. According to Goffman, this is what holds small groups together. It is a promissory note that a person can be trusted and establishes good rapport with others who may one day return the favor. This seemed to make perfect sense; by jumping in before another person's fall-off became too noticeable, rappers were shielding people from the embarrassment that comes from not being able to freestyle without stopping.

But I soon learned that there were some key problems with my analysis. One day, I met up with Big Flossy and explained how I was interpreting the data. He listened carefully and then started laughing, adding:

> I mean, it ain't really about that. I mean, it is sometimes, but really it's you just tryin' to keep the cipher going, ya know what I'm saying? If you let it die, then everybody loses, because you out there just tryin' to have fun with your friends and if it's really hot, you don't want it to die.

The microsociological perspective gave me a close and nuanced picture of the interaction, but I was misreading people's intentions.

While rappers at Project Blowed were generally friendly with each other, people didn't typically jump in because they were trying to save others from embarrassment. As Big Flossy would explain, people jumped in because they felt the shared responsibility of keeping the cipher afloat. In other words, jumping in had much less to do with saving a peer from ritual embarrassment than with saving the entire interaction from coming to a halt. Big Flossy's account helped contextualize the act of jumping in. And more important, he showed me the necessity of always contextualizing micro-level observations in a local cultural milieu.

Similarly, those who use video recording devices for data collection must find unobtrusive ways to do so in the field. Videos are not present in every setting, and their use can transform the way people interact with each other and the researcher. This situation should be avoided. And in the end, videos cannot replace field notes or interview transcripts. Although they give us a raw picture of "what happened" in an interaction, our ability to make sense of interactions is still shaped by the juicy backstories, life histories, and larger community life that inform our analyses.

As such, ethnographers can think of the microsociological perspective as a way to deepen and enrich understandings of recurrent interactions within one's field site. These insights can provide a building block for understanding the larger community and context of our observations.

Conclusion

There are many ways in which microsociology impacted my work. In a broad sense, it helped me go beneath the surface appearance of the social world I was studying. It pointed me to the messy and sometimes surprising ways that people interact with each other. While zooming into the unfolding action of streetcorner ciphers, I uncovered collaborative work that rappers were doing to make the cipher flow smoothly.

Beneath the surface appearance of ciphers as proving grounds where rappers battled each other over moments of disrespect, I began to see a world of micro-level practices and maneuvers that made up these recurrent interactions. More important, I saw what few were saying: ciphers and battles were interactions that depended on collaboration. While rappers talked about trying to outshine each other and wanted to seize the emotional energy of these interactions, they were also working together in subtle ways. Rappers were collaborating when they took turns in the cipher, whenever they borrowed lines or phrases from another person's rhymes, and whenever they mutually agreed to *not* escalate battles into violence.

In all, the microsociological lens promises to enhance ethnographic work. It is a perspective that shines a light on interactional processes that are often invisible to outsiders and taken for granted by insiders. It also gives the researcher an appreciation for close, comparative analyses of data. The microsociologist works diligently at uncovering small and often imperceptible variations in how different interactions unfold. This perspective, if nothing else, is one that inspires a degree of humility. Once you're down there with that lens, you begin to see how much we have not yet uncovered about communication and interaction. And, most important, this approach allows one to see that interaction is not simply the site where larger social forces are instantiated—social order is generated *through* interaction.

References

Anderson, Elijah. 1999. *Code of the Street: Decency, Violence, and the Moral Life of the Inner City*. New York: Norton.
Clayman, Steven and John Heritage. 2002. *The News Interview: Journalists and Public Figures on the Air*. Cambridge: Cambridge University Press.

Collins, Randall. 2008. *Violence: A Micro-Sociological Theory*. Princeton, NJ: Princeton University Press.
Contreras, Randol. 2012. *The Stickup Kids: Race, Drugs, Violence, and the American Dream*. Berkeley: University of California Press.
DeLand, Michael. 2013. "Basketball in the Key of Law: The Significance of Disputing in Pick-Up Basketball." *Law & Society Review* 47(3): 653–685.
Fine, Gary and Corey Fields. 2008. "Culture and Microsociology: The Anthill and the Veldt." *Annals of the American Academy of Political and Social Science* 619: 130–148.
Garot, Robert. 2010. *Who You Claim: Performing Gang Identity in School and on the Streets*. New York: New York University Press.
Goffman, Erving. 1967. *Interaction Ritual: Essays on Face-to-Face Behavior*. New York: Doubleday.
Goodwin, Charles. 2003. "Pointing as Situated Practice." In *Pointing: Where Language, Culture and Cognition Meet*, edited by Sotaro Kita, 217–241. Mahwah, NJ: Lawrence Erlbaum.
Heritage, John. 2005. "Conversation Analysis and Institutional Talk." In *Handbook of Language and Social Interaction*, edited by Kristine Fitch and Robert Sanders, 161–184. New York: Academic Press.
Heritage, John and Douglas Maynard. 2006. "Problems and Prospects in the Study of Physician–Patient Interaction: 30 Years of Research." *Annual Review of Sociology* 32: 351–374.
Humphreys, Laud. 1975. *Tearoom Trade: Impersonal Sex in Public Places*. Chicago: Aldine.
Jackson-Jacobs, Curtis. 2013. "Constructing Physical Fights: An Interactionist Analysis of Violence among Affluent, Suburban Youth." *Qualitative Sociology* 36(1): 23–52.
Jerolmack, Colin. 2013. *The Global Pigeon*. Chicago: University of Chicago Press.
Jerolmack, Colin and Shamus Khan. 2014. "Talk is Cheap: Ethnography and the Attitudinal Fallacy." *Sociological Methods & Research* 43(2): 178–209.
Katz, Jack. 1999. *How Emotions Work*. Chicago: University of Chicago Press.
Kelley, Robin. 1998. *Yo Mama's Disfunktional!: Fighting the Culture Wars in Urban America*. Boston: Beacon.
Lee, Jooyoung. 2009. "Escaping Embarrassment: Face-Work in the Rap Cipher." *Social Psychology Quarterly* 72(4): 306–324.

Lee, Jooyoung. 2016. *Blowin' Up: Rap Dreams in South Central.* Chicago: University of Chicago Press.

May, Reuben. 2001. *Talking at Trena's: Everyday Conversations at an African American Tavern.* New York: NYU Press.

Maynard, Douglas. 1984. "The Structure and Discourse in Misdemeanor Plea Bargaining." *Law & Society Review* 18(1): 75–104.

Pollner, Melvin. 1982. *Mundane Reason: Reality in Everyday and Sociological Discourse.* Cambridge: Cambridge University Press.

Sacks, Harvey, Emanuel Schegloff, and Gail Jefferson. 1974. "A Simplest Systematics for the Organization of Turn-Taking for Conversation." *Language* 50(4): 696–735.

Schegloff, Emanuel. 1992. "Repair after Next Turn: The Last Structurally Provided Defense of Intersubjectivity in Conversation." *American Journal of Sociology* 97(5): 1295–1345.

Schloss, Joseph. 2009. *Foundation: B-boys, B-girls, and Hip-Hop Culture in New York.* New York: Oxford University Press.

Smith, R. Tyson. 2014. *Fighting for Recognition: Identity, Masculinity, and the Act of Violence in Professional Wrestling.* Durham: Duke University Press.

Chapter 2

Capturing Organizations as Actors

KATHERINE CHEN

At summer's end in 2015, more than sixty-seven thousand people celebrated the arts and community at Burning Man in the Nevada Black Rock Desert.[1] They camped together, with some braving extreme temperatures and dust storms for more than a week, in a horseshoe-shaped temporary city composed of art installations, recreational vehicles, tents, and homemade shade structures. In this remote, harsh expanse ringed by mountains, these desert denizens practiced a gift economy, engaged in radical self-expression, participated in interactive, artistic, and voluntary endeavors, and upheld other countercultural principles. Their activities culminated in a bonfire of the Man, a more than forty-foot-tall wooden and neon sculpture anchoring the city's center.

In 1998, when the event was in its thirteenth year and drew a population of about fifteen thousand persons, I started observing the Burning Man organization's preparations in San Francisco and attending the event as an organizational ethnographer. After finding a Burning Man organizer's email address on the Burning Man

---

1. Population figure from http://burningman.org/timeline/#!/2015.

website, I contacted Marian Goodell to ask permission to study the organization and its event; in my email, I briefly explained my research question, plan, and reasons for studying the organization.[2] After conferring with her fellow organizers, Goodell granted me access on the condition that I volunteer for Media Mecca, a department under her oversight. Despite my lack of public relations experience, I started volunteering with others, vetting and assisting the media covering the event. I also observed other departments' gatherings and meetings, including organizers' meetings that were closed to outsiders and rank-and-file members. With this dual role as researcher and member, I joined the estimated two thousand volunteers whose efforts help Burning Man unfold as an arts festival.

When I embarked on this research, my choice felt high-risk but compelling. At the time, most people were not familiar with Burning Man or its organization. Even now that Burning Man is better known, people are still surprised to learn that the self-described "spontaneous" event requires a year-round organization. While the original Burning Man, a bonfire around which twenty friends gathered on a San Francisco beach, involved minimal organization, growing coordination challenges encouraged organizers to establish its first formal organization, a legal partnership, to run the event. Following an accidental death and injuries at the 1996 event, organizers disagreed about whether Burning Man should continue. After the legal partnership dissolved, the remaining leaders regrouped

---

2. While my entry was smooth, some organizations erect high barriers to entry, requiring long negotiations for access, or they may outright refuse access. Ethnographers thus have different approaches to gaining access. Some have trusted public figures write a letter of introduction (Watkins-Hayes 2009). Others have used their institutions' alumni networks to identify and approach potentially receptive gatekeepers. Chambliss (1996) first had informal conversations, usually over lunch, with potential informants before asking for formal permission to study a hospital. In other studies, researchers decide they can conduct their research only via covert participant-observations. Using a temp agency, Ogasawara (1998) began working as a secretary at a firm; when asked about her involvement, she disclosed that she was interested in learning how companies worked.

as the Black Rock City, LLC, to continue running the event.[3] This organization, which I call the Burning Man organization, enabled Burning Man to survive setbacks that once threatened to end the event (Chen 2009).

Burning Man is now in its third decade, and its "Burners" have formed groups, organizations, and gatherings built on its principles across the United States and around the world (Chen 2011). Burning Man's colorful aspects, including its interactive artwork (Bowditch 2010; Chen 2012b; Clupper 2009; Kristen 2003, 2007), gift economy (Kozinets 2002; Turner 2009), spiritual rituals (Sherry and Kozinets 2007; Pike 2001; Gilmore 2010), and revelry (St. John 2009), draw most public and scholarly attention.

So why use an organizational lens to study Burning Man? Compared with other phenomena in the social sciences, organizations have attracted less scholarly attention. With their ubiquity, organizations seem mundane, or they are viewed with dread and derision, as depicted by *The Office* TV show and the Dilbert comic strip. Moreover, scholars are less familiar with applying an organizational perspective to phenomena; with the migration of organizational researchers to professional schools in education, business, and nonprofit management, fewer courses on organizational theory and behavior are offered regularly in disciplinary programs outside professional schools. In many sociological studies, organizations tend to recede into the background.

This inattention to organizations is much like neglecting to study the water in which fish swim: much societal action takes place within organizations, and much societal action is driven by organizations. Thus, a fuller understanding of many social phenomena involves taking the organizational dimension into account or, even better, studying organizations as actors. In contemporary society,

---

3. This for-profit organization became a subsidiary of the nonprofit organization (Burning Man Project) in 2014. http://journal.burningman.org/2014/03/news/global-news/burning-man-transitions-to-non-profit-organization/.

organizations are everywhere, and they impact our lives from birth onward. They govern, educate, and employ us; they foster fellowship, and they provide goods and services. They reflect and substantiate certain values and goals, from the mundane to the life-altering (Chen, Lune, and Queen 2013). Organizations offer one form of social order that is legally recognized and taken for granted in contemporary society.

Before delving into how to study organizations, let's differentiate organizations from other collectivities. So what are organizations? Among other features, organizations usually have defined boundaries about who are members, specifications about who has authority to make decisions, rules that govern how activities are undertaken, and procedures for what activities are monitored and documented (e.g., Ahrne and Brunsson 2011). Many organizations are small and informal; they have not yet obtained legal status as nonprofit or for-profit organizations. Several organizational forms—like the mob, triads, cults, and some social movement groups—are considered illegitimate by the state and operate in the shadows. Other organizations are accepted, formal institutions where people collectively endorse particular values and pursue goals; these include nonprofit organizations that are religious (churches, synagogues, mosques, etc.), educational (schools and universities), professional (associations that promote professionals' interests), and voluntary (charities and volunteer-powered groups). For-profit organizations, from small mom-and-pop enterprises to multinational conglomerates, are also major players in society. The state has its own constituent organizations, from those charged with protecting and studying the physical environment to those (e.g., law enforcement and military) that can legitimately exert physical force to enforce their mandates. In the United States, the government additionally contracts with for-profit and nonprofit organizations to provide goods and services, thereby connecting a complex patchwork of organizations.

When examining organizations, laypersons and practitioners usually consider utilitarian, "measurable" aspects, like a for-profit organization's profitability, a nonprofit organization's effectiveness, or a governmental organization's efficiency. While some organizational researchers study organizations with such practical concerns in mind, most have more expansive research questions that view organizations through a particular theoretical perspective. Their questions examine, for instance, how organizing practices and outputs impact the experiences of members, customers/clients, and the public; how pursuing certain organizational imperatives—particularly, organizational survival—can direct efforts away from other goals; why people obey (or resist) organizations; how members form relations that can help or hinder activities; and how organizations interact with the state and other organizations.

Why Ethnography?

Depending on the research question, organizations can be studied through a variety of methods, including analysis of organizational documents, network analysis of members and relations among organizations, surveys of members or organizational representatives, and interviews with members. Of the possible ways of studying organizations, organizational ethnographies are especially effective for unveiling how organizations actually operate (Morrill and Fine 1997; Schwartzman 1993). By revealing the "black box" of organizations, organizational ethnographies allow us to examine their activities in situ. With ethnographies, we gain fine-grained insight into what organizations do, how they do it, and how they shape or are shaped by people, other organizations, and the state.

In particular, organizational ethnographies can capture both formal and informal organizing structures and practices, revealing both how organizations are supposed to operate and how they actually operate in practice. Many organizations, especially those that are older and more established, document their formal structures in handbooks, rules, and organizational charts that can be consulted or communicated during orientations and trainings. However, informal organizing structures are usually tacit and often can be learned only through observations of activities, hands-on experience, or mentoring or coaching by peers. Ethnographies can examine these informal dimensions, including how informal relations animate organizations. Friendships, enmity, and even romantic relations are not reflected by members' official organizational positions, but they can bolster collegiality and citizenship among members, as well as ignite friction (Hodson 2001). Furthermore, ethnographies can reveal the interplay between the formal and informal, shedding insight into, for example, how organizations can exacerbate inequalities or promote equality (cf. Tomaskovic-Devey 2014).

Ethnographies of Organizations as Contexts versus Drivers

Before delving into examples of how to study organizations using the ethnographic gaze, I first distinguish between ethnographies where researchers study phenomena within organizations but do not examine organizations as entities and ethnographies where organizations are the foci. The former researchers treat organizations as contexts in which their actors interact; in such studies, organizations are "sites" of action (Powell and Brandtner 2016). These researchers might portray people as "primed" by their organizations to act, think, or emote in particular ways. However, such researchers concentrate more on how status characteristics like age, race, ethnicity, and gender foster particular interactions and outcomes, or they identify processes, such as racialization and stratification, as explanations for discourses and behaviors they observe.

Contemporary ethnographies that follow people in the context of organizations are increasingly prevalent. This is partly because people spend much of their time in organizations; they attend educational institutions, labor in workplaces, seek assistance in governmental offices, and commune together in voluntary associations. For example, in an ethnographic study of low-income teenagers living in New York City, Newman (1999) and a team of graduate students examined how these teenagers learned skills while working ostensibly low-skilled jobs at fast-food restaurants. While Newman described aspects of these workplaces, her findings focused on the limited upward mobility of these workers in the labor market. The fast-food restaurant's division of labor and routinization limited workers' opportunities to learn skills beyond their assigned responsibilities. Since their personal networks were limited, workers had few contacts with persons in other, desired occupations and workplaces that could foster alternative career prospects. These conditions consigned the teenagers to "dead-end" jobs. On the flip side, Khan's (2011) ethnography of students at a private boarding school revealed how the collective experience of elite schooling created among students a sense of privilege, one that emphasized hierarchy and "earned" achievement. In this heady milieu, students learned from their older peers, faculty, and staff how to articulate certain values and perspectives about their positions. In such studies, organizations reside in the background rather than the foreground; organizations serve as picturesque backdrops where researchers happen to arrive at certain realizations.

In contrast, organizational ethnographies view organizations as actors in their own right, as "drivers" of action (Powell and Brandtner 2016). In other words, organizations are the unit of analysis. People are important, but their presence is transient—they graduate, switch affiliations, drop out, are pushed out, or die. Despite this member turnover, most organizations continue, with a few enduring for centuries. Organizational structures ease such transitions; mission statements, positions, written rules and standard operating procedures, and organizational histories provide guidelines on what (or, more often, what *not*) to do. These specifications ensure stability and continuity, making organizations appear to be immutable monoliths. Nonetheless, organizations are animated by people's activities, and they also must contend with pressures from the state and other organizations.

Ethnographic depictions of organizations as drivers have made important contributions to our understanding of how organizations shape and are shaped by people's activities. For example, through the participant-observation she conducted as an employee at a McDonald's, Leidner revealed how this fast-food restaurant embedded control in its division of labor, routines, and specialized machinery. By narrowing workers' and customers' choices of actions down to standardized, "idiot-proof" steps, McDonald's cultivated efficient processes and uniformity of outputs (1993: 72). While workers found this routinization monotonous and the workplace unbearably frenetic, they also found that routines offered protection from unusual customer demands. Similarly, in an ethnography of a high-tech firm, Kunda (1992) showed how managers wielded organizational culture, reinforced through trainings, meetings, and symbols such as slogans, to motivate employees to work long hours. While some employees relished the camaraderie cultivated by this strong culture, other workers, particularly those burned out by the company's hard-driving milieu, withdrew and criticized these practices as exploitative.

Since organizational ethnography excels at revealing the black box of organizing, its rich data contributes to our understanding of how organizations operate as actors vis-à-vis people, other collectives, and society at large. To form such an understanding, ethnographers can observe or undergo the experience of becoming a member, thereby gaining insight into how organizations acculturate new members. By making repeated observations, ethnographers document daily activities, as well as unusual situations such as disruptions by disasters or economic downturns, that can reveal shared understandings of how organizations work.

Organizational ethnographers also pay attention to seemingly inconsequential, taken-for-granted organizing activities. Researchers can start by identifying repeated instances of activities. Since most organizations have set routines, rules, and roles, these offer easy starting points for ethnographers to document. Ethnographers can also compare official structures against what actually happens, including members' rules of thumb, workarounds, and personal routines. In addition, ethnographers have access to moments when people collectively reflect on their organizations' efforts and aims. For instance, besides water cooler talk, after-work drinks, and online discussion, meetings are occasions when members and leaders talk about these issues. Through such venues, ethnographers can identify emergent organizing themes or dilemmas, including those that might never be resolved.

Like other ethnographers, organizational ethnographers enter the field with a particular research topic and question in mind. But they also must be open to reconceptualizing their research questions as they gather and analyze data; research questions invariably change once researchers realize that some or even all of their assumptions are incorrect or inapplicable. My research experiences attest to such recalibration. When entering the field, I aimed to document how a temporary organization initiated and shut down organizing activities. Once in the field, I realized that this research question was relevant years before, but that the Burning Man organization had recently passed that stage, with people working year-round to organize the annual event. Instead, my research captured a crucial turning point as the organization struggled to continue coordinating Burning Man. The organization faced various pressures to end or alter the event, including financial shortfalls, opposition by local organizations, and members' differing opinions about what to do. During multiple several-months-long stints observing meetings and trainings, I struggled to pinpoint what exactly I was studying.

With the richness of ethnographic data, a phenomenon can feel amorphous and ripe with a multitude of analytic possibilities. The danger is that an organizational ethnographer tries to describe everything and, in doing so, reveals nothing. Theories—existing ones or emergent ones—provide the hooks upon which ethnographers can organize the presentation and analysis of their data. With a theoretical orientation, ethnographers can fine-tune their research question and focus on certain, rather than all, aspects of their phenomena.

For my research, determining "what is this a case of?" was a long process of honing the appropriate research question. Burning Man's colorful, oddball aspects made it difficult for me, as a then-novice ethnographer, to discern the underlying phenomena. I spent much time considering what audiences and literatures my research addressed. Eventually, I realized that by studying an unusual, extreme case (Chen 2015), I could delve into various organizing challenges that confront most organizations, not just ones that produce yearly temporary communities. Since Burning Man members had to discuss organizing dilemmas and weigh organizing options more explicitly than they would have done in mainstream organizations, such issues were more visible for study.

Turning to organizational theories and prior organizational research, I broke my research down into organizing challenges, using the Burning Man organization to examine in-depth dilemmas that confront all organizations. In my book (Chen 2009), I focused on the ways the organization handled how to recruit and retain members, how to coordinate relations with other organizations, including ones that sought to suppress or exploit Burning Man for their own purposes, how to teach members unfamiliar norms and practices, and how to integrate multiple perspectives on the process of organizing. The Burning Man organization relied on collectivist or democratic practices, such as authority based on members' adherence to a collective mission, decision-making by consensus, and letting members choose responsibilities by interests rather than by skills and experience. These practices were intended to encourage members' input and engage their interests. At the same time, the Burning Man organization also incorporated bureaucratic practices, including a division of labor and hierarchy. In my articles, I examined how different groups within the Burning Man organization grappled with power and authority (Chen 2012c) and how leaders and members used storytelling to reinvigorate meaning, model unfamiliar norms, advance their interests, and connect with others (Chen 2012a, 2013, 2016).

To show readers how an organizational ethnographer can train her eye on organizations, I walk readers through several examples drawn from my field notes. In each of the following sections, I highlight how the ethnographic gaze can document and critically examine organizing activities.

Recruitment, Placement, and Training of Members

Manuals and other written materials document the designated procedures that organizations follow to recruit and place people into roles and prepare them to assume assigned responsibilities. However, ethnographic observations allow researchers to identify the otherwise implicit rationales underlying these procedures, as well as the practical steps of enacting these procedures. In particular, trainings and orientations are ideal observation points, as organizations most explicitly display their organizing structures and beliefs during these occasions. In these instances, people share illuminating details that animate procedures. For example, during a training of volunteer managers, organizer Harley Dubois explained her volunteer recruitment and placement philosophy as allowing newcomers to discover their interests, rather than guessing what their interests are or intervening in an overt top-down manner. She suggested, "Wouldn't it be best if you let people repurpose themselves? Let people screen themselves out . . . Let them decide that they're not right for the job." At another observed training for leaders of Burning Man offshoots, Dubois suggested adopting a long-term outlook by cultivating leadership from the rank and file. By watching volunteers in action, she identified "who would be a good candidate to watch" and stated, "I am going to groom them" for leadership positions.

Organizations, particularly established, relatively large ones, usually have routines for acculturating newcomers. By observing or undergoing training and orientations, ethnographers can gain insight into how organizations transform newcomers into members. During a training of Greeters, a group responsible for welcoming and acclimating arrivals to Burning Man, I recorded field notes while a volunteer nicknamed "Z" went over a paper handout. Summarizing the Greeters' mission as "greet, gift, gab, and guide," Z explained the importance of the first aspect for first-time Burning Man attendees: "The objective is to make them comfortable [and feel] welcome to the community." Similarly, at a Black Rock Rangers training, experienced Rangers shared tips that highlighted how they distinguished their roles as volunteer "community mediators" from those of law enforcement. Leaders showed how they had personalized their khaki-colored costumes with fun accents, and they also demonstrated how they physically positioned themselves—crouched, at eye level, and to the side, with hat and sunglasses off—during interactions with event-goers to elicit conversations rather than confrontations. Such observed efforts illuminated how people enacted their departments' ethos through interactions with others.

Participant-observation offers extended opportunities for ethnographers to experience such trainings firsthand and then try out the taught practices. In the field, "exceptions" to procedures allow researchers to probe members' understanding of how to handle situations. To illustrate this, I share an extended example from my participant-observations as a volunteer at Playa Info, a question-and-answer service located at the city's center. Playa Info's name came from the Spanish word *playa* for a seabed turned desert that periodically floods; besides referencing the event's physical locale, it aptly described the streams of people patronizing this service. For my shifts at Playa Info during the 2011 Burning Man, I joined a small crew of volunteers in the air-conditioned trailer housing the Found unit. Underscoring how its volunteers specialized in reuniting found items with their owners, Found deliberately dropped the first half of the expected "Lost and Found" name.

To orient me to my duties, "Lead Infomaniac" (members coined their own creative titles to describe their positions) Lauren Carly instructed me to read the laminated sign of steps taped to the wall and to return with any questions. The sign outlined three steps: (1) ask people to describe their lost item, coaching them as needed to elicit details that would help with identification; (2) do not allow people into the trailer to search for found items themselves; (3) hand unsuccessful item-seekers informational cards about how to search for items after the event. In a growing queue outside the trailer, people waited their turn to describe their lost items to attentive volunteers, who scribbled down notes for reference. Those in line had their own sign outlining what steps they should follow, which included the exhortation, "no whining."

Worried about expensive electronic items that lacked owner identification, I asked Carly what to do with items that could not be definitively confirmed as belonging to a particular item-seeker. She advised stating that an item fitting the description "is not present and to check back later." I soon learned the drawbacks of deviating from this procedure when I shared details about failed searches. One search ended with a bystander berating me for not allowing a sobbing woman to inspect a drained cell phone. Another search deteriorated with an item-seeker shrieking, "You gave someone else my iPod?" after misunderstanding my statement. After these experiences, I asked other volunteers about how they handled such exchanges, reaching realizations that would not have emerged from interviews or observations.

As this extended vignette illustrated, learning for both members and ethnographers continued through "doing," including making mistakes. Participant-observations offered opportunities—often through inadvertent missteps rather than calculated foresight—for ethnomethodological testing of collective understandings. Finally, while the observations I made documented interactions among people, these were oriented toward capturing my unit of analysis: the organization. I examined provided guidelines and interactions not because they reflected something about the involved persons or those situations, but instead because they helped reveal organizational rules and expectations, formal or informal.

Integration of Members' Multiple Interests

Most people are acutely aware of one major motivation for joining organizations: having to sell one's labor for a living. Nonetheless, the motivations for joining and contributing extend beyond instrumental considerations, as evidenced by the panoply of altruistic associations powered by volunteer labor. Moreover, even workplace organizations deploy an array of carrots, including bestowing honorifics and running contests that reward top performers, and sticks, such as removing privileges and public shaming, to encourage people to contribute. These all attest to how members enter organizations with their own interests and experiences, which may or may not coincide with their organization's aims. Ethnography is particularly effective at pinpointing how organizations juggle members' interests.

My observations underscored that Burning Man organizers were especially attuned to how they could accommodate members' interests, given the organization's and the event's dependence upon volunteers. For example, at a training session, Dubois recommended that managers talk with each new volunteer about his or her interests, as motivations differed among volunteers: "That's its own conversation, and it's complicated. Motivation is about one person." At meetings, people constantly discussed how to manage volunteers. For instance, during one such meeting, two organizers went over what motivated one longtime volunteer. They concluded that both the urgency of the project and matching his interests were factors in securing his valuable skills and attention:

MARION GOODELL: Sam [*name changed*] is random unless it's at the last minute; [then] he's the best firefighter.

MICHAEL MIKEL: He loves to do stuff that is fun for him.

GOODELL: ... He picks and chooses.

At times, organizers realized that volunteers could not always complete work according to the organizers' deadlines and standards. These difficulties prompted debates about whether organizers should pay people to increase accountability for certain tasks:

LARRY HARVEY: He works up to the deadline; he wanted to be independent... I'd temper criticism of Daniel [*name changed*]. In a way, he's almost a volunteer.

MARIAN: The problem is the accountability issue; he says he doesn't want money... Daniel is not the problem, but it is a problem with Daniel.

In other instances, organizers had to redirect members' activities. One year, a reporter wrote a letter to Dubois complaining about being hazed by a shift of overzealous Greeters who welcomed new arrivals by commandeering their cars as a "valet parking" prank. With this letter and similar accounts in hand, Dubois investigated and reprimanded those responsible, threatening to ban repeat offenders. At a meeting with other organizers, she noted the rise of such activities as "what happens when you get people empowered." She explained, "Things start to escalate; they [volunteers] get too into it." However, members did not always share or appreciate organizers' perspectives. Some complained that such introduced rules and guidelines were overly restrictive and ruined the event's free-spiritedness. The nicknames "The BMorg" and "The Borg," as aficionados and detractors called the Burning Man organization, and contention over how to organize departments and activities pointed to the tensions and ambivalence that people experienced in the day-to-day coordination of the event. These all provided rich data on how people conceived of organizing options vis-à-vis their interests.

Ethnography excels in revealing not only managerial understandings of the rank and file, but also members' collective understandings of their organization and the tensions among these different perspectives. In the Burning Man organization, the principle of self-expression and the organizational practice of decision-making by consensus allowed conflicts and disagreements to surface for discussion. Such understandings can also be documented in organizational silences (Anteby 2103); the absence of discussion or contention can reveal issues that are taken for granted. To fully do an organizational ethnography, it was essential for me to capture a range of perspectives, often on the same topic, from differently situated actors. The organization does not consist only of what its managers do or think. Instead, it encompasses coordinated and yet at times contradictory perspectives and actions. Understanding an organization means observing it across its variety of levels, and seeing how widely shared some perspectives are and how tensions among perspectives can create opportunities, as well as enormous challenges for organizations.

Deciding on and Communicating an Organization's Purpose and Activities to Insiders and Outsiders

Through their specified goals and practices, organizations narrow down choices of actions (Simon [1945] 1997). Nonetheless, even organizations that have well-defined missions and long-standing practices must periodically assess whether their activities and their goals match, particularly when considering new practices or expansion. Organizations also must constantly communicate their missions and efforts among their current and prospective members and to those outside their organization, including customers or clients, other organizations, media, and the state.

While interviewees can recall aspects of past discussions about organizing practices, especially when assisted by meeting minutes, emails, or other documents, they have difficulties reconstructing the nuances of such discussions from memory. Ethnography excels at capturing subtle distinctions as stances evolve, particularly during interactions among individuals and groups. At the Burning Man organization, discussion continually arose about whether proposed or ongoing organizing activities violated or upheld Burning Man's ten principles. At one meeting, organizers debated whether selling videos via a newsletter sent to event-goers violated Burning Man's value of decommodification. This discussion started with one organizer's acknowledgment of another organizer's skepticism of these sales.

MARIAN GOODELL: Crimson has a furrowed brow on this.

CRIMSON ROSE: . . . It seems like we're going forward towards selling stuff.

LARRY HARVEY [*pointing out that selling is not inconsistent with mission*]: We sell tickets.

ROSE: . . . Why would it [advertisement of goods] go into the newsletter?

HARVEY: I would like to get rid of the other stuff; I want to go marketing on the Internet.

ROSE: . . . We had this conversation that we were going to dump everything—"

GOODELL: . . . Juicy Danger has twenty videos left; he wants to know [what to do with them]. [Dave] Thorney [office manager] has pointed out that the fulfillment process is a burden.

MICHAEL MIKEL: Farm it out.

GOODELL: We should probably discuss it . . . Thorney should be on it [the discussion].

At the end of this exchange, Rose asserted that sales by the Burning Man organization were not about maximizing profits: "Us selling products is not about making big bucks." Such observations showed how members grappled with values and unveiled countervailing views about what people considered appropriate undertakings for their organization.

Organizational ethnography can also capture meaning-making at the individual and group levels. Using Ahrne's (1994) centaur metaphor, we can view an organization's members as part "individuals" and part "organization." Because organizations channel participants' activities within specific values and practices, people can act differently within organizations like Burning Man than they would in other contexts, such as the family or neighborhood. While researchers can capture some aspects of organizational meaning-making by observing discourse, other aspects are evident in circulated organizational symbols, such as logos, slogans, chants, informal traditions, and mascots, that are intended to unify members around a central, if not all-encompassing, identity. Within an organization, ethnography can further identify multiple subcultures, where groups have distinct languages, values, and customs that they use to differentiate themselves from other groups or even the larger organization (e.g., Martin 1992). This means that doing an organizational ethnography does not necessarily mean looking for unity or the things that are central to all aspects of the organization. Instead, researchers can also explore intra-organizational variation and difference in order to understand both the creative potential and points of fracture within organizations.

Field Negotiations and Struggles with Other Organizations

The preceding section segues into another aspect of organizations: no organization can operate as an independent island. Like people, organizations are embedded in a larger milieu: other organizations supply them with resources or acquire their outputs; competitors can take away their business, while cooperators can help sustain them; professional organizations disseminate norms; and the state regulates their activities. Organizational researchers are interested in understanding how organizations operate within their larger organizational fields. Ethnographies can vividly capture the dynamics of these relations.

These dynamics can appear in members' humor and self-reflection about encroaching rationalization. For example, at a meeting, organizers discussed having new members of the Department of Public Works sign liability waivers before they could camp at the "Ranch" while preparing the temporary streets and infrastructural service shelters for the event.

> MICHAEL MIKEL: Make sure that anyone else who comes to the Ranch signs a waiver.
> WILL ROGER: Remember, you can't sign away liability, just acknowledge risk.
> MIKEL: It helps...
> LARRY HARVEY [*joking*]: We're going to rename the Ranch "Waiver City."

Observations also offer a window onto how organizations view other organizations' goals and actions. At an observed meeting of organizers, Harvey fretted aloud that the media had the "potential to perpetuate lies and attract the wrong people. We feel we have a mission to [share with] the world, that's why we communicate." After the meeting, we paused to watch fifteen minutes of footage of Burning Man intended for local cable access in Reno, Nevada. After the video ended, viewers agreed that they could show this short documentary to their moms, as it lacked other documentaries' fixations on nudity and drugs that stoked what organizers viewed as sensationalist controversy. This audience applauded the clip's factual narration as journalism that supported, rather than detracted from, Burning Man's art and community.

In addition, observations can capture an organization's efforts to engage other parties. I draw on two sets of sequential meetings to illustrate how ethnography can reveal the way organizations manage relations with other organizations, particularly agents of the state. During interactions among agencies and Burning Man, Burning Man organizers recognized that each organization had its own interests and procedures. They proposed an alternative approach that incorporated multiple interests, rather than just deferring to an agency's pressures to accept their preferred practices. Ethnographic data documented the tensions that arose when organizations attempted to coordinate activities. In particular, observations captured how Burning Man organizers came up with "solutions" during their rehearsals of anticipated interactions with representatives of other organizations.

At a meeting, Burning Man organizers discussed the actions of agents from the federal Bureau of Land Management (BLM). This agency was responsible for overseeing the public lands that Burning Man paid a large fee to use:[4]

> DUANE HOOVER: There were a couple of incidents on Friday and Saturday night; the BLM sprung it. It was [BLM agent] Mike Bilbo's job, but he got stuck, so [another BLM agent] Barb Keleher had a ticket book [and patrolled] with two gun-toting BLM people. Every time they saw a fire, they would check the list; if it [the fire] wasn't on that, they would write tickets . . . They are bureaucrats.
> LARRY HARVEY: That will come up in the cooperator's meeting.
> HARLEY DUBOIS: We'll just make a list of junk.
> HOOVER: A definition of an approved burn, we have it on the list.

---

4. In 2015, the Special Recreation Permit fee for Burning Man was $3.6 million, exclusive of other costs.

> CRIMSON ROSE: Ranger Reed brought over [artist] Kal Spelletich and asked if he was ok, kept harassing them. If someone has a laminate [indicating that the person is an artist], leave them alone.
> DUBOIS: That is one more thing they have to do.
> HOOVER: With the BLM, we need to co-opt them.

At a subsequent meeting in Reno with the BLM and state agencies, Burning Man organizers raised the issue of monitoring and ticketing fires with the responsible agent:

> MARIAN GOODELL: Barb had a ticket book in hand and was being escorted.
> BARBARA KELEHER: It was not related to burn platforms [that protect the desert from burn scars] but art burns. I need items twelve hours beforehand. I saw twelve incidents and told people to move to burn platforms. The guys I was with didn't write a ticket.

Such exchanges revealed how organizations negotiated their interests and procedures. Keleher urged Burning Man to follow a bureaucratic process, thereby upholding her work protecting the land as a BLM agent. Her expectations of documentation and scheduling was counter to the spontaneity of bonfires; the Burning Man organization wanted to protect an artistic tradition that enacted the Burning Man principle of self-expression. While the people involved may have been able to generate interpersonal solutions, their positions within organizations made certain pathways more or less possible. Observing the interactions ethnographically allowed me to watch parties continually negotiate efforts during meetings, attempting to align inter-organizational activities with their respective missions and interests.

The Burning Man organizers were particularly cognizant of how state organizations were subjected to their own pressures, which in turn placed pressures upon Burning Man. In preparation for a town hall meeting with Burning Man supporters, organizers discussed how to address relations with law enforcement. Burning Man organizers acknowledged attendees' dismay at law enforcement's uniformed agents patrolling the event in Humvees, helicopters, cars and by foot. Nonetheless, Burning Man organizers wanted attendees to understand law enforcement's perspective, that local sheriffs and other officials had to assert their presence because of a widely circulated, erroneous news report of drug cases at Burning Man. Since the media coverage implied that Burning Man—and by extension, law enforcement—was permissive of drug use, officials had to demonstrate otherwise.

> MARIAN GOODELL: I need to talk in there with the why . . . the why is that the media reports seem to indicate that we are tolerant of drugs.
> LARRY HARVEY: We want to sympathize with them [law enforcement].
> HARLEY DUBOIS: Our next topic will go into that.
> ANDI GRACE [*reading the question*]: Why do the cops treat all of us as if we were on drugs? . . . It makes me mad that this is what Burning Man is all about.
> GOODELL: I'll talk about the mistaken AP [Associated Press] report of seventy drug cases a year.

At the town hall meeting, when answering a question about what to expect regarding law enforcement at Burning Man, organizer Larry Harvey made a finer distinction between drug selling and usage. Drawing on the Burning Man principle that encouraged decommodification, Harvey emphasized how Burning Man would cooperate with law enforcement regarding drug dealers.

> This comes down to communication. This probably comes from the idea that big drug trafficking [is happening at

Burning Man]. What dealers? This is a self-sufficient community. In the past, we had individuals or groups to try to empty drugs [at the event]. I have no problem with throwing them in jail. I have no patience with someone making thousands from selling drugs. We can talk to them and educate them, alter their perception; this could be a perception that we're letting drug trafficking [happen]. The war on drugs is not appropriate here.

Burning Man organizers also sought to educate attendees on how to interact with the media, which was eager to document deviance. As Goodell stated to attendees at the town hall meeting, "It's your responsibility to watch what you say to the media." During such discussions, the Burning Man organization highlighted the interplay of relations with the media and law enforcement, each of which had their own imperatives guiding their actions.

To understand the organizational field and how organizations navigate relations within the field, organizational ethnographers need to map the players. Once these players are identified, researchers can use observed meetings within an organization or inter-organizational gatherings to gauge their interests and their procedures. Weaker organizations—those who are dependent upon resources that they cannot procure elsewhere—are likely to concede to other organizations' demands for particular practices. In contrast, organizations like Burning Man, which have access to resources and the social capital to mobilize relations, as well as the motivation to defend interests, are apt to try other actions. They are more likely to openly challenge and contest other organizations, as well as propose alternatives that incorporate multiple parties' interests. One of the advantages of doing ethnography when studying organizations is the researcher's capacity to observe and compare "insider" conversations and activities within an organization and interactions with "outside" organizations, people, or groups. Understanding how organizations maintain their boundaries, as well as the alignment of or divergence between how they understand and act internally versus externally, is a key feature that organizational ethnographers explore.

Special Considerations for Organizational Ethnographers

To collect data, ethnographers enter organizations with a specific role defined by certain responsibilities and expectations. Some ethnographers assume a formal role as a paid employee, an intern, or a volunteer. Sometimes researchers may be enlisted to take formal organizational responsibilities, such as recording meeting minutes or constructing, administering, and analyzing surveys. Researchers may also offer or be asked to contribute other services to the organization—those requiring expertise, like grant-writing for nonprofit organizations, or even grunt labor—in return for access to their site. Managing these roles and responsibilities requires some finesse, to ensure that researchers can undertake their research (including observing organizations from multiple perspectives) and that organizations, particularly less resourced ones, get what they need. Since payment or salary for services can require accountability that may interfere with researchers' responsibilities, ethnographers must weigh the pros and cons of such financial arrangements.

In addition, organizations have a particular temporality involving workday rhythms. Capturing informal relations may require after-hours socializing at venues outside the organization. Some organizations follow project-driven cycles; Burning Man had its big event once every year, so organizers spent most months of the year ramping up for this endeavor and devoted the following months to recovering and assessing those efforts.

Finally, organizational ethnographers face a breadth versus depth issue. Particularly in large organizations, because of time constraints, an organizational ethnographer may be able to closely follow only one or two departments. A team ethnography approach can facilitate wider coverage of an organization and offer different insights depending on the researchers' positions and characteristics.

Conclusion

In the utopian community of Burning Man, organizing issues come to the forefront that are latent or taken for granted in conventional organizations. Organizational ethnographies impart insight into the puzzles of how to convince people to contribute to common goals and how to coordinate efforts that may or may not accomplish stated and desired objectives. In other words, members breathe life into their organizations through their actions, and their values and perspectives shape and are shaped by their organizations.

Most of this chapter described what organizational ethnographers do. I conclude by highlighting what specifically organizational ethnographies allow the scholar to see, as compared with other kinds of ethnographies. As before, I draw upon my own work as an example. If one studies just the Burning Man *event*, an ethnographer will observe many seemingly freewheeling activities, from spontaneous interactions among strangers to elaborate rituals at art installations. Yet without knowledge of the *organization* behind the event, at best she will just skim the surface of the rich variety of perspectives and actions that enable those activities to take place, as well as the dilemmas that shape and alter the event's trajectory.

What will she gain by doing an organizational ethnography? She will see the underlying organizational routines honed over the years, along with the experiments and mistakes made. She will also understand how organizers created the enabling framework for this event: by melding both bureaucratic and collectivist practices—modes of organization that often are considered antithetical rather than complementary—the Burning Man organization allows creativity to ferment.

In addition, she will gain a deep sense of different groups' struggles over power and authority. For instance, the organizational approach allows for a fuller appreciation of why the Department of Public Works parades its sunburned, tattooed, and dreadlocked corps on Mad Max–like art cars and construction machinery throughout Black Rock City for all to see. While at the event, she might run into representatives of the various governmental organizations involved with Burning Man. But without observing their activities preceding and following the event, she will not know how these interconnected actors attempt to regulate or redirect activities for their goals and interests, or how the Burning Man organization has parried these efforts to protect the mission of producing an artistic community.

In short, the organizational ethnographer captures the rich dynamics of the organization as an actor that interfaces with other organizations and shapes people's experiences. With organizational ethnographies, we take organizations as the fundamental unit of analysis. In doing so, we gain insight into how much of contemporary societal action is coordinated, and how many of our societal values are carried out, via organizations.

Acknowledgments

The author is grateful for comments and discussions with Howard Lune, Howard Mandiberg, Jacqueline Olvera, Celina Su, and Curtis Chan, as well as for comments from this anthology's editors and contributors.

References

Ahrne, Göran. 1994. *Social Organizations: Interactions Inside, Outside and Between Organizations*. New York: Sage.

Ahrne, Göran and Nils Brunsson. 2011. "Organizations Outside Organizations: The Significance of Partial Organization." *Organization* 18(1): 83–104.
Anteby, Michel. 2103. *Manufacturing Morals: The Values of Silence in Business School Education*. Chicago: University of Chicago Press.
Bowditch, Rachel. 2010. *On the Edge of Utopia: Performance Art at Burning Man*. Calcutta: Seagull Press.
Chambliss, Daniel. 1996. *Beyond Caring: Hospitals, Nurses, and the Social Organization of Ethics*. Chicago: University of Chicago Press.
Chen, Katherine K. 2009. *Enabling Creative Chaos: The Organization Behind the Burning Man Event*. Chicago: University of Chicago Press.
Chen, Katherine K. 2011. "Lessons for Creative Cities from Burning Man: How Organizations Can Sustain and Disseminate a Creative Context." *City, Culture and Society* 2(2): 93–100.
Chen, Katherine K. 2012a. "Charismatizing the Routine: Storytelling for Meaning and Agency in the Burning Man Organization." *Qualitative Sociology* 35(3): 311–334.
Chen, Katherine K. 2012b. "Artistic Prosumption: Cocreative Destruction at Burning Man." *American Behavioral Scientist* 56(4): 570–595.
Chen, Katherine K. 2012c. "Laboring for the Man: Augmenting Authority in a Voluntary Association." *Research in the Sociology of Organizations* 34: 135–164.
Chen, Katherine K. 2013. "Storytelling: An Informal Mechanism of Accountability for Voluntary Organizations." *Nonprofit and Voluntary Sector Quarterly* 42(5): 902–922.
Chen, Katherine K. 2015. "Using Extreme Cases to Understand Organizations." In *Handbook of Qualitative Organizational Research: Innovative Pathways and Methods*, edited by Kimberly D. Elsbach and Roderick M. Kramer, 33–44. New York: Routledge.
Chen, Katherine K. 2016. "'Plan Your Burn, Burn Your Plan': How Decentralization, Storytelling, and Communification Can Support Participatory Practices." *Sociological Quarterly* 57(1): 71–97.
Chen, Katherine K., Howard Lune, and Edward L. Queen II. 2013. "'How Values Shape and Are Shaped by Nonprofit and Voluntary Organizations': The Current State of the Field." *Nonprofit and Voluntary Sector Quarterly* 42(5): 856–885.
Clupper, Wendy. 2009. "The Erotic Politics of Critical Tits: Exhibitionism or Feminist Statement?" In *Political Performances: Theory and*

Practice, edited by S. Haedicke, D. Heddon, A. Oz, and E. J. Westlake, 251-267. New York: Rodopi.

Gilmore, Lee. 2010. *Theater in a Crowded Fire: Ritual and Spirituality at Burning Man*. Berkeley: University of California Press.

Hodson, Randy. 2001. *Dignity at Work*. New York: Cambridge University Press.

Khan, Shamus Rahman. 2011. *Privilege: The Making of an Adolescent Elite at St. Paul's School*. Princeton: Princeton University Press.

Kozinets, R. V. 2002. "Can Consumers Escape the Market? Emancipatory Illuminations from Burning Man." *Journal of Consumer Research* (29): 20-38.

Kristen, Christine. 2003. "The Outsider Art of Burning Man." *Leonardo* 36(5): 343-348.

Kristen, Christine. 2007. "Playing with Fire." *Leonardo* 40(4): 332-337.

Kunda, Gideon. 1992. *Engineering Culture: Control and Commitment in a High-Tech Corporation*. Philadelphia: Temple University Press.

Leidner, Robin. 1993. *Fast Food, Fast Talk: Service Work and the Routinization of Everyday Life*. Berkeley: University of California Press.

Martin, Joanne. 1992. *Cultures in Organizations*. New York: Oxford University Press.

Morrill, Calvin and Gary Alan Fine. 1997. "Ethnographic Contributions to Organizational Sociology." *Sociological Methods and Research* 25: 424-451.

Newman, Katherine S. 1999. *No Shame in My Game: The Working Poor in the Inner City*. New York: Vintage Books.

Ogasawara, Yuko. 1998. *Office Ladies and Salaried Men: Power, Gender, and Work in Japanese Companies*. Berkeley: University of California Press.

Pike, Sarah M. 2001. "Desert Goddesses and Apocalyptic Art: Making Sacred Space at the Burning Man Festival." In *God in the Details: American Religion in Popular Culture*, edited by E. M. Mazur and K. McCarthy, 155-176. New York: Routledge.

Powell, Walter W. and Christof Brandtner. 2016. "Organizations as Sites and Drivers of Social Action." In *Handbook of Contemporary Sociological Theory*, edited by Seth Abrutyn, 269-291. New York: Springer.

St. John, Graham. 2009. "12 Noon, Black Rock City." *Dancecult: Journal of Electronic Dance Music Culture* 1(1): 127-136.

Schwartzman, Helen B. 1993. *Ethnography in Organizations*. Newbury Park, CA: Sage.

Sherry, Jr., John F. and Robert V. Kozinets. 2007. "Comedy of the Commons: Nomadic Spirituality and the Burning Man Festival." *Consumer Culture Theory* (11): 119–147.

Simon, Herbert A. (1945) 1997. *Administrative Behavior: A Study of Decision-Making Processes in Administrative Organizations*, 4th ed. New York: Free Press.

Tomaskovic-Devey, Donald. 2014. "The Relational Generation of Workplace Inequalities." *Social Currents* 1(1): 51–73.

Turner, Fred. 2009. "Burning Man at Google: A Cultural Infrastructure for New Media Production." *New Media & Society* 11(1/2): 73–94.

Watkins-Hayes, Celeste. 2009. *The New Welfare Bureaucrats: Entanglements of Race, Class, and Policy Reform*. Chicago: University of Chicago Press.

Chapter 3

Macro Analysis

Power in the Field

LESLIE SALZINGER AND TERESA GOWAN

What does it mean to be asked to be the "standard-bearer" for a "macro" perspective? For researchers committed to challenging the hoary micro/macro binary, that is a complicated request indeed. Nonetheless, if to do "macro" ethnography is to act on the belief that, seen from any particular social location, there are structures that constrain, impel, and impress themselves on its occupants—then yes! For us, to be sociologists at all is to recognize the relational, scalar, power-drenched world of the social and to locate the people and fields we study in those structuring practices, relations, and discourses. In this context, ethnography emerges as a privileged method, one that provides a ringside perch on the processes through which subjects act and are made in the asymmetrical interactions of daily life.

All this suggests that one's "analytic lens" is not a methodological issue in a narrow sense, but an attitude toward one's data that reflects political and theoretical investments. For us, that means a primary focus on questions of power and domination, and on the possibilities of instability and critique. Given this attention to how hegemony is made—or not, macro analysis in ethnography focuses on the intense force fields between larger structures of power and the subjects they constitute, and who make them in turn. That is, we are interested in making manifest and understanding the interface between the self and discourses of subjectification, where the social—with its accompanying inequalities of power, access, and voice—is actually made in practice. As people move into action as social beings, their need for meaning drives them to make (or remake) sense of what they're doing, whether they take on hegemonic formulations or innovate their own frameworks. Thus, we take the processes through which meanings are made to be a primary focus of empirical investigation, in which we can see power relations being made and unfolding in real time.

There are of course many modalities of power, organized around varied intentions and understandings and backed by equally varied iterations of force, control, and knowledge. Too often, in analysis that takes the notion of structure seriously, capitalism and state power count as "macro," and formations of gender, race, and sexuality are lumped together with "culture" and read as "micro." This habitual framing misstates every element. Capitalism and state power are as much discursive as material, and gender, race, and sexuality themselves are material as well as cultural relations (Foucault 1975; Gilmore 2007; Omi and Winant 1994). These theoretical formulations lead us to methodological practices that always seek to situate observations in constitutive frameworks, in which discourse and selfhood are always within the frame. This does not mean that our field notes are full of vanilla interactions, to which we then simply apply distant Marxist, feminist, or Foucauldian frameworks. To the contrary, we seek to identify power as it operates in the field, focusing our ethnographic eye on those relations in practice and, only once they are identified, seeking to situate them in constitutive structures. Among other strategies, this leads us to prioritize comparison across both situation and subject, as focusing on meaningful practices across varied contexts makes it easier to grasp both the specificities of each case and the commonalities driven by discursive or economic forces shaping the field.

Our interest in how power works up, down, and through social space has led us to investigate not only the situations of those located lower down in society's many hierarchies, but the constitution of the forces they encounter as well (Burawoy 1998; Burawoy et al. 1991, 2000). In shifting our lens from those with less power (e.g., the homeless) to those with more (e.g., financiers), we are not alone. Since Laura Nader's (1972) prescient call for anthropologists to "study up," anthropologists, and increasingly sociologists, have begun to study the powerful. In recent decades we find sociological ethnographers in labs studying the development of knowledge (e.g., Latour and Woolgar 1979) and on trading floors studying finance (e.g., Knorr Cetina and Bruegger 2002), focused on understanding the workings of scientific and economic knowledge. What is striking about many of these works, however, is how little they discuss power. Our own aims in following Nader's call, then, are to undo the essentializing distance that has produced objectifying images of social forces, while retaining the broader question of social relations of power, thus locating these ethnographic descriptions of power in hierarchical social space.

In the following two sections, we turn to our empirical work, looking at subjectifying processes and fields of power up close. For an ethnographer interested in power, subjectification has a magnetic draw. As we move through the field, we pay close attention to the ways that people come to be the subjects they are in social space. How do they identify, whether explicitly or implicitly, across the varied social contexts, spaces, and moments they inhabit? What does this emergence and variety show us about the intimate, institutional, and cultural discourses and practices that summon them as particular kinds of subjects (Althusser 1971)? What kinds of interests—both near and far—might this local subject-making serve, and what are its intended and unintended consequences? In the accounts that follow, we show the process through which, in very different projects, we each investigate fields where discursive power addresses, forms, and bring subjects to life, and where subjects repurpose and reshape larger discourses in turn. And we demonstrate that ethnographic practices focusing on the relationship of self and context lead us out to structuring discourses and their obdurate material manifestations. These in turn bring us back again to subjects and daily practices, enabling the endless, hegemony-producing looping of power relations to be made visible.

The first of these sections focuses on subjects situated at the bottom of the power relations under investigation. The second section sees us both looking for more traction on how power itself is established within our respective fields of inquiry, and so in quite different ways we each turn our lens from the constitution and more limited agency of those on the receiving end of capitalist and governmental power to those who exercise those forms of power or who make up social universes whose power is felt far away. That is, as previously noted, we move from "studying down" to "studying up." However, we retain our focus on situating what we study vis-à-vis macro forces, thus limning the political culture of social inequality and grappling with the constitution of power as well as its consequences.

Constituting Subjects

To be a social actor requires social recognition, hence the fundamental polysemy of the noun "subject," with its apparently contradictory referents: object of study, object of power, agent (Foucault 1982). Much sociological research (e.g., surveys) comes late to the action, working with "subjects" whose identities are already established and interpreting outcomes within seemingly fixed and self-evident categories (e.g., race or socioeconomic status). However, here the ethnographer has an advantage, as she can watch identities as they emerge in social space, tracking the discursive processes within which subjects are recognized and constituted, and within whose logic they act on the world. Thus, the trick of fieldwork is to catch those subjectification processes in action, to identify the multiple addresses—in language and practice—through which intelligible subjects are made, and thus to delineate the mutating relations of power in which action takes place. In the brief descriptions below, we each take a core sample from a larger project to show that process as it unfolds, demonstrating the method of identifying discursive power at work in real time and space as an integral aspect of macro analysis.

Making Productive Subjects

Leslie: In the early 1990s, when I first entered the export processing plants (*maquilas*) that were to become the center of my first book (Salzinger 2003), I was interested in the gendered composition of the workforce: Why were men replacing women in certain sectors of the industry and not others, and what were its implications in production? However, my work as an ethnographer—immersed in the daily labor of production on the line, feeling the sharp and anxious eyes of supervisors, responding to the teasing, confessions, and competition of co-workers—brought me to a different set of questions about gender itself. Why did it feel so different for me to be a (young, US born) woman in some plants than in others? Why did masculinity and femininity look so different across plants located in the "same" cultural space? How were these meanings related to the striking quiescence of workers at three of my four sites and to the entertaining chaos of the fourth plant? And how was all this related in turn to the swashbuckling success of the maquila industry overall, with its skyrocketing efficiency and profits?

It was ethnographic immersion that brought me from the original question of workforce composition (workers as objects) to making workers (workers as subjects), from gender as a question of numbers to the question of gendered meanings, from taking "woman" and "man" as fixed categories to looking at their constitution in local process. The move to subjectification was not a move into "micro processes," however, but instead an attempt to understand that crucial border between capital and labor where working subjects are produced (or refuse such production), and thus where profits are ultimately secured or lost.

By my arrival in Juárez, shrinking global distances had long since unleashed a race for cheap labor that converged on a single desired object, the reputedly "docile and dexterous" young third-world woman, whose nimble fingers would build the circuit boards guaranteed to produce profits back home. In interviews and conversations throughout the city, managers expounded upon the virtues of a female workforce, composed of hires who were "by nature" inured to boredom and frustration and in need of only minimal wages. This structuring assumption, which I came to call the "trope of productive femininity," organized the mechanics of hiring and shop-floor production, as well as the laboring conditions of industry workers. However, over the decades since the industry's 1965 founding, managers' obsession with women workers had led to periodic shortages of not only female bodies, but feminine docility, as tight labor markets predictably undermined shop-floor compliance. Thus, by the early 1990s, although the desiring discourse about the predominance of women workers persisted, the gender composition of factory floors varied widely and some companies began to look farther afield for assembly workers.

To grapple with this fragmented production arena, I embedded myself on the shop floors of four maquilas from three production industries, working on the line, hanging out, and chatting with workers and managers alike. The plants proved to be sharply different social universes, despite their similar embedding in a transnational system of production and in the culture of Mexico's northern border, thus making it possible to investigate both local subjecthood and the specific discourses that produced those distinctive selves. In the TV production plant that I called "Panoptimex," sexy, self-conscious young women—trope come to life—populated the shop floor, models of productivity in every sense. Across town, in

"Andromex," a sterile hospital goods plant, masculinized men and women alike jockeyed for respect and remuneration in a highly productive fencing match with management. The last two plants I studied were both owned by the auto parts maker "Autoworld." "Anarchomex," a nearby plant, stood out for its shop-floor disarray, with catcalling young men and interested young women concerned more with each other than with quality indices and assuaging managerial frustration. And in Anarchomex's sister plant, "Particimex," three hundred miles to the south in "Santa María," responsible, avowedly "nontraditional" young women ran the shop floor, to the enthusiastic applause of their successful young Mexican managers. Comparison thus made structuring forces more visible, and these differences in turn became the project. Who were the gendered selves that emerged on each shop floor? What shop-floor practices, rules, and forms of address explained the specifics of their enactment? How did these management decisions relate to the unforgiving competition over profit margins that had established this corner of global production to begin with? What was it about the specific imperatives, contradictions, and tensions of production on each shop floor that led to local managerial discourses, and how did these in turn enable the idiosyncratic gendered subjectivities I found in each plant?

Of the four plants I studied, Particimex was perhaps the most surprising. A bright new building set alone amid *chile* fields, it owed its very existence to the problems I'd seen at Anarchomex, which managers at "Autoworld" headquarters attributed to their inability to obtain the docile maidens whose promise had enticed them to Juárez to begin with. The Santa María plant was thus their solution—greener pastures in every sense. But the plant I encountered was full of surprises. As the young, enthusiastic Mexican manager took me around my first morning, explaining the plant's innovative participatory team structure and "auto-control" mechanisms, I was struck by scattered groups of young women workers sitting around tables, chatting among themselves. Unlike workers caught chatting in other plants I'd seen, they made no move to return to work at our approach. To the contrary, they watched with open curiosity as we passed by, some calling out casual, first-name salutes to my guide, then returning to their conversations. "We're not traditional here," he commented pointedly. Wandering the shop floor a few weeks later, I noticed a woman packing finished goods—a job generally described as too "heavy" for women workers in Anarchomex. She explained that she was part of an all-women team, and team members wanted to keep it that way. They rotated jobs. "We had a man on the team . . . He just wanted to . . . order everyone around. We called him *el influyente*. He left . . . and we told the supervisor we want only women. We can do all the jobs." These internal practices had repercussions for how women workers discussed life outside the plant as well. A young woman speaking of being bossed around by her husband commented, "Here, really, they don't order you around. You are responsible for your own work, for what you do." A co-worker mused, "Maybe I won't get married. They [husbands] don't let you do anything . . . Now that we work here, we're different than before."

These assertive "nontraditional" versions of womanhood were surprising in a rural area in which the lives of these young women outside the plant were structured through the ritual of asking for permission to do almost anything, whether from fathers or young husbands. And they were especially surprising in a factory built for the express purpose of getting access to a conventionally docile female workforce. But I realized that they were part of a highly effective labor control system, in which rhetorics of empowerment drowned out discussions of low wages, and the plant reliably turned out some of the highest productivity numbers in the company worldwide. Given my interest in capital and profits, I couldn't but be struck by the contrast between Anarchomex's chaos and Particimex's acclaimed productivity indices. And as a scholar of gender, I couldn't help but wonder about its links with the unusually assertive versions of femininity I found on the shop floor.

So why here? To the frustration of the iconoclastic head of organizational development in Autoworld's Juárez headquarters, Anarchomex's US-born managers had categorically refused to try participatory management strategies, but then, they weren't prepared to work in Santa María either. On the other hand, not only were Particimex's Mexican managers willing to relocate, but, they told me, they saw these systems as enabling them to put themselves on the company map. In a large US corporation in which what they had to offer was their knowledge of "their people," participatory management leveraged that knowledge, highlighting their particular strengths for their sometimes dismissive US bosses. And in an American corporation in which they were always in danger of being lumped with local workers rather than US managers, gender became a terrain in which women could articulate their own modern difference from "traditional" Mexico, producing the surprising femininities I found at work on the Particimex shop floor.

Shop-floor subjectivities are inescapably local and particular, and as in any locale, they can be analyzed in isolation. However, to ignore the macro context in which they actually emerge—at the fulcrum of capital's attempt to create surplus value—would be to misunderstand their origins, their implications, and the many and complex roles they play. The assertive, invested, independent young women of Particimex stood out as a group, not only among the many maquila workers I had met in other plants, but against the background of daily gendered practices in Santa María as well. This ethnographic observation led me to seek explanations beyond local norms. Immersed in daily life in the plant, I found subjectifying discourses that emerged from a transnational structure whose origins were both distant—in global capitalist competition and in the offices of Detroit—and nearby—in the professional ambitions of their bosses and the shifting gender mores of the community of Santa María. The distinctively "feminine" subjects I found on the shop floor therefore made social sense only *within* these overlapping contexts.

The multiple power structures at play on the shop floor—of capital, US domination, and gender—thus become visible not because of some prior theoretical claim, but through the always interpretive work of ethnographic observation and its iterative analysis. As Cynthia Enloe (1990: 3) so concisely says, the basic feminist (and, I would add, sociological) question is, "how was this made?" It is in thinking about the idiosyncratic local subjects that ethnographic immersion makes visible and asking not just "who is here?" but "what are the forces in and through which they emerge?" that we can more fully grasp power's crucial constitutive edge.

Producing "the Homeless"

Teresa: As we shuttle between analysis and fieldwork, the challenge for the would-be macro ethnographer is to *let the field speak*—that is, to remain flexible enough to focus and extend the case in the most pertinent directions—without flying off in centrifugal chaos. A constant eye on subjectification and its effects helps us to hold the center, when other lines may be shifting.

Galvanized by the example of Leslie and other fellow Burawoy advisees, my study of homeless men in San Francisco opened with a macro extension to capital—namely, situating the increasingly ubiquitous homeless recycler with his shopping cart full of bottles within the return of large-scale informal labor produced by deindustrialization and the radical retraction of the social state.

Burawoy's (1998: 16) call to "begin with our favorite theory" has been characterized as imposing a theory-driven rigidity on field investigation that precludes "surprises" (Timmermans and Tavory 2012: 173). Yet as both a scholar and a teacher, Burawoy emphasizes theoretical reflexivity and flexibility with the motto "Be Bold, Be Wrong!"

No two cases are likely to be identical (Sayer 1984). If we initially brainstorm the academic and "commonsense" assumptions we are bringing to the field, subsequent anomalies will likely show that the case is on the move. "Wrongness" may lead us to modify or extend existing theory, but often, as in my case, this is not enough. Early on in a project, especially, our attempts to extend our cases meaningfully may propel us into new questions, theories, literatures, and, ultimately, sites. Here, I'll sketch this process drawing on a research crisis toward the end of my first year of fieldwork.

I had started out with some assumptions about dumpster diving as a "survival strategy" that would be experienced as stigmatizing. This turned out to be mostly wrong. While all sorts of very poor people collected bottles and cans for money, in San Francisco most prominent were a core group of "pros" who had created an intense web of meaning and pride around an activity they eagerly constructed as "work."

After publishing my first article, which described this construction of scavenging as a blue-collar job, I had the sense of following an increasingly obscure target. Limiting the context to the labor process and macroeconomics of the recycling industry felt increasingly disingenuous. The recyclers' routine was punctuated by comments to housed people that mobilized their work as evidence that they were neither criminal nor incapable. "I ain't hanging out, I'm resting!" "At least some people are working for a living." "It's good to know you are cleaning up the neighborhood." The crucial role of the work in stigma management was further underlined by men's conspicuous physical performance of the work, imperiously holding up traffic to roll their loaded carts across busy intersections.

As I adjusted to these messages and we started talking more about the experience of homelessness, some people said directly that psychic survival was as much at stake as economic rewards. "You lose that sense of getting through the days, that's the worst thing . . . With us recyclers, it's different—at least you are doing something and you can live with yourself," said a middle-aged Latino, Anthony.

If this "dirty job" was not only about the homeless getting cash but about surviving the master status (and social death) of homelessness, I was faced with tough decisions about how to extend my case differently, and eventually how to reconceptualize my sampling. If case extension is about moving beyond local processes to macro structuring forces, it seemed that pervasive cultural discourses about homelessness held enormous force over these men's lives. How was it that people on the street seemed increasingly molded as stock homeless archetypes, such as the withdrawn service recipient, the friendly panhandler as public character, the wily drug tout, and the pro recycler? Did entering such roles represent fleeting or lasting shifts in subjectivity?

"If you ain't here, you ain't no idea," commented Derick, an energetic, defiant African American in his early thirties, about his commitment to recycling. "So I got my hands dirty. Right, but I didn't have to deal with any bullshit poverty pimps to get my money; I've got my own. No police, no questions asked, no supervisor, no motherfucking workfare jacket."

Derick explicitly referenced both the carceral state (which threatened to reimprint the status of criminal) and the degraded social state or "poverty pimps," who would medicalize and individualize his poverty with their probing questions. And indeed, once I retooled my fieldwork around the more holistic questions of *what defined the experience of homelessness for different men, and how*, what seemed ubiquitous was wholesale criminalization and pathologization. As Derick suggested, the city's closely entangled punitive and welfare functions played a viscerally immediate role in their lives. Regular police clearances, with tickets for "camping" and other status offenses, corralled thousands toward the purgatorial shelter system, leaving the men constantly disrupted and on the defensive.

Whether trying to get shelter beds for more than a night, to retain General Assistance, or to keep out of jail, men on the street were endlessly burdened with "questions asked," demanding ritual excuses for indigence combining modest claims to "deserving poverty" with admissions of personal failings.

Within this messy field, overlaid by complex and sometimes conflicting images of criminality, mental illness, and drug compulsion, how might I draw together the most fruitful macro trails? Rather than sticking with favorite theories about labor informalization, I was led by my field experiences in the direction of a discourse analysis of homelessness, contextualized by the history and sociology of homelessness, criminalization, and poverty management.

My questions now turned on the ways men experienced homelessness on the street and in the poverty agencies. What new kinds of subjects were being made? To what extent did the pro recycling scene create an anomalous homeless reality, and how?

I developed a schema highlighting three institutionalized discursive logics constituting contemporary homelessness—sin-talk, sick-talk, and system-talk. Rooted respectively in criminal justice, the shelter system, and the radical advocacy movement, these discourses created different structures of coherence with antithetical causal stories about homelessness and potential solutions. Sin-talk summoned the twin strategies of exclusion and punishment to deal with "street people," sick-talk called for treatment for "multi-problem individuals," and system-talk turned the lens outward, demanding reform, or even transformation, of the broader society.

Methodologically, this turn entailed retooling both samples and sites. I continued to study men, given their separation from women, but went in and out of poverty agencies and other institutions with my street companions wherever possible. I broadened my sample on the basis of the working schema to include men who identified more closely with the strong agency of criminality or with the moral reprieve of disability and addiction, trying to keep a demographic breakdown roughly typical of the city's homeless population.

I found that the way men were "doing homelessness" led them to converge in different spaces, leading me toward new naturalistic samples, such as the self-identified hustlers of the Tenderloin skid row neighborhood—who refused to see themselves as victims and never used the language of "homeless" or "on the street," instead claiming the streets as their own turf. How different groups understood poverty and homelessness became key, but so did the gathering of intimate life histories, revealing the relationship between durable dispositions and the making of homeless subjects in the present.

In order to understand the making of the field, though, I needed to extend up through its institutional structures, grasping the larger processes producing, mediating, and culturally coding male homelessness. Here is not the place to recount that entire journey, but one point seems important to emphasize: the question of how far the macro extensions of my San Francisco case could be generalized.

We ethnographers are often quizzed about generalization. Our capacity to generalize from our cases depends, I argue, on the scale and character of the structural forces involved. For example, there are strong correlations between deindustrialization, economic depressions, and homelessness across the world. Of course, these are highly mediated across places and demographic groups by different social welfare systems, housing prices and tenure, the strength of kinship ties, and many more factors. However, in other aspects, far more uniform effects can be seen. For instance, during the middle to late 1990s changes in federal homelessness policy transformed shelter programs all over the United States. A general professionalization led by changes in federal funding stipulations shifted toward substance abuse counseling, changing the character of case management and consolidating sick-talk as the institutional lingua franca. As programs offered more services to clients in return for much deeper levels of compliance, substance abuse became the default "problem" for able-bodied people who could or would not offer other justifications for their homelessness.

Many men complained that the new programs assumed every able-bodied man was homeless because he was an addict. One skilled construction worker, Carlos, finally found some painting work only to be told, "Nuh-uh. No way. It's not work you need right now. You need to work on your recovery."

Carlos called me from the shelter, nearly crying from frustration. "I don't know what to do. They are going to kick me out the program if I take the job. It's so fucking stupid. [Wayne] is so sure that it's all about drugs, you know . . . 'You've got to work on your issues,' he says. All I know is, for me, work is a big fucking issue, the biggest. I came to this town for work, and this is the first decent work I find, and they won't let me stay in the shelter if I don't go to fucking AA every day." Carlos was about to blow. "Jesus Christ, it's like, it's like all the change has got to be you. You're the asshole, everything thing else is just fucking dandy. Well, maybe it's not that simple!"

The shelter's focus on substance abuse and other "sick-talk" meant that Carlos's admission to some cocaine use (in common with many successful tradesmen and professionals) foreclosed his "system-talking" attempt to maintain his identity as a carpenter, firmly constituting him as a "street addict."

As a "macro" ethnographer, I could have continued to focus on the political economy shaping Carlos's experience, highlighting his subaltern position in the trades as a man of color, then following his increasingly desperate migration coinciding with regional construction busts starting in the East. This story was well worth telling, but given that I was deeply embedded in various street scenes, it made more sense to explore the *erasure* of such a way of seeing across the whole homelessness industry. By turning from political economy toward the institutionalized discourses that generated radically different constructions of extreme poverty, the project settled into a different kind of macro.

Fixing Power in the Gaze

In the first half of this chapter, we explored the constitution of subjects subordinated by capital and state power. However, such analyses too easily reify those impinging structures, imagining a set of relationships between thinking subjects as a geometric edifice that operates beyond human reach. This is both inaccurate and politically unhelpful, as it suggests a kind of power immune to intervention or even critique (Gibson-Graham 2006; Salzinger 2004). For an ethnographer, "studying up" is one way to short-circuit that objectifying dynamic, to get more traction on the constitution and operation of dominant structures as well as their consequences. In different ways, we have each taken on that challenge, looking to describe from up close some of the structures that shape the world we inhabit. That is, rather than studying the constitution of only those whose agency is most circumscribed, in this section we describe ethnographies focused on subjects who themselves make up structures of power with far-reaching implications.

Spinning Nationality into Capital

Leslie: Shortly after I finished the fieldwork for my maquila study in 1994, the peso collapsed and the entire Mexican export-processing industry went through one of its periodic restructurings in response. Looking up from the shop floor, I decided my next project should turn from production to finance, from those constituted by the vagaries of capital to the traders who made up the market itself. From that thought to the research itself was a long journey, but in the early 2000s, I began fieldwork on the New York and Mexico City trading desks of "Globank," a major, US-owned transnational bank that dominated peso/dollar exchange.

Seen from the vantage point of the maquila sector, foreign exchange markets were an external force, shifting the conditions under which production occurred with breathtaking speed and finality. However, viewed from up close, from the perspective of the Globank trading desks, these same markets are themselves made up of individual agents, every move a gesture in a cultural field defined by economic assumptions, national and corporate goals, market norms, and tropes of appropriate masculine, national, and "professional" (i.e., disinterested) performance. That is, the market itself is made of these discursively produced gestures; although the agency of individual traders is of course sharply circumscribed, there is no pre-social "market" to which they are added: they *are* "the market." Thus, traders are both cogs in and producers of a discursive structure with formidable consequences beyond their own realm. To take a macro approach to studying up in this context, then, is to document the many structures that impinge on specific sets of traders in specific market locations—domestic economies and politics; workplace-level incentives and hierarchies; Forex market norms; discourses around masculinity and appropriate forms of national affiliation and professional distance—and to document their consequences for the exchanges that emerge. In so doing, we can begin to limn an economic "force" (Burawoy et al. 2000) we more typically view from afar.

Between 2001 and 2006, I did six periods of ethnographic research, ranging from two weeks to three months, on peso/dollar exchange bank trading desks in New York and Mexico City, spending most of that time in Globank. On trading desks in both cities, I sat next to any trader willing to put up with me for the day, chatting, questioning, being teased, taught, and lectured, writing and writing, and then jumping out of the way whenever a trading rush hit. Here I will focus on a single locale, Globank's Latin American "emerging markets" desk in the United States, as its function as the administrative hub of Globank trading desks throughout the Americas makes the complex and asymmetric power relations that typify the market easier to spot. For similar reasons, I will concentrate on a specific set of interpellatory discourses within that locale—the reiterated citation of nationality and its unmarked other, "professionalism"—as nationality threads through the market, linking traders' personal identities to the national objects they trade and making visible the power relations that structure both. The descriptions to follow thus demonstrate how ethnographic observation of the way subjects turn up in social space, attuned to the pressures and invitations within which that occurs, can illuminate both local processes and their consequential links to cross-cutting discourses around nationality, workplace hierarchy, and market power.

The "New York desk" is in lower Manhattan, a cramped island of eleven young, mostly Latin American men. The group's small size belies its outsized reach. The desk is the fiber optic hub for currency exchanges that ricochet across the United States and Latin America, and sometimes across the globe. Linked directly to Globank offices in all the major Latin American capitals, this group trades many millions of dollars a day, in constant internal interaction, not only with their multiple screens and with each other, but in real time over open mics with their compatriots in branches throughout Latin America's major cities. At every moment, they live and function at the nexus of transnational and national space.

Globank's "comparative advantage" in these markets is the access to information provided by its local trading desks throughout Latin America. However, local trading desks are far away and can be mired in "local viewpoint." This was made explicit when a Globank economist told me flatly, "Local treasury may be reluctant to go short because they've got to live there." So how could they leverage that local knowledge, that privileged access to information, without having to pay for it in inconvenient allegiances and sensibilities? The New York desk is Globank's answer to that question: populated by traders circulating up from "home" offices for several-year stints, work on the desk provides on-the-job training in "objectivity" in the trade, cultural performance in the rich social life surrounding it.

Globank's New York traders work for a transnational corporation, live outside their countries of origin, speak fluent English, and are casually, unthinkingly mobile. That is, they are precisely the sort of rootless global elites so frequently invoked by academics (e.g., Castells 1996) and media alike. Except, in practice they are not. Watching them over time on the Globank desk revealed that they constantly indexed nationality in daily interactions. This, I soon realized, is because they are hired *as* Mexicans or Brazilians, expected not to erase their nationality but to use it to financial advantage.

Effective trading in these markets requires the capacity to read between the lines in political developments and find information in a context where asymmetries of access abound. Latin American traders are frequently the first to hear rumors of impending shifts and shocks in their own country's currency. New York traders' relationships with those back "home" and their commitment to returning make these information flows possible.

Access to information is only part of what nationality brings. Being Latin American itself is a kind of currency, and although most of the traders' English is flawless, Spanish marks boundaries. A Latin American salesman, annoyed at the spreads provided by the lone Anglo on the trading desk, says loudly to his client in Spanish, "It's a gringo who's giving us those prices. The Ecuadorians, the Mexicans, they all give us good prices." The other traders laugh approvingly, despite the fact that they *agree* with their colleague's pricing. When an Anglo salesman complains to an Ecuadoran senior trader that he doesn't understand a conversation just forwarded to him, the trader yells across the aisle, "It's emerging markets! Learn Spanish!" Although the financial heart of electronic transactions is always written and confirmed "professionally," that is, in English, I'm struck, as I look over shoulders, at how Spanish marks technically unofficial conversation. This is where the market's lifeblood—news, rumors, gossip—flows, and this is where allegiances are cemented and rifts marked.

The nationality claimed here is also a prized cultural object. When I tell Diego I'm planning to go to Globank in Mexico City, he answers in English, "You'll like it . . . It's very 'folkloric.'" What it is not, however, is an expression of either material stakes or political belonging. For one thing, the New York–based traders' pay comes in dollars. The Brazil trader makes explicit the effects of these practices as I push him on how he feels about the persistently falling Brazilian currency. "Sure, if I were being paid in reales [I'd worry]." He shrugs. By pulling Latin American traders out of their countries of origin and paying them in dollars, Globank gets access to their local expertise, without having to worry about countervailing personal interests.

All this is part of the active constitution of an appropriately market-oriented attitude among traders whose friends, families, and futures lie in the countries whose currencies they trade. Discussions on the desk and in meetings are packed with critiques of home governments and jokes at their expense. Over time, I'm especially struck by the unusually harsh treatment meted out to a young trader up from Brazil for a training visit who keeps betraying an inappropriately citizen-like concern for Brazilian policy. All month, the other traders school him, correcting not his assessments but the vantage point from which he makes them. One day he makes clear that he disagrees with the substance of some new policies at home, not because of the way they affect his position in the market, but as someone who has to live with them. The room is uncomfortable, and following him out after the meeting, Diego, uncharacteristically brusque, tells him he talked too long. Later they hear the Argentine president is threatening to resign. "Is that good or bad?" he asks. "Are you flat?"[1] "No." "Then it's bad."

Focusing on the discourse of nationality as an ethnographic object allows us to look at one slice of the three-dimensional space that is the global foreign exchange market. Discourses of national identity, produced both inside and outside the bank, interpellate traders, who use those discourses in turn not only to make money but to make the market itself. Far from obliterating national identity, participation in Globank reconstitutes it in productive terms, sidelining political issues and bringing cultural tropes to the fore, allowing Latin American traders to use knowledge and connections, with feeling!, without being weighed down by conflicting interests

---

1. "Flat" is a market term signifying that a trader does not have a speculative position in the currency he's trading. In this case, not being flat meant that the trader was financially at risk if the Argentine peso collapsed.

or distracting loyalties. On a daily basis, they perform a market in which "culture" produces affiliation and alliance but "professionalism" enables buying and selling "Mexico" without reference to the lives lived within the country itself.

Pace economists' descriptions of currencies as self-evident objects of speculation, it takes a particular kind of social actor—one who is simultaneously engaged enough to be knowledgeable while disengaged enough to literally sell his [sic] country short—to make such a market function. Studying these exchanges up close makes it possible to demystify their operations and reveal their cultural underpinnings. At the same time, locating these subjectifying processes in institutional structures of transnational capital reveals the connections between these cultural processes and power and inequality more broadly, thus linking culture to political economy. Ethnographic immersion, sensitized to the question of power and politics, can illuminate the quotidian practices through which elite, (re)nationalized selves make a market, and thus identify a crucial site and set of processes in which a "developing nation" is transformed into an "emerging market" and a country is made into a commodity, for sale like any other.

Manufacturing Addicts

Teresa: As I witnessed numerous homeless men without serious drug or alcohol problems being placed by default in mandatory substance abuse groups in San Francisco, it became clear that they could stay in the primary "transitional housing" available to them only if they accepted the addict label and entered highly disciplinary residential rehabilitation facilities. An emerging professional consensus was compelling poverty agency staffers all over the country to read successive waves of dispossession purely in terms of addiction and mental illness, and their academic counterparts were now producing more work on "the homeless" and their personal pathologies than on poverty and inequality.

When time came to design my next large project, I aimed straight for what seemed to be a central engine of this "medicalization" of poverty, the rapidly expanding world of court-mandated drug rehabilitation. This time, I wanted to get deeper into the constitution of a field itself, and thanks to my collaboration with Sarah Whetstone and several others, I was able to gather a treasure trove of both field notes and life history interviews across several sites.

If processes "live in relations," argues Matthew Desmond (2014: 565), "then studying them requires a dynamic approach, abandoning the group or place as the locus classicus of ethnographic exploration and taking processes themselves as the fundamental units of analysis." To what extent this strategy means abandoning long-term personal or spatial intimacy depends, of course, on the chosen process, but Desmond argues for tracing social process through new contexts, knitting together diverse spaces and agents.

Our project unpacked the process of a new temperance crusade among (and against) the poor that has taken off over the past twenty years through the archetype of the "criminal addict." Rather than hold tight focus on one place or group, we moved through a set of institutions in which this iconic subject is locally identified, disciplined, converted, and punished. In other words, rather than staying with one group or site and using subjectification as a productive launching pad for extending the case, we took a key modern subject—the criminal addict—and followed the ways that subject was constituted, looking far "up" into crucial national policy shifts but focusing the ethnographic research "across" a field of governance. Even more than insured rehab, strong-arm rehab "succeeds," even in the short term, only with a minority of clients. We retained a strong focus on how the subjects of these interventions themselves took up (or refused) this identity in different ways—strategically, passionately, reluctantly, or creatively, turning it back on itself.

From the jail and city drug court we pursued the clients into the strong-arm rehab we called Arcadia House, which serves as one of the primary sites of subjectification for court-mandated clients. Another key site was Victory Ministries, Arcadia's powerful evangelical equivalent. Like other conversion-based rehabilitation facilities, Victory Ministries had steadily expanded in size and influence since the various changes in federal law known as Charitable Choice (1996–2000) started to promote government contracts for faith-based social services and drug treatment. Here we shifted laterally again to fieldwork in the churches that provided their performative outlet and much financial support. Finally, we talked to former clients trying to launch new lives, sat in on the AA meetings that reinforce recovery discourse and community post-treatment, and studied the experience of the "sober houses" (both AA and evangelical) that have become a primary source of cheap housing for single adults. In what follows, I focus on one part of the process—the attempted creation of the criminal addict through the collaboration between drug courts and strong-arm rehab.

The war on drug users and dealers has been a primary driver of the threefold increase in the US prison population since 1980, incarcerating many for the first time and steadily increasing the flow of angry, often traumatized men and women from what are often already troubled families and communities. Over the past twenty years, public worry about the expense, harshness, and volatility of this strategy of social control has swelled, giving rise to renewed interest in mandatory rehabilitation. The response has been the explosion of drug courts, which operate on the principle that those charged (or convicted) of drug crimes should give up their rights to due process in favor of "therapeutic justice." Based on the idea that individuals are incapable of acting in their own interest (by stopping their illicit drug use) without the criminal justice system's involvement, drug courts turn defendants into clients, with the entire legal team (including both prosecutor and defender) working with the judge and treatment personnel to provide a supportive, firm, and consistent message. Clients are usually sent to residential treatment, but most end up under the harsh discipline of what we call strong-arm rehab, rehab for the uninsured, which emphasizes excising criminality (Gowan and Whetstone 2012).

In the dull wood and beige of the drug court, Donnie, an African American man in his late twenties, was called to the bench. His short braids fell back from a high forehead over bright eyes and a narrow mustache, his light voice and vivacious style at odds with an oversized sweater with large orange and navy stripes. He slouched against the lower shelf of Judge Paak's bench, but valiantly threw himself into the heavy banter characteristic of court appearances framed around "doing okay."

> JUDGE PAAK: How are you doing, Donnie?
> DONNIE: Doing okay, doing good! Like the sweater? [*He smiles goofily up at the judge.*]
> JUDGE PAAK: Any time you're wearing a sweater it's a good day! [*Forced laughter all around.*]

The judge asked the counselor for an update. (In fact, the more significant team discussions and decisions about clients were all made prior to the court session, in backroom consultations where the treatment staff's assessment most strongly determined the outcome.)

> COUNSELOR: He's been back almost a week now. He's doing pretty good. Last week he had a few behavioral issues but he's on track, doing all right. [These "issues" were typically minor, such as eating food in a room where food was not allowed.]
> JUDGE PAAK TO DONNIE: So do you know what happened last time and what's gonna be different this time?
> DONNIE: Oh, *everything's* gonna be different . . . I'll take it *one day at a time*. Evidently *I can't do it on my own* so I asked my brothers and my peers for help.

JUDGE PAAK: You've got it in your head. I hear you say it, so you can use it.

Hindsight is 20/20, and in the light of Donnie's relatively quick abandonment of the program after this episode, his performance feels less than wholehearted. He made an unorthodox differentiation between "brothers" and "peers," which marks a refusal to fully enter Arcadia's color-blind "family" construct. And despite Paak's encouraging statement that now he had "it" in his head, Donnie appeared on the edge of satirizing this same received wisdom, claiming total renewal all over again (only one week after returning from the street), then stringing together one clichéd AA motto after another. Yet performing these lines was in fact what the theater of drug court demanded, and the clients knew that the line between performing and mocking the script was fine indeed. Indeed, "Fake it till you make it" is a motto of its own, speaking to the uncertain place between force and consent, between going through the motions and the slow distillations of those new motions into habit.

Yet there is no doubt that Donnie had learned how to "talk the talk" to some extent. The first priority in Arcadia is to get clients to take on the identity of the criminal addict. In a typical exercise comparing and contrasting addicts with sober people, clients called out that addicts were "selfish, greedy, manipulative, monstrous, dirty, irresponsible, and arrogant." Sober people, on the other hand, were canonized as "selfless, giving, accountable, lovable, clean, responsible, and humble."

Strong-arms like Arcadia are not in the business of saving people from damaged aspects of themselves, but of making brand-new people. Backed up by criminal justice, they required the intensive reprogramming of behaviors and attitudes, not rehabilitation but "habilitation." *Re*habilitation would imply the preexistence of a socially adjusted adult, whereas "criminal addicts" needed to start from scratch, acquiring the disciplined behavior and life skills that they had never learned. This project allowed very limited attribution of honor or rationality to the pre-recovery persona, and statements to the contrary were inevitably interpreted as "stinking thinking," a sign of the addict who had not been transformed.

It was mostly the African American clients, generally the least drug-dependent in reality, who were paradoxically the targets of the most confrontational makeover attempts. Young African American Lamar reflected:

> Sylvia threatened to make me wear some rainbow suspenders because she says my pants are too low. Stupid shit . . . When I went to jail I got treated better than this.

Anchored by the diagnosis of criminal addict, Arcadia staffers slipped easily between biological, therapeutic, moral, and ultimately racial-cultural frames. Given Sylvia's focus on the tightness of Lamar's belt, it's not surprising that Donnie and Judge Paak emphasized the wearing of the sweater in the court's treatment theater.

"The bus to prison is always waiting," the counselors would tell the Arcadia men. "It's right outside your door." And indeed, some weeks after the "sweater" day Donnie returned in cuffs and an orange jumpsuit. With a beatific smile he assured a stern Judge Paak that no, he did not want to return to Arcadia but would rather serve out the rest of his sentence in jail.

"You understand that you are done with drug court and are now doing straight time?" asked the judge.

"Yup," Donnie grinned quickly, his former slouch and ingratiating jokes a distant memory, along with the ill-fitting stripes. He radiated electric energy, feet apart and shoulders square. "Straight time."

Donnie was evidently unconvinced, but the project of becoming a new subject seemed to resonate with some of the clients. Those who stayed the course duly learned to present themselves as new people. Cory, a white methamphetamine user in his early twenties, told his "brothers" that he was trying to leave behind his "criminal-thinking mind": "I never want to be my old self again, because that was my demon self."

For the minority who graduated and stayed sober, a cohort heavily skewed toward white men, the makeover continued to feel worth it. "You just gotta take it, and take it, and take it, till you start to get it," said Steve, a white forty-five-year-old who had lost his livelihood as a city parks worker to his alcohol and cocaine use.

Jimbo, a white man in his mid-forties who had been sent to Arcadia after doing some time on a weapons charge, insisted that for him the turning point had been calm advice and the promise of family, rather than severity.

> Counselor Mike takes one key from his hand and drops it in the other hand, and he says, "You know the key is gonna fall. And the more you do it, you know that . . . that you're gonna get the same outcome. Sobriety is the same way. The more you do it, the better your life will get." And then I [Jimbo] was like, Wow, that makes sense . . .
>
> It wasn't sitting on the bench [which combined public humiliation with solitary confinement], because I already did all that bullshit from the military. You can beat me, you can stick me out there and do push-ups all day and say whatever you're gonna . . . But it was the little things that really helped me."

Jimbo had spent his teens on the street stealing and selling sex, and the next decades crisscrossing the country, in and out of the military and precarious jobs, haunted by alcoholic bingeing and sudden rages. He had never found peace in regular family situations, and Arcadia's (and AA's) promise of an alternative family structure became increasingly compelling. Jimbo had now been living at Denham halfway house for an unusual six years, firming up the habits of peaceful sobriety with the help of AA, Wicca, and learning the guitar. Like other successful graduates, Jimbo expressed gratitude that "the system" had forced him into serious treatment, commenting that his military background helped him deal with the harsh discipline.

While a minority of clients of mandatory treatment struggle through into new sober lives, well over half disappear before the halfway mark, walking out or kicked out. Yet in the process of cycling between precarious employment and poverty management institutions saturated with strong-arm's "criminal addict" construct, even the recalcitrant learn to present themselves as well-meaning but helpless creatures in strong need of firm external discipline. They simultaneously learn that pointing to experiences of chronic unemployment, racial discrimination, poverty, and isolation represents "not taking responsibility." Within the increasingly hegemonic construct of poverty as (criminal) addiction, I learned that the word "structure" means only one thing. Far from being a vital concept for critical analysis or critique, it refers to the bridle that substandard Americans "need": necessary systems of accountability enforced by the muscular state or the low-wage labor market.

The Necessary Politics of Macro Ethnography

So what does macro analysis mean for ethnography? Like Andrew Sayer (1984: 122), we take the social world to be inherently complex, each research site a node within an infinitely open system riven by all sorts of flows of economic, discursive, and institutional power. Sure, each scholar has to choose a focus for her research, but too much bracketing of larger-scale power relations mutes the vitality of the sociological imagination. In order to understand power in the fluid, multi-scalar way that the great twentieth-century theorists teach, "micro" and "macro" have to be understood as linked by and infused with cultural structures "all the way down" (Geertz 1973: 28–29), whether our terminology centers on discourse, racial formation, hegemony, heteronormativity, or governmentality. For us, a good ethnography should explore at least some of these flows.

For many years, Burawoy's version of the extended case method has come to stand for macro within US ethnography, sometimes with respect, sometimes as caricature. Both of us continue to value it as a framework that highlights the social as a dimensional space and that places power and social critique at its center. Like many scholars who have engaged productively with this work (e.g., Eliasoph and Lichterman 1999), we give cultural structures a more central place than earlier iterations that focused more narrowly on political economy. However, the perennial potential for both capital and the state to throw ordinary people's everyday lives into crisis has been demonstrated yet again over the past decade, as the 2008 financial crisis nearly brought down the world financial system, leaving massive food and housing shortages in the global south and increased unemployment, debt, and precarity everywhere (Desmond 2012; Weinstein 2014). At the same time, the United States' long turn toward criminal justice as the foremost principle of and institution for the social control of poorer Americans has been met with successive waves of revolt, from Occupy to #BlackLivesMatter, inspiring sociologists to maintain vigorous engagement with both those "on the ground" (Haney 2010; Rios 2011) and those in more powerful locations, such as city lawyers, police captains, and leaders of prison guards' unions (Beckett and Herbert 2009; Page 2011).

Both the above-mentioned crises and the multiple social refusals and revolts they have engendered suggest the continuing centrality of power to any form of social analysis. They also make clear that power always lies both beyond and within any site we study. Yes, some of the processes of domination that shape the field are beyond the view of the ethnographer (and often of the participants). However, vital strands of power related to these "external" structures run through all of life, as powerful or hegemonic discourses, as ingrained practices, and sometimes, indeed, as overt moments of economic domination or authoritarian despotism. As ethnographers, our aim is to make these strands visible and to draw out their links to larger structures.

Perhaps because the increasing political and economic polarization of the past few decades has made elite power so evident, ethnographers are increasingly not content to study consequences but have turned instead to "studying up" (Nader 1972)—to focusing directly on power itself. Yet this has proved to have its own pitfalls. For instance, a project like Leslie's, in which she spent informal time over a long period with elites, creates a powerful temptation to "go native." After all, Leslie is more like an elite trader than she is like a maquila assembly worker! The general expansion of economic sociology and science and technology studies motivates highly educated middle-class intellectuals to do fieldwork with people with whom they have a lot in common (e.g., Beunza and Stark 2004). In some cases they gain rare intellectual recognition and financial rewards from the field itself.

Given that sociology's political traction has shrunk in tandem with declining commitment to the social state and the regulation of capital, such enticing conditions tempt us to lose critical distance and to underplay power relations altogether (especially as domination is usually the least popular topic among powerfully situated field informants!). However, in the current conjuncture, it is more essential than ever that ethnographic work at the managerial and elite levels remain truly macro, attuned to the complexity of subjectification in a world where those with more privilege tend to have bigger, better selves and to be oblivious to the ways that their "smartness," dynamism, charity, or autonomy may be predicated on the helplessness, drudgery, or routinization imposed on others (Sherman 2007). Ethnography has a long tradition of empathy for the subject, which has often flowed seamlessly into sympathy for the "underdog" (Gouldner 1973). In the context of "studying up," however, it is all the more important to separate the ethical and political, avoiding the seductions of becoming "traditional intellectuals"

(Gramsci, Hoare, and Nowell-Smith 1972: 5–23) for the market or punitive state.

Of course, the notion of studying "up' or "down" feels rather crude in a post-Foucauldian academy. "Up" seems to imply simply more raw power, and "down" its endpoints or results, with "culture," or the workings of race and gender, relegated to the everyday. In practice, many ethnographers seem to be doing away with this divide (e.g., Haney 2010; Mahmood 2011). Leslie details the on-the-ground production of purportedly traditional gender hierarchies in the maquilas, and Teresa the individualization and medicalization of poverty within homeless shelters and strong-arm rehab. In such cases, the everyday practices of middle-class professionals, whether in factories, social services, or the legal system, play a vital part in developing or maintaining projects of intimate control and productive power. In so doing they indeed serve various "higher-up" imperatives to increase productivity or pursue new disciplinary targets, but they also draw deeply, in specific ways, on the existing patterns in which race, class, and gender work to mark bodies and constitute subjectivity.

To further complicate the picture, the workings of power are often unstable or unpredictable. People fight domination in all sorts of ways, from refusing eye contact to flipping dominant discourses, from working slowly to building large-scale social movements (which become power structures of their own). Ethnographers, like other scholars, are now more likely to theorize agency as a new form of subjectification than as pure "resistance" (e.g., Mahmood 2011). The women of Particimex claim new dignity and autonomy, but at the same time help their managers achieve record productivity. But we could equally write the sentence the other way around. The limited dignity and autonomy allowed within one setting may break new boundaries in others, and new possibilities may emerge, sometimes even revolutionary ones.

Whether we are studying authoritarian settings or social movements, subjectification—the making and remaking of people under different social conditions, the meaning that they make of these conditions, and the action that ensues—should be a core analytic of ethnographic investigation. And given that we all live within complex global webs that interweave economy, culture, politics, and ecology, it makes sense to extend our cases where the lines of connection are most charged for the lives of our participants and those they affect. When working with people experiencing oppression, ethnography should not just serve as a field guild to the exotic, but follow these charged lines of connection "up" and "out" into linked structures of domination. Similarly, work within sites or fields of privilege should trace how privilege is made and exercised—by extending the case to implicated others near and far (e.g., Sherman 2007).

Subjectification isn't the only form that power takes, of course. A drone dropping a bomb on a wedding party, a sudden layoff, a cancer due to asbestos exposure—such disasters are not fundamentally discursive. But the strength of macro-oriented ethnography lies in its ability to see the processes whereby meaning is created, becomes power, and sets humans in action. This means that, for us, all micro is inherently macro, and vice versa. We look for the most interesting and important ways that people's lives are being shaped by hegemonic projects and assess the success or failure of this subjectification. Or we travel up lines of power to take apart the constitution of social "forces" (Burawoy 1998: 15–16), excavating the ways that the small day-to-day practices of those in powerful locations make, shake, or break the life worlds of the rest of humanity. Sometimes we do both. Whatever the case, we center our research within a multidimensional and "macro" vision.

References

Althusser, Louis. 1971. "Ideology and Ideological State Apparatuses (Notes Towards an Investigation)." In *Lenin and Philosophy and Other Essays*, edited by L. Althusser, 127–186. New York: Monthly Review Press.

Beckett, Katherine and Steve Herbert. 2009. *Banished: The New Social Control in Urban America.* Oxford: Oxford University Press.

Beunza, Daniel and David Stark. 2004. "Tools of the Trade: The Socio-Technology of Arbitrage in a Wall Street Trading Room." *Industrial and Corporate Change* 13(2): 369–400.

Burawoy, Michael. 1998. "The Extended Case Method." *Sociological Theory* 16(1): 4–33.

Burawoy, Michael et al. 1991. *Ethnography Unbound: Power and Resistance in the Modern Metropolis.* Berkeley: University of California Press.

Burawoy, Michael et al. 2000. *Global Ethnography: Forces, Connections and Imaginations in a Postmodern World.* Berkeley: University of California Press.

Castells, Manuel. 1996. *The Rise of the Network Society.* Cambridge, MA: Blackwell.

Desmond, Matthew. 2012. "Eviction and the Reproduction of Urban Poverty." *American Journal of Sociology* 118(1): 88–133.

Desmond, Matthew. 2014. "Relational Ethnography." *Theory and Society* 43(5): 547–579.

Eliasoph, Nina and Paul Lichterman. 1999. "'We Begin with Our Favorite Theory . . .': Reconstructing the Extended Case Method." *Sociological Theory* 17(2): 228–234.

Enloe, Cynthia H. 1990. *Bananas, Beaches & Bases: Making Feminist Sense of International Politics.* Berkeley: University of California Press.

Foucault, Michel. 1975. *Discipline and Punish.* New York: Pantheon.

Foucault, Michel. 1982. "The Subject and Power." In *Michel Foucault: Beyond Structuralism and Hermeneutics*, edited by H. Dreyfus and P. Rabinow, 208–226. Chicago: University of Chicago Press.

Geertz, Clifford. 1973. "Thick Description: Toward an Interpretive Theory of Culture." *Culture: Critical Concepts in Sociology* 173–196.

Gibson-Graham, J. K. 2006. *The End of Capitalism (as We Knew It): A Feminist Critique of Political Economy.* Minneapolis: University of Minnesota Press.

Gilmore, Ruth Wilson. 2007. *Golden Gulag: Prisons, Surplus, Crisis, and Opposition in Globalizing California.* Berkeley: University of California Press.

Gouldner, Alvin W. 1973. *For Sociology: Renewal and Critique in Sociology Today.* London: Allen Lane.

Gowan, Teresa and Sarah Whetstone. 2012. "Making the Criminal Addict: Subjectivity and Social Control in a Strong-Arm Rehab." *Punishment & Society* 14(1): 69–93.

Gramsci, Antonio, Quintin Hoare, and Geoffrey Nowell-Smith. 1972. *Selections from the Prison Notebooks of Antonio Gramsci*. New York: International Publishers.

Haney, Lynne A. 2010. *Offending Women: Power, Punishment, and the Regulation of Desire*. Berkeley: University of California Press.

Knorr Cetina, Karin and Urs Bruegger. 2002. "Global Microstructures: The Virtual Societies of Financial Markets." *American Journal of Sociology* 107(4): 905–950.

Latour, Bruno and Steve Woolgar. 1979. *Laboratory Life: The Social Construction of Scientific Facts*. Beverley Hills, CA: Sage.

Mahmood, Saba. 2011. *Politics of Piety: The Islamic Revival and the Feminist Subject*. Princeton, NJ: Princeton University Press.

Nader, Laura. 1972. "Up the Anthropologist: Perspectives Gained from Studying Up." In *Reinventing Anthropology*, edited by D. H. Hymes, 284–311. New York: Pantheon.

Omi, Michael and Howard Winant. 1994. *Racial Formation in the United States: From the 1960s to the 1990s*. New York: Routledge.

Page, Joshua. 2011. *The Toughest Beat: Politics, Punishment, and the Prison Officers Union in California*. Oxford: Oxford University Press.

Rios, Victor M. 2011. *Punished: Policing the Lives of Black and Latino Boys*. New York: New York University Press.

Salzinger, Leslie. 2003. *Genders in Production: Making Workers in Mexico's Global Factories*. Berkeley: University of California Press.

Salzinger, Leslie. 2004. "Revealing the Unmarked: Finding Masculinity in a Global Factory." *Ethnography* 5(1): 5–27.

Sayer, Andrew. 1984. *Method in Social Science: A Realist Approach*. London: Routledge.

Sherman, Rachel. 2007. *Class Acts: Service and Inequality in Luxury Hotels*. Berkeley: University of California Press.

Timmermans, Stefan and Iddo Tavory. 2012. "Theory Construction in Qualitative Research from Grounded Theory to Abductive Analysis." *Sociological Theory* 30(3): 167–186.

Weinstein, Liza. 2014. *The Durable Slum: Dharavi and the Right to Stay Put in Globalizing Mumbai*. Minneapolis: University of Minnesota Press.

Chapter 4

People and Places

DOUGLAS HARPER

Ethnography was first thought of as the in-depth study of a definable space, where the researcher develops deep relationships with the people she or he is studying. Ethnographers participate; they observe; they speak and listen; and to some limited degree, they gain the perspective of their research partners.

In the meantime, ethnography has come to mean many things: studies of what Marc Angé (1995) called "non-places," studies of the abstract experiences of neoliberalism (e.g., Greenhouse 2012), studies of disembodied human interaction carried out in the digital world (e.g., Underberg 2013), or autobiographical stories (e.g., Adams et al. 2014), to name a few examples from a very broad literature. I remain committed to the original conception, at least in terms of studying talking, snorting, farting people in a specific place—that is, one with rocks, grass, and human constructions. It is not the only kind of ethnography, but it has been my emphasis and is what I shall talk about in this essay.

Ethnography originated in social anthropology in the era of Malinowski, and in sociology during the 1920s at the University of Chicago. Malinowski (1961) spent nineteen months between 1915 and 1919 doing ethnographic fieldwork among the Trobriand

Islanders to produce *The Argonauts of the Western Pacific* and several subsequent books based on this fieldwork. The sociological ethnographies done at the University of Chicago also involved close observation, in-depth interviewing, and immersion with one's subjects and locales, producing a spate of books and an enduring tradition.

For several decades, the Malinowski-style ethnography was the rite of passage for a PhD in anthropology. In sociology, ethnographic studies became a less consequential but always vital part of the discipline.

In this essay I look backwards at my research, in the spirit of the original definitions of ethnography. More than most ethnographers, I concentrate on small numbers of people who become central characters in my ethnographic narrative; in fact, in two instances (*Good Company* and *Working Knowledge*), I focused on single individuals in the contexts and cultures surrounding them. To varying degrees, these studies allowed me to write and photograph nuanced portraits of the people I studied. Because I worked on most projects for several years, I came to see the people who inhabit my ethnographies in deep and complex ways, with contradictions showing and dreams revealed. I sought to understand them in terms of their actions, motivations, and beliefs, but also in the context of history, economy, legal systems, and other structural forces that influence their lives. More simply: I sought to write and photograph the idiosyncrasies of individual persons in relation to the sociological forces that provided the context of their lives, honoring both dimensions of social existence. That said, the more time I spend with people, the harder it is to fit them into tidy social types or explain the regularities of their behavior solely in terms of abstract mechanisms.

"Place" is also a crucial factor in all the studies I've completed. Places have traditions that might come from climate (Bologna, where I studied food culture, is so hot and humid that only a soft wheat grows there, which influences every aspect of the way Italians from that region define their food) or from particular forms of urban life. Homeless men so typically inhabited certain parts of cities that for decades these regions had their own name, "skid row." Willie, a mechanic I studied, depended on the "looseness" of a rural northern environment with a very low population density to work as he wanted to. He could never have gathered or used materials as he did in a regulated urban scene, and in fact he had chosen to live in this isolated place precisely to be "under the radar" of the bureaucracies he wanted to avoid. The men in the halfway house where I recently filmed are almost all from very poor neighborhoods that are also oddly isolated due to urban development policies and patterns of industrial deterioration. Their addictions cannot be reduced to these places, but they can be understood as a natural part of the deep alienation that comes with that turf. These are but a few of the ways "place" figured in my ethnographies.

The challenge in focusing on "people and places" is not to get lost in a hyper-individualized portrait of a person or locality, but to ground each of these in sociological themes that the people and places develop, and that develop them.

There are also wonderful opportunities afforded by focusing on people and places. It is an excuse to abandon the arid language of sociology and embrace description, emotion, and detail. Photographs, for me, become meaningful not as the adjunct of words but as a way to communicate nuanced meanings. My orientations and skills pointed me in the direction of people and places; doing so had both intellectual and artistic rewards.

Place in Ethnographies

Once, the *place* of ethnography was a village or a neighborhood; that has changed. In his book *Ethnography through Thick and Thin*, George Marcus (1998) argues that the traditional sites of ethnography—the isolated village or small community—are disappearing, and to keep ethnography relevant, its focus must expand to the modern world system and relationships between the center and periphery. Ethnography must become *multi-sited*. Traditional forms of knowledge are also increasingly influenced by world media (and, in the meantime, traditional forms of communication are increasingly supplemented or replaced by the digital). As a result, the isolated, "pure" community or the village is simply not as relevant as it once was. People leave the village for the center, often continents away; cultures blend and adapt. Thus, the ethnographer must follow.

I believe that, despite all this change, there remains a justification for the original formulation, an ethnography situated in place, focused on humans making culture.

Place in the Practice of Ethnography

"Place" is integral to the very idea of ethnography. The assumption is that deep knowledge of situated social practices, beliefs, behaviors, and rituals reveals insights into comparable situations in different settings, and ultimately that they show what culture is and how it operates. One of the best-known examples is Geertz's (2005) study of the Balinese cockfight. The fifty or so cockfights that Geertz observed took place in one of several tiny lots in a small village: social action located in a handful of square feet, moved throughout the villages to avoid police raids. Geertz learned how the cockfights, including the betting that surrounded them, were organized, performed, and experienced. Geertz argued that "attending cockfights and participating in them is, for the Balinese, a kind of sentimental education" (2005: 83); from deep knowledge of place-bound cockfights, Geertz created a theory of Balinese culture-in-miniature. Of course, for Geertz *place* served as the backdrop for his more central analysis of ritual. But it was integral to the analysis and reminds us that social action is indeed emergent from specific and defined locations.

The Place of Tramps

Understanding place and culture was crucial in my ethnographic studies of the tramp (Harper [1982] 2015). The project began when my anthropology professor James Spradley invited me to make photos for a follow-up of his study *You Owe Yourself a Drunk* (1969). At first my photographs were about *place*, the skid rows where homeless men congregated and lived.

I photographed these neighborhoods (primarily in Boston, but also New York and Minneapolis) for a hundred or more days over fifteen months. Most American cities in the post–World War II decades had similar regions with similar establishments: greasy-spoon restaurants, single-room-occupancy hotels, flophouses, missions, pawnshops, daily employment centers, and woebegone bars and liquor stores. I photographed the human casualties I found there against the background of the material dereliction of these urban spaces (figure 4.1).

As my involvement in the project deepened, Spradley encouraged me to make it the focus of my graduate studies. Thus, in my first year of graduate school I spent two weeks without money living on the same homeless streets I had photographed, during a frigid mid-February, as an assignment for a fieldwork course. I stayed in a mission in a rough Boston neighborhood that housed over four hundred men, and wandered the streets during the day, learning the routines that produced food, relative safety, and shelter.

From this experience I came to see the skid rows as *places of failure*. Most of the men were alcoholics and their lives were in steep decline. From my brief experience I sensed little communication among the men I met aside from the sharing of commonsense survival strategies.

The *place* of homelessness changed its meaning when I traveled with tramps in the American West over the next three years. The tramps were, by external measure, the same as the skid row men—that is, homeless, largely unconnected to families, and with a

FIGURE 4.1

Homeless men on Skid Row, circa 1970

complex relationship with alcohol. But the *place* represented by the hobo "jungles" and the freights was entirely different from the skid row neighborhoods I had seen. Tramp routines were about movement, mastery, and even adventure. Who, indeed, does not love a trip and all it promises? Thus, after two summers of short trips and preliminary work, I set out on the trains from Minneapolis toward the apple harvest in the Pacific Northwest and "buddied up" with a tramp who was coming down from a several-week drunk. The boxcar was his place to dry out and re-sort his life, and it was also the setting of our momentary relationship on the road. The tramp, Carl, master of the tramp culture, at first treated me as a clueless acolyte. He taught me how to handle the trains and how to deal with uncertain characters and, more important, how to be in a tramp relationship: how to keep one's distance while becoming close; how to be trustworthy; how to move on when it was time.

I think the freight train ride was to the tramp what the cockfight was to Geertz's Balinese. It was vividly real, dangerous, and unforgiving, and it was complicated. But more fundamentally, it was the symbolic universe through which the tramp defined himself. Men on the freights sorted themselves into status hierarchies, including tramps, home guards, riffraff, and jack rollers (etc.), and this was based on how well they managed their alcoholism, their gear, and their own physical being—whether they were as clean as one could be on the trains—and, critically, whether they would join a bottle gang to get drunk when wine was brought into the car. In all these ways, the tramp negotiated the possibilities that announced his selfhood: a member of a culture the men identified with in a very strong way.

Tramps and trains had a near mythic role in American history, and it was a history that they knew and celebrated. One day in western Montana my companion stood in a boxcar door pointing at a family traveling comfortably in a Winnebago, close to the train as the highway paralleled our tracks. To Carl their comfort on the road was un-American, but his rough experience on the road was not. Tramp workers, after all, had ridden freights to the intermittent, difficult, and dangerous jobs in logging, mining, and other frontier industries a hundred years before. Through this arduous process the freight car had become a place of identity, rooted in history and vividly real (figure 4.2). In Geertz's language, the train rides were a text; and the fact that the tramps spent hours of most days in the company of others, retelling their stories and listening, comparing and judging the others around the jungle fire, made the texts alive and meaningful.

It was also the case that because the then extensive sociological research on homeless people was centered on skid rows (the only *place* where homelessness was imagined), there were no studies of the railroad tramp in the literature, and thus no understanding

FIGURE 4.2

A tramp named Strawberry atop a flatcar, Western Montana

that homelessness could have the cultural reality that I described. Most studies of homelessness were based on surveys: researchers found captive audiences on skid rows; clients were often coerced into filling out questionnaires by mission or social service staffs, and the researchers retreated to their homes and safe communities after their research activities were completed. There was very little actual ethnography in the early studies of homelessness,[1] and I came to see that it was the missing but necessary corrective. Thus, I entered the tramps' cultural places and asked, at first, simple questions like "How do you find the train, avoid the police, tell when a rider is a thief?" Later, I asked more open-ended questions about

---

1. In the meantime, that has changed; now ethnographers of homelessness are common, if uneven in quality. A recent masterpiece of this literature was written by Teresa Gowan (2010), a contributor to this volume.

life histories and cultural norms and practices. Entering the places occupied by the tramp meant giving up of the security of home for the field, destabilizing my own sense of security in order to be open to what I was learning. It offered an understanding of place from the point of view of the tramp, and I learned how grounding their identity in these places—as opposed to the marked "places of failure" (e.g., skid row) occupied by traditional homeless populations—enabled tramps to reject the stigma associated with vagrancy, if not the label of vagrant altogether.

In the years after I completed my field research, the material basis of the tramp culture completely changed. By and large the tramps' work shifted to others or disappeared; when I wrote the second edition of the book, I queried orchard owners in the region where I'd worked as a tramp, and the response was unequivocal: tramp workers had been replaced by Hispanic families. Other dangerous or undesirable work previously done by tramps had been assumed by illegal immigrants recruited into the sub-proletariat via informal labor pools.

The tramp and the skid row alcoholic were produced by and dependent on various *places*: small neighborhoods in pre-gentrified cities and jungles in rail yards tolerated by rail police, freight trains themselves, and work situated in places where workers had to arrive and depart on schedule. Both cultures—of the bum and the tramp—were lodged into place and could be understood only if they were situated in relation to these places, not just in relation to larger structural forces.

Clearly, place is not central to all ethnographies, but an awareness of its potential meaning is always useful because all social action is emplaced somewhere. Places are often the center around which identities, social relations, meaning-making, and routinized interactions orbit, and so even if one decides to study something like "culture" or an occupation or "social role," one would do well to locate it in places that are bound to matter for how it is instantiated. Places often embody tradition and culture in ways that encourage certain kinds of interactions and social relations and discourage others.

Place on the Farm

I now reflect on meanings of place in an agricultural community composed mostly of dairy farmers. In this study (Harper 2002), *place* was a neighborhood consisting of 120-acre farms that had remained nearly consistent in size from their settlement to the historical moment I studied. I was interested in how these farms were revolutionized by new technologies, farm practices, agricultural culture, labor availability, and changing rural communities of post–World War II America, and how the change inaugurated in that era was further revolutionized by a second stage of technological and social revolution that I was seeing in the 1980s.

The culture of farming had originally been based on families who took care of animals (primarily oxen and horses) that pulled implements for planting, weeding, and harvesting crops, as well as cows, sheep, chickens, and other animals that provided food. The *place* of farming implied a system of labor, technology, family structure (gender- and age-based division of labor), and also, crucially, forms of shared work the farmers called "changing works" (a term I used for the title of my book). This was not by choice; agriculture was defined, and one can say limited by, the tools by which it was done. By the end of the nineteenth century, the first stage of machine-powered mechanization had occurred; a few decades later, tractors and other gas-powered machines initiated an inexorable transition to the modern systems.

I studied this history as a neighbor. At first the farmers were exotic strangers; I saw them on their massive tractors and waved from the road; they waved back uncertainly. As I watched them working the land, I wondered about the history of this particular soil and the implications of that history for the future of farming and rural communities. It took several years and several research strategies to turn my interest into an ethnographic study. I first worked unpaid for a neighbor for several weeks to experience farmwork close up; I later did photo elicitation interviews with elderly farmers with photos made in the era when they were young (post–World War II). I completed a survey of forty-eight farms immediately contiguous to ours and visited each of those farms for follow-up interviews and daylong visits. I also photographed agricultural work for several years from eye level as well as from a small airplane I hired to fly me over the farms in order to gain a structural view of contrasting agricultural systems and practices (figure 4.3).

The history of this study seems methodologically haphazard at first glance. But it reflects my evolving orientation to the same question—that is, how had people created agriculture on the same

FIGURE 4.3

Family farmstead from 2,000 feet, St. Lawrence County, New York. The degree to which the farm has industrialized is shown in the layout of the buildings

pieces (*places*) of land? My first instinct was to "become" a farmer as I had briefly become a tramp, but I quickly saw that was both impossible and, I am chagrined to say, not very interesting. Several days atop a huge tractor pulling big machines across the land did not attract me to the insider experience. My first interviews with farmers about the "meaning of land" also fell flat on their faces. The "land" was too general, too abstract. Only when I discovered the old photos and encouraged farmers to remember their own experiences in circumstances similar to those depicted did the study come alive. Finally, through the twists of fate, I met sociologists at Cornell who encouraged me to contextualize my understanding with a quantitative survey, which provided a frame for the entire study. The final project included elements from each stage of these efforts.

I began the fieldwork in 1980 and published the book in 2001, and while I did not work on it the entire time, it was an ongoing internal conversation. I realize it is daunting to imagine keeping a project alive for this amount of time, but this was real-life ethnography, merged with my personal life and several other projects. It should also reassure young ethnographers that the back burner is always there, and often the best soup is that which is simmered.

When I studied farming on this local place, I learned that the earlier system had balanced land, animals, technology, and labor and had produced interdependent communities. By today's thinking, the agriculture was incredibly inefficient, requiring a great deal of human labor. Crops grew at the same rate as weeds, and if there were no herbicides they had to be removed by humans wielding hoes. Cow, pig, and chicken manure had to be removed from barns with rudimentary tools and spread on fields with horse-drawn spreaders of the small first-generation tractors. Hay was cut by hand, and a skilled worker could cut only a few suburban-yard-sized fields in a day; harvesting grains (oats, wheat, and corn) required several people working together. What was remarkable, however, was that with all the human labor, the caloric input required to create food was roughly equal to the output, and the new systems based on chemicals and gasoline-powered machines required vastly more caloric energy than they produced in food.

The old system was inefficient by the measure of food produced per acre and human effort required, but the land was physically nourished and cared for. The ratio of animals (cows, sheep, pigs, and chickens) to acreage was such that farm production of manure was about what the typical acreage of a farm needed for soil replenishment. In the past, farmers knew each field and its idiosyncrasies and potential, and ploughed and harvested in attentive and informed ways; now farmers are typically far too busy to see or experience the land that is the basis of the system. "Land" (place) went from living dirt to an input in a cost/benefit analysis.

With this technological change came new forms of social relations. Long-term, face-to-face associations among farmers (embodied in the "changing works" crews that drew upon the labor from about seven farms) gave way to solitary time on a powerful tractor or in a milking parlor where cows were, in one farmer's words, reduced to "teats and feet" (figure 4.4). It was very unusual for farmers to visit or experience the lives of their neighbors. It is not a stretch to say that farm life, celebrated by the elderly farmers I interviewed as they viewed photographs made in the post–World War II era, had been joyful because it had been collective, but it had evolved to the kind of alienated life often associated with cities. Their neighbors were now mostly strangers, interacting with each other through formal contracts rather than custom and friendship.

In this transition, the farmers' relationships with animals and the land itself had also been transformed. In the old system, farmers kept cows for up to twelve years and knew them individually (and made breeding decisions based on their personalities as well as their milk production); in the new system, cows were milked hard for a year or two before they were slaughtered to become fast-food hamburgers. Their lives were brutal and short in the modern free-stall barns, where they were rarely if ever allowed the natural pleasures of pasture.

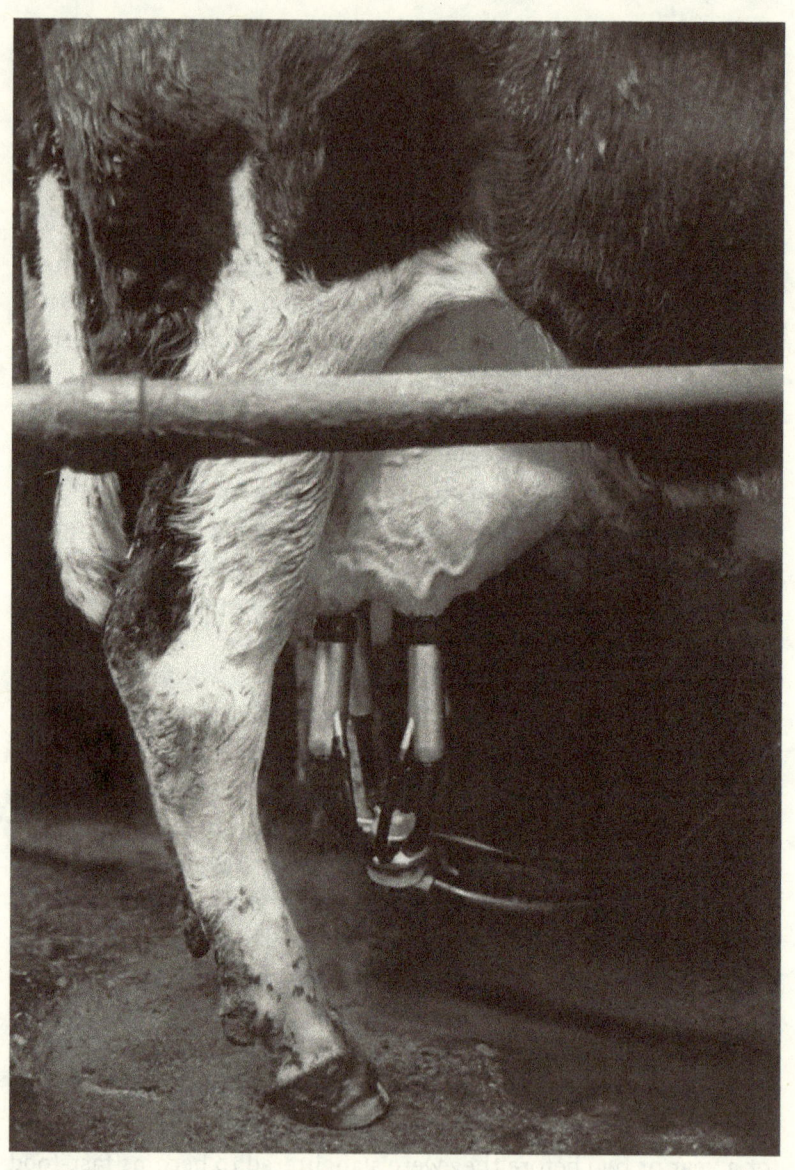

FIGURE 4.4

"Teats and feet," the cow as experienced on an industrial farm

In the case of land, a farmer told me that in his earlier life the land had been alive with natural nutrients supplied in manure and straw; it was plowed to avoid erosion and planted with rotated crops to rest and restore the land. Now, he said, the land was a reservoir holding seeds, insecticides, pesticides, and chemical fertilizer, abused by huge tractors, and generally treated as inert and even dead.

In terms of this essay, *place*, in this case land itself, is a site of culture, where people act in collective and mutually understood ways because they are motivated by shared meaning and values. The land stays the same as the human actions change, and as new forms of work and technology replace the old, new values and meanings emerge.

The neighborhood I studied in northern New York resembled agricultural regions in several parts of the United States where the climate, crops, and animals were similar. It was a case study of one type of agriculture in a large and varied agricultural landscape. But however different these regions and their agricultural systems were, at least some of the general features I noted—attitudes and practices relating to land, chemicals, technology, community, and animals—were likely found to one degree or another in virtually all farms of industrializing, rationalizing hyper-capitalist America.

I don't think until I volunteered to write this essay that I realized how grounded all my ethnographies have been in place: my coauthored book on Italian food (Harper and Faccioli 2009) was a study of the food system in and around Bologna, a region with a tradition of growing food, creating recipes, and following customs for eating that reaches back more than a thousand years. For example, the soft wheat that grows around Bologna will fall apart if worked with spaghetti presses, but there have always been chickens—thus, eggs plentiful enough to mix with pasta dough ... and presto! *sfoglia* (dough rolled into sheets) that is cut into the rich pastas of that rich land. Willie's shop in *Working Knowledge* (Harper 1987) was a tiny lot off a forlorn back road, but his work made possible the work of neighboring farmers who were scratching out a living in their own marginal places. And so on. Beginning with the study of agriculture, I began to use aerial photos to understand culture, and in assignments now I ask students to frame an aerial photo using Google Earth of a *place* where they grew up that had special significance for their socialization, development, and identity.[2] The results are often remarkable. Identifying a *place* with an aerial photo demarcates boundaries in which culture, biography, and lifestyles were defined and experienced.

So despite our understanding that culture appears in "non-places," in digital interaction, virtual communities, institutions, and other non-placed settings, these do not make a serious treatment of place obsolete for ethnography. In fact, I often ask students to study the sociology of a place with an initial two or three hours of close observation and extensive field notes. This might be a courtroom, a student bar, or an Italian piazza. It is often useful to see these places comparatively: students in research teams sent to ten piazzas in Rome report that social life within varies tremendously from one piazza to another. The variation may be based on something as elemental as shape, size, architectural accruements, or other material, place-bound aspects of place. What this says is that particular places have a singularity that must be understood if one is to explain the behaviors that occur within them, since no two places host identical social scenes.

People in Ethnographies

Bronislaw Malinowski's research among the Trobriand Islanders in New Guinea produced one of the first modern ethnographies. Malinowski made the case for deep involvement with his research

---

2. This was a variation of the "self-portraiture without self" assignment I developed for visual sociology courses. See Harper (2012).

subjects and close observation with the "real people" of his research. His books, particularly *Argonauts of the Western Pacific* ([1922] 1961), remain some of the most important studies in the history of anthropology. In *Argonauts,* Malinowski redirects anthropology away from social Darwinism, making the persuasive point that so-called primitive people create culture that is in every way as complex, interesting, and important as the culture of developed societies. In this way, his work appeared to be steeped in respect for difference. He wrote himself into his accounts and offered narratives that blended observations, anecdotes, interview segments, and analysis. Malinowski's ethnographies, for the first time in anthropology, demonstrated that material, emotional, and psychological separation between observer and observed was antithetical to ethnography's identity. He produced books that defined anthropology at an important crossroads; he had distinguished professorships, and his work has endured.

Yet when his second wife, Valetta Swann, published his diary from his fieldwork twenty-five years after his death (Malinowski 1967), a storm of controversy followed. The impact of the publication in 1967 still reverberates through the discipline and, in fact, is partially credited with having set in motion the "reflexive turn" that revolutionized ethnography (see Forrest Stuart, chapter 8, this volume).

It is astonishing to confront the diary, which reveals his lustful fixation on native women and his embrace of forced sex, as well as his reference to "deflowering" a woman as a "favor." Most shocking are his attitudes toward the natives he interviews and observes. He states his "general aversion for niggers, for the monotony-feel imprisoned" (1967: 162). And "As for ethnology: I see the life of the natives as utterly devoid of interest or importance, something as remote from me as the life of a dog" (167). Most famously, he writes (and it is fair to note that he is reading Joseph Conrad at the time), "On the whole my feelings toward the natives are decidedly tending to "Exterminate the brutes" (169).

Malinowski's diary does not describe insights he is gaining that will forever earn him a place in anthropology. He describes sailing, reading novels, and socializing with other Europeans, missionaries, officials, and visitors, while yearning for his European lovers and his mother as he paws native women when he has drunk too much. He mostly eats tins of European food and has trained a native to be his manservant. He is judgmental and arrogant and seems the opposite of what one would imagine an anthropologist to be, and certainly not the author of his many ethnographies that emerged from the fieldwork covered by the diary.

The publication of the diary became part of an emerging ethnographic sensibility in which "reflexivity"—telling the story of the research as part of the research—took a central place. Reflexivity acknowledges that gaining knowledge among humans is a social process. Malinowski's diary told us that empathy is not automatic or simple; researchers and those being studied may be indifferent to each other; they may feel superiority or inferiority, distaste or hatred; or they might feel affection or even love for each other. But despite the human complexity of ethnography, the purpose is to learn about the deep meanings of human interaction, symbols, language, kinship structures, and all else; in other words, to remain distant and in some defensible way "objective." In order to reconcile these contradictory commitments, ethnographic writing and films should, as much as possible, weave the story of their creation into the ethnography itself. This seems especially important in ethnographies that focus on people and places rather than social structure or abstract mechanisms, as the ethnographer's very human relationships—sometimes friendships—with those they study impact what we can learn about the particulars of their lives and sometimes shape those particulars.

Malinowski's dirty laundry led anthropology to a deep examination and a new commitment to transparency. This impressed me; the social sciences suddenly seemed countercultural: facing off against that which was dehumanizing and dishonest. I could get into that.

This inspired me to study individuals or small groups and to find novel and humanistic ways to vividly describe what I'd learned. I did my best to be open about my values, interpretations, and assumptions, and I considered it a central part of my job to give voice to those who appeared under my pen or before my camera—not just present my own interpretations of them. This also meant seeking forms of collaboration, such as photo elicitation (to be described), where the roles of researcher and researched are reversed. In the end, reflexivity in ethnographies based on people and places is rooted in the understanding that knowledge draws from relationships, interactions, reactions, interpretations, and appreciation of the Other.

Homeless People

At the beginning of my project, homeless men were simply a human surface I photographed. A year later, when I stayed in missions and on skid row, I had just the barest encounters in which I discussed mundane issues regarding food, shelter, and safety with the men I met. I never felt more alone, though in the company of many. To invigorate the study, I hitchhiked through the West the following summer, looking for tramps in freight yards in the Dakotas, Montana, and Washington. Though I met tramps, conversations were again limited. It was not until I began to ride the trains that tramps began to open up to me. Our conversations were first based on solving problems: how to avoid railroad bulls (police); how to find the right train in miles-long yards; how to actually ride trains. Eventually these conversations became deeper. I told the tramps what I was doing, and at least some of them found that interesting. I could tell that many of them saw me as just another idealistic dreamer, about as likely to accomplish what I hoped to accomplish as they were to realize their imagined cabin by a stream, far from the encroachments of society.

To get more deeply into the culture, I planned a trip of a month or more in which I would ride the freights from Minneapolis toward the apple harvest in Washington State. I left with about twenty dollars; I carried a change of clothes, a tape recorder about the size of two packs of cigarettes, a tiny Leica camera, about ten rolls of film, and notebooks. I had a bag of food, and after that was gone I would eat what I could find or come up with. In other words, I would not be Malinowski with his pith helmet, manservant, tinned European foods, and steady company of missionaries, traders, and others from his life off the field. I would try for immersion and write about my experience as well as what I learned from tramps on the road. Indeed, I discovered that going deeply into the culture opened me up to those I met; it also made me confused about my own identity as the days and weeks went on. My growing understanding seemed genuine because it applied to what I was experiencing as well as to the experiences of others.

I was more than a little apprehensive when I entered the freight yards on that late August afternoon. I'd been on the freights enough to know how easily one could be hurt or killed; the trains were punishing, and many of the men I'd met were violent, unpredictable, or just plain mean. But I had also met those who fit my expectations of "the tramp," and I certainly hoped I would find the perfect informant: a sage, wizened man just waiting to engage meaningfully with an eager student. Naive, but true.

That first night in Minneapolis I searched for a train and met Carl, coming down from a three-week drunk, filthy, stinking, and swaying from his inebriation. He was decidedly unfriendly and made it clear I was not welcome in his freight car, where he would, that night, end his binge with his last quart of cheap Canadian whiskey. He seemed hardly the tramp I was looking for.

We met up, however, the next day in a Montana freight yard, both having ridden the wrong train, and spent the next month together. We rode trains across the country, found jobs in the apple harvest in Washington State, and eventually shared a workers' cabin. We camped in hobo jungles or in weeds behind buildings, and eventually under apple trees in the orchards where we would work. We finished my food in a couple of days; then we ate stews with odd ingredients made in hobo camps and food we'd found on our own. I watched Carl transform his definition of himself as a homeless man living in filth on skid row, drunk and out of control, to that of a worker who was justly proud of his work ethic. He was a World War II combat vet who had never settled back into society, and at about fifty years of age he looked like an ancient, beaten man. Our momentary relationship had a name—buddying up—that defined what one expected from a tramp and what was not expected. It was OK to share a trip and to look out for each other, but when you were ready for a change you walked away, and you walked away alone (figure 4.5).

Carl's stories filled the hours we spent waiting for trains, sharing a hobo jungle, or camping under apple trees. The stories that animated my book *Good Company* (Harper 2015) emerged from our experiences: waiting for a job led us, naturally, to talk about work; coming down from a hangover led him to talk about drunks he'd had and how other tramps handled, or did not handle, alcohol. We met tramps Carl knew, and these conversations revealed how and what they exchanged or offered, how their reputations were made and ruined, and how they accepted who they had become. The conversation below took place between a tramp Carl had known for several years named Boston Blackie; we were in a hobo jungle near the apple region of Washington State, waiting for a train to take us toward the harvest:

"Yeah, well, I get so dee-sgusted with myself," Blackie said out of the blue, "I don't know what to do. I can have a hundred dollars this mornin'..."

Carl interrupted, "An' you won't have a dime tomorrow—I know, I know. I'm the same way."

FIGURE 4.5

Carl in a boxcar, coming down from his three-week drunk

Carl nodded at me: "Well, when you saw me I was drinking a quart of Grand Canadian, wasn't I?"

"Yeah, that you were."

"That's pitiful," Blackie said seriously; "you ought to be ashamed of yourself. But who's kidding who—it's the same with me."

He looked Carl straight in the eye and bent forward to emphasize his point: "Several times lately I found myself wonderin'—just what the hell's going to become of me!"

They began to laugh, and they laughed and laughed; I thought they'd roll on the ground. Then Carl said: "I had a dollar; and a few pennies left—that's all I had left from that last job. Here I am, couple days later, fucked up on an old train!" (Harper 2015: 31)

The conversation came out of nowhere and led to recollections of pathetic moments in their lives, delivered with humorous introspection. When we parted ways with Blackie I thought, "How great, old tramps who genuinely care about each other and affirm each other's complex identities." But then Carl told me backstories, and all the suspicions, bad deals, manipulations, and pure bullshit came to the surface. The story would only have come from a shared moment in a hobo jungle, and it taught me about the *performance* of the jungle meeting where a lot of the camaraderie is faked, the shared pathos of repeated failures, and just a tiny bit of acceptance and hope.

I had the sense to understand that my time with Carl would constitute the central drama of my ethnography: our trip to the harvest and our work there was a typical story of the culture; the men we met on the road were the normal cast of characters, and I borrowed on Carl's identity to observe it from close up.

My feelings toward Carl evolved, and I suspect his feelings toward me did as well. As our ride across the American West unfolded, I felt we became strongly attached, and I think he momentarily and partially shed his usual tramp role. He was worried about my naïveté and seemed to enjoy being something of an older brother or even a father figure to me. When we finally settled at a campsite after several days of travel, he made a fire and I demanded toast; it was breakfast time after all, and I still had some bread left. Figure 4.6 shows Carl handing me the toast in the dim light of predawn; he had fashioned a bread holder from a green branch and toasted it perfectly. The photo captures the essence of that moment in our relationship.

When we moved into an orchard cabin and began our career as apple knockers, he tired of my questions. By the time I left it was clear he was done with our relationship. When I left the cabin to hitchhike east, he admonished me not to ride the freights; the trains would be crawling with thieves looking for my wages (in cash in my pocket). But he said this with weary resignation; I would never learn (and, in fact, I was nearly robbed when I decided at the last minute to catch a freight out of Spokane). More than a month together ended in a couple of sentences and a nod implying goodbye.

When I embarked on the writing, I was faced with a quandary. I was interested in how tramps' lives were structurally created, but I also wanted to communicate the feel of the trip and the emotional ups and downs I'd experienced. The narrative voice came naturally because the fieldwork itself was a typical story of the culture: Carl finished a drunk, as he had many times before, found his way to the freight yard, where he departed with spare change for an imagined job thousands of miles away. He made the trip while buddying up with a neophyte who happened to be a PhD student, and after a month they parted. I expected that when he finished his harvest job

FIGURE 4.6

Toast prepared and offered in a tramp jungle

he'd drink up his wages on a binge and begin again; his life history was built on a series of identities—worker, traveler, drinker—each with a logic of its own. I had come to see Carl as a *tramp*, with all the warts and contradictions of that identity.

Of course, I also realized that Carl was but one example, and I questioned whether I could present the culture through his individual experience. But as we talked to other tramps for often interminable hours waiting for trains, waiting for the harvest, and just waiting, variations of Carl's stories were told and retold. Each tramp presented himself as a trickster who had fucked up again and again, but had also survived. Although at first I had seen Carl as the wrong informant because he was so clearly at the low moment of the tramp life, I later came to understand that he was the perfect representative of a culture with status hierarchies, clear expectations, and myriad ways to mess up. I found myself thinking that were I studying assistant professors attempting to achieve tenure (as I was when I wrote the book), we'd all have very different stories, but they would reduce to very similar variations on a theme. I would approach the study of the striving trickster professors much as I approached the tramps.

Willie

During my first job as a university professor in far northern New York, I lived many miles from the university on an old farm. I met a neighbor, Willie, a mechanic in a small shop he owned who fixed cars, agricultural equipment, stoves, and other appliances, sewing machines, and virtually anything based on mechanical parts. He often made new parts and re-engineered machines as he repaired them. In this poor neighborhood of small farms, everybody wanted to make use of Willie's skill (including me), but he worked if and when he was motivated to do so, and that was normally because a job interested him or he owed a favor in the complicated social web in which he lived. Though he lived in a capitalist society, he did not have capitalist values. Very often he adjusted his fees to the value of the object being fixed rather than the amount of time he'd spent on a job. And he often fixed things in the process of a repair simply for the pleasure of making it "right," and of course he never charged for these repairs.

As a sociologist, I found Willie very interesting and eventually came to see him as a "bricoleur" in the sense meant by Lévi-Strauss (1966). Like Lévi-Strauss's "savages," Willie drew upon different skills to solve novel problems in usually new ways. This became a theoretical frame on which much could be hung, but there had to be a method, a way of learning.

At first I tried to describe Willie in photos and field note observations, but it was soon evident that my understanding of his working knowledge was superficial at best. Eventually, I came across a method that was little known at the time called "photo elicitation" (PE), which reversed our roles and made Willie my teacher. The anthropologist and photographer John Collier (1967) coined the term in the 1950s; in essence, PE was an interview method based on a discussion of photos that the research subject understood far more deeply and in a different (culturally informed) way than did the researcher.

Thus, we launched into photo elicitation research. I photographed details of Willie's work as well as the shop and its vast universe of objects; I also photographed the other men who regularly came by the shop. I tape-recorded thirty-some hours of discussions of these photos as Willie took me on tours of his working consciousness. Because we were fast friends, this was a wonderful experience. We felt we were accumulating knowledge about problem solving, webs of affiliation in the poor neighborhood, and identities; the implications from our observations and interviews reached from Willie's modest neighborhood to Marx, Weber, Lévi-Strauss, and Durkheim.

The book that emerged from this research needed new strategies, just as the project had. I distinguished conversations, analysis, and field notes in the text with different font styles, and positioned images across from textual passages to make precise points. Some pages of the book contain a single image, others up to six; these choices were made due to the mutual unfolding of textual and visual information. This was before Photoshop, Pagemaker, or InDesign; I made photos in my darkroom at the size my design called for, photocopied them, and pasted them into a dummy across from the text they related to. If I didn't like the results, I reprinted the photos at a different size and started over. My editor, Doug Mitchell at the University of Chicago Press, accepted that the design was part of the message and that specific means of expression were needed to lend nuance to a complex portrait of a person and place.

PE provided a way to ground textual knowledge. Willie might tell the history of a piece of metal that he used in a repair, like a piece of a smokestack from a stripped-out factory, unsuccessfully fashioned into a stove part by a neighbor, who then traded it to Willie (figure 4.7). Having the photo present in the interview encouraged Willie to dwell upon it in detail, and it became a door opening to cultural understanding. The gestalt of images mated with explanatory and theoretical text was far greater than any of the parts standing alone.

Every author has a favorite project and *Working Knowledge* is mine, in part because I feel that the book communicated what I asked it to and in part because it brought real rewards to Willie. He became a local folk hero and put his half share of the royalties to good use. It is likely true that I overidentified with Willie because I had the opportunity to study a person I admired greatly, and it is also likely that my perspective clouded some of the darker aspects of the ethnographic tale: the poverty, the sheer difficulty of his life, and the occasional bad deals with neighbors born of their desperation.

Willie was notable, however, because he was individually interesting. He was a character. One day, he mentioned that he'd played guitar with Hank Williams. I dismissed this as crazy, but later

FIGURE 4.7

Willie adapts a piece of metal from a smokestack from a derelict factory into a bumper for his tractor

I found an 8 × 10 photo of Hank under a pile of bills on the desk inscribed, "To Willie, my best rhythm guitarist." While I began to think of Willie as a "social type"—the bricoleur—he continued to surprise me by expanding beyond the analytical box I had placed him in: fixing a sewing machine to sew his daughter's confirmation dress, which he designed on the spot and was stunning; rebuilding a sawmill when it was −25 degrees to cut his wood because he gave all of his to his ill neighbor.

Though it may seem ironic, dedicating an entire book to developing a single character in all his humanity also produced a sociological portrait that captured the essence of a *kind* of historically and geographically situated person. When the book was published, I heard from a great number of people from many places far from the North Country who said, "Willie is also my neighbor, my uncle, my friend . . ." These were letters from regions where the environment nursed a kind of intelligence into existence and created people probably very much like Willie.

Photography, People, and Places

This essay features eight images from several tens of thousands I've made as part of my ethnographic research. Often, photographs in sociology are eye candy in our introductory textbooks, simply restating obvious points in clichéd ways (fathers holding babies in a chapter on the "new family," for example). An intellectual movement devoted to visual sociology, institutionalized as the International Visual Sociology Association, has existed since the early 1980s and does have an increasing impact on our thoughts about images in research and about the visual aspect of society and culture in general. In the spirit of the gradually growing acceptance that images are rightly key to doing and presenting ethnography, I'd like to add the following thoughts about photographs, people, and places.

Photographs generally contain specific, identifiable information. They exhibit a wonderful tension by reproducing the world concretely while subjectively creating it. In other words, there is usually information in a photograph that we recognize as "true" or "actual," yet we also recognize that our interpretation of that truth or actuality is due to a long list of choices (some unconscious) that frame, focus, expose, modify, and otherwise actually create the image.

The "actuality" of photographs means that we can use images to communicate precise information about what we are writing about that is often much more than any words can offer. Carl's offer of toast (figure 4.6) seems unlikely: a tramp in the predawn carefully preparing toast with a green branch and offering it over a jungle fire. The setting, the fire, a jungle on the edge of a train yard, the junk littered around, Carl's dirty work uniform, and his expression all become a gestalt of cultural messages that are also about fieldwork and the relationship between two unlikely traveling companions. The tramp Strawberry (figure 4.2) stands brazenly in full view as if he owns the yards, common when the photo was made but impossible now. And so on. Once one becomes attuned to creating ethnographic understanding via images, one becomes a different kind of photographer—one bent on making images that illustrate ideas rather than simply being visually captivating. (Of course, it's nice to do both.) Figure 4.8 shows this well. There are two nicely dressed older Italian women, sisters who are enacting the weekly Sunday family dinner and offering desert made from chestnut flour, a reminder of WWII poverty. The walls of Francesca's flat are covered with family photos, all elegantly framed. We are sipping desert wine from an unlabeled bottle, made by friends. But it is the energy of the moment that the photo most importantly captures. I was writing about the sociology of food (Harper and Faccioli, 2009) when I made the photo; I'd been at many of these Sunday dinners at Francesca's, and the photo captures the easy friendliness of the moment and their willingness to carry on as though things are perfectly normal while facing my large negative camera. The image captures a moment of "truth" that is also a fiction; it happened this way time and time again, but never while facing a large and imposing camera.

Photographs also offer perspectives that don't translate easily into words. The best example in this essay is figure 4.3, the aerial image of a farmstead. I studied forty-eight farms to generate a typology of farms, and seeing them from the air revealed aspects of their organization, technology, and "structure" that eye-level viewing would not.

Finally, there is the matter that ethnographies tell a great deal about place and people. There was no way to hide Willie's poverty (figure 4.7), whether or not it was a matter of some degree of choice. His shop was what some called a glorified junkyard, no matter the genius or the complex social world behind it. Willie was identifiable in my study, and in all of my books the central characters and

FIGURE 4.8

Francesca offers dessert at the weekly Sunday dinner, Bologna

their settings are identifiable. His reputation was affected by what I wrote and photographed about his life. There are institutional review boards that would approve of these methods and many that might not. For me, however, the issue transcends the bureaucratic approval that our work must justifiably garner. The ethical issues are bound up, I believe, with an obligation to tell a story that is consistent with in-depth, sociologically informed learning. In other words, I suggest that part of the "right" to tell the story with identifiable people and places comes with having the confidence that what we offer is, to the degree it is possible to determine, "true." Our visual telling must be based on deep research rather than a fantasy, a prejudgment, or a momentary visit by a news reporter.

This discussion opens a Pandora's box, but since images are so bound up with my own ethnographic analysis of people and places, a brief introduction to some of the issues is necessary.

Final Thoughts

There is no best way to do ethnography. From my perspective, ethnography must provide deep knowledge about its immediate topic, and it must be relevant to larger ideas about society. I think the ethnographer has the license to experiment with methods and writing (photography, etc.) because it is artful rather than technical, improvised and creative rather than formulaic.

While an approach to ethnography that foregrounds people and places may seem anachronistic given the reality of global interconnectedness, and the contemporary social scientific emphasis on mechanisms and generalizability, this tradition remains alive and well (see, for example, Duneier 1999).

In summary, the approach to ethnography espoused here allows people and places to breathe, embracing rather than glossing over their peculiarities. While it recognizes the ethnographer's responsibility to link one's case study to larger social processes, it also recognizes that no two places are the same and that people's motivations, aspirations, and trajectories in life cannot be entirely contained in "institutions," "mechanisms," "social types," or whatever other analytic box social scientists employ to bring order to the chaos of social life. Our subjects are themselves often cognizant of the social forces that surround them and can occasionally circumvent or alter them; this warrants an approach that highlights the idiosyncratic and the contingent. Developing characters and places is not simply a rhetorical device (though it does tend to produce fine narratives!). After all, who among us would be convinced that the significance of our grandmother's house, or of our own hopes and dreams, could be fully captured and explained by concepts, theories, and forces invented by social scientists?

References

Adams, Tony E., Stacy Holman Jones, and Carolyn Ellis. 2014. *Understanding Qualitative Research: Autoethnography*. New York: Oxford University Press.
Angé, Marc. 1995. *Non-Places: Introduction to an Anthropology of Supermodernity*. New York: Verso.
Collier, John. 1967. *Visual Anthropology: Photography as a Research Method*. New York: Holt, Rinehart and Winston.
Duneier, Mitchell. 1999. *Sidewalk*. New York: Farrar, Straus and Giroux.
Geertz, Clifford. 2006 (1973). "Deep Play: Notes on the Balinese Cockfight." *Daedalus* 134(4): 56–86.
Gowan, Teresa. 2010. *Hobos, Hustlers, and Backsliders: Homeless in San Francisco*. Minneapolis: University of Minnesota Press.
Greenhouse, Carol. 2012. *Ethnographies of Neoliberalism*. Philadelphia: University of Pennsylvania Press.
Harper, Douglas. 1987. *Working Knowledge: Skill and Community in a Small Shop*. Chicago: University of Chicago Press.
Harper, Douglas. 2002. *Changing Works: Visions of a Lost Agriculture*. Chicago: University of Chicago Press.
Harper, Douglas. 2012. *Visual Sociology*. London: Routledge.
Harper, Douglas. (1982) 2015. *Good Company: A Tramp Life*, 3rd ed. London: Routledge.
Harper, Douglas and Patrizia Faccioli. 2009. *The Italian Way: Food and Social Life*. Chicago: University of Chicago Press.
Lévi-Strauss, Claude. 1966. *The Savage Mind*. Chicago: University of Chicago Press.
Malinowski, Bronislaw. (1922) 1961. *Argonauts of the Western Pacific*. New York: Dutton.
Malinowski, Bronislaw. 1967. *A Diary in the Strict Sense of the Term*. London: Routledge.

Marcus, George. 1998. *Ethnography Through Thick and Thin*. Princeton: Princeton University Press.

Spradley, James P. 1969. *You Owe Yourself a Drunk: An Ethnography of Urban Nomads*. Boston: Little Brown.

Underberg, Natalie. 2013. *Digital Ethnography: Anthropology, Narrative, and New Media*. Austin: University of Texas Press.

Chapter 5

Mechanisms

IDDO TAVORY AND STEFAN TIMMERMANS

While "mechanism based explanations" have become widespread in the social sciences,[1] for many ethnographers, they are accompanied with some angst. Talk of mechanisms evokes the image of the factory in which social processes are identically stamped, instead of appreciating the messiness and abundance of protagonists' lives and narratives. The world seems too complex to capture in the language of mechanism-based explanation. There is just too much going on. And even if we could capture it mechanistically, ethnographers may fear that we would lose the distinct voices of the people we spend time with. After all, if one of ethnography's most powerful warrants is its humanistic appeal, don't mechanisms substitute this voice for a more experience-distanced language?

Drawing on pragmatist and interactionist ideas, this chapter puts mechanism-based explanations at the center of ethnographic work. We point out that ethnographers necessarily think causally. Although focusing on mechanisms may decenter observed

---

1. See, e.g., Gross (2009), Hedström (2005), Hedström and Swedberg (1998), Hedström and Ylikoski (2010), and Tavory and Timmermans (2013). For an important discussion of mechanisms in ethnography, see Vaughan (2009).

protagonists in the written narrative, focusing on processes constitutes a powerful warrant for ethnography. Regardless of whether ethnographers are ultimately interested in the micro-level dynamics of the situation or in globalization, mechanisms are the implicit levers of ethnographic work that provide analytical torque.

To exemplify how mechanism-based explanations work in action, we outline interactional mechanisms where actors negotiate and co-construct the definition of their situation, as well as explore the effects of being routinely misaligned about what is going on. To further unpack this approach, we then provide two excerpts from our own work, showing how we can identify such mechanisms through "coding-in-motion"—taking the interactional back-and-forth among actors as our primary unit of analysis. We end this chapter with a reflection on the utility of mechanisms for answering one of the trickiest ethnographic questions: What is this a case of?

Ethnographers Think Causally

Since identifying mechanisms is a form of causal thinking, the first issue we need to establish is whether ethnographers even want to make causal statements. Isn't it ethnography's warrant to provide "thick description" of social action by showing the webs of meaning that the people we study are suspended in? If thick description is our marching order, isn't causality best left to positivists? We think not.

Theoretically, thick description and causal reasoning are not mutually exclusive. If we want to understand why someone acted in a particular way, it would be strange *not* to ask how they understood their situation. And by the same token, writing about people's lives and narratives does not absolve us from trying to figure out the causal processes implicated in such stories. Causality and interpretation are two sides of the same coin (Reed 2011). As humans, we live in a meaningful world, and our actions—and thus the structure of causality in the social sciences—almost inevitably include such meanings.[2]

Even ethnographers who are reluctant to use the term "causality" routinely make causal claims. Think, for example, of Clifford Geertz's (1973) classic paper on the Balinese cockfight that helped consolidate the mandate for thick description. He explains the meanings of the fight, but as a matter of course he also uses these meanings to explain who bets on which bird and when—people usually bet on their village's rooster against another village, on their families' cocks against another family, and so forth. The point is clear—if we understand *how* people make meaning, we gain a better appreciation of *why* they do the things they do. Thick description embeds causal claims.

Geertz is not the exception. Abend et al. (2013) show that across all examined North American ethnographic publications, writers employ causal language. Of course, not everyone uses words like "cause" or "necessitate" in their writing. Sometimes, they use verbs like "structured," "shaped," "gave rise to," and other weaker formulations that imply causal claims (see also Vaidyanathan et al. 2015). Even in the most protagonist-centered ethnographies, researchers claim that the social forces they show through the stories *shape* or *structure* the narrative.

Making causal claims, however, is not necessarily the same as making mechanism-based explanations.[3] What, then, distinguishes

---

2. This, incidentally, does not mean that there are no causal narratives that disregard the explicit meaning-making hailed by thick description. Some arguments rely on the structure of networks or on demographic pressures that are invisible from any one point of view. Some causal claims may rely on a misunderstanding, and still others on routines or deeply embodied action that never becomes explicitly meaningful. The point is simply this: if you are worried about forsaking meaning for causality, don't be.

3. There are counterfactual accounts (where we establish causality by arguing that if X wouldn't have happened, Y wouldn't have either), there are regularity accounts (where we simply say that, usually, after X happens we see Y), and there are

a mechanism-based explanation? We define a mechanism-based explanation as a causal argument in which, ideally, (a) we can show how a change between states A and B happens continuously, from beginning to end; (b) this change can be described on a low level of aggregation, so that, as Elster (1989) puts it, we can see "the cogs and wheels" of the causal process; and (c) these processes can be generalized from a specific set of observations.[4] The emphasis on the ongoing action necessary for a mechanism-based account is particularly compatible with ethnographic work. More than any other method, ethnographic work traces action as it occurs. The level of aggregation of the data is also extremely fine-grained—after all, we have access to actual people as they live their lives.

Thinking in terms of mechanisms forces us to explicitly consider the shape and structures of the phenomena that move processes along. But what do the basic building blocks of a mechanism look like? One of the key insights found in much of sociology, and in ethnography in particular, is that collective acts do not need to be reduced to the action of the individuals in the scene: the micro-level foundations of sociology need not be located on an individual level. An interaction cannot be simply reduced to the actions of one person *plus* the actions of another—interaction is not additive, but emergent and collective.

Underlying this insight, the founder of American pragmatism, Charles S. Peirce, advanced an approach that emphasizes meaning-*making*, rooting meaning in action. Meaningful action ties together the sign we use, the object we are referring to, and the effect the sign-object produces. Simply put, we can't talk of meaning-*making* unless it has some kind of effect upon actors—an emerging understanding,

---

interventionist ways to establish causality (where we show that our intervention in the world has patterned effects; see, e.g., Reiss 2009). For the relationship between mechanism-based and counterfactual accounts of causality see Woodward (2002).

4. See, especially, Elster (1989), Gross (2009), Hedström and Ylikoski (2010), and Machamer, Darden, and Craver (2000). See also Tavory and Timmermans (2013).

emotion, or action. We propose that this vision of meaning-making should be considered the basic building block of a mechanism-based explanation. Following the ongoing construction of meaning as ethnography's elementary unit of analysis could involve examining countless actions, thoughts, and emotions in one individual or, alternatively, one action, shift in perception, or realization across a collectivity. The meaning is no longer interpreter-bound but exists as a distinguishable stand-alone ethnographic object.

Of course, meaning is not made from scratch. Interpreters bring their own habits of thought and action into a situation. Seeing a "cheerleader," for example, is possible only because we immediately attend to certain clues about people's attire, where and how they move through space, and so on. We do not puzzle out our world from scratch every time we confront it, but build on habits of thought and action to make sense of the situations we face. These habits, in turn, change as we go through our lives. Each interaction we have leaves a small mark, engraving some habits even deeper, changing others in ways that may be quite radical.

This pragmatist vision of meaning thus implies a temporal perspective. This "moving perspective" has also been the inspiration for later interactionism (Blumer 1969). Think about a conversation: each turn-of-talk becomes the ground for the next turn, closing some possible interpretations and opening others. Similarly, meaning-making moments are strung together in chains. Conceptualizing ongoing action in terms of such chains allows us to think not only about the basic building blocks from which mechanism-based explanations are made, but also about the actual shape of these mechanisms. In some ethnographic observations, we can take one instance of meaning-making as the fundamental unit of analysis. There are indeed singular moments of choice and action that may serve as a mechanism-based explanation as they become aggregated into larger social effects. These are mechanisms that take individual *action* as its basis.

And yet even these seemingly singular moments of action are but the endpoint of a chain of action and interaction that shaped them. What a Peirce-inflected interactionism makes us realize is that if we want to understand the social mechanisms through which action takes shape, the most basic building block that provides us such understanding would not be a moment of action severed from its context, but the concatenation of several iterations and multiple layers of meaning-making in *inter*action. Meanings are co-constructed, changed, played with, and amplified not through addition but through the back-and-forth of irreducible interactional processes.

Mechanisms in Interaction

Ethnographies that remain attentive to the interactional unfolding of worlds implicitly point to mechanisms. In this section, we draw out some ethnographic examples of a mechanism-based approach, even if their authors did not present the work in these terms. We begin with examples of interactional mechanisms that include the negotiation, shifts, and amplifications of shared meaning. Arriving at an intersubjective definition of a situation is a collective act (Blumer 1969). As we show, mechanism-based explanations do not force ethnographers to ignore their protagonists' narratives or to think in either micro or macro terms. Focusing on mechanisms, however, does mean that ethnographers emphasize transposable patterns rather than specific biographies and narratives, and that they focus on the emerging contours of action as the basic building blocks of analysis—whatever level of aggregation it ends up being.

Alignments

A first example of a mechanism-based explanation that shows the irreducibility of interactions can be found in Forrest Stuart's (2016) book, *Down, Out, and Under Arrest*. The book traces the community effects of zero-tolerance policing on the inhabitants of Skid Row, a Los Angeles downtown area that has become the place of last resort for people when they're down on their luck. Stuart documents an intensive form of policing in which people are at risk for arrest for minor infractions and violations (e.g., sitting on the sidewalk, jaywalking).

In one of the many poignant moments in the book, Stuart shows that this form of intense policing results in men and women on the street policing each other's actions. As Stuart writes:

> The constant threat of police interference forced the vendors to adopt the gaze of the police and to act as surrogate officers, thus engendering a perverse mode of privatized enforcement that undermined the commonly theorized benefits of informal control, undercut the possibilities for rehabilitation, and worsened the social and economic marginalization of Skid Row residents. (2016: 166)

The mechanism that Stuart depicts here consists of a repeated iteration of meaning-making: first, one of the unforeseen effects of intensive policing is that people who constantly get stopped, frisked, and arrested begin to "see like a cop." Thus, one reaction to intensive policing is the attempt to modulate one's behavior to fit the assumed perceptive schemas of police officers. Because this reaction is modeled after repeatedly observed police actions, residents integrate the contextual aspects typical of police modus operandi: if police officers stop someone in your vicinity, they are likely to also ticket you for some infraction, real or imagined. Here, then, emerges a second part of the mechanism Stuart describes, where some men and women begin to themselves enact modes of "third party policing" in order to keep their environment safe from police presence.

The irony is not only that third party policing emerges from fear rather than a spirit of collaboration, but also that these men and women react to *perceived* infractions. For example, since white men (unless they are extremely disheveled) seem out of place, the residents police them away; since women are assumed to be sex workers, a few men forcefully removed a man from Skid Row who was trying to keep his drug-addicted wife with him. When enforcing the anticipated police perspective, the men on the street ended up replicating some of the most repressive and unjust forms of such policing.

Even more troubling is that the efforts of people on Skid Row necessarily fall short. For police, the framing of Skid Row citizens as "social problems" does not disappear with these behavioral modifications. Instead of becoming more lax in their policing, they continue to find more fine-grained infractions, which leads to further behavioral modifications (or, alternatively, some people simply give up).

An interactional model then locates the injustice of Skid Row citizens' plight in the iterative response between police action and citizens' anticipatory behavior and the continuous shaping of both parties' reactions.

Colin Jerolmack's (2009) article "Primary Groups and Cosmopolitan Ties" employs a similar interactional sensibility that implicitly contains the elements of a mechanism-based explanation (see also Jerolmack 2013). Jerolmack is interested in the question of how mundane leisure practices bridge interethnic ties between groups that are usually set apart. He shows that Italian working-class men created ties with black and Latino youth in a Brooklyn neighborhood through pigeon-keeping. What are the set of interactional mechanisms that explain this outcome of turning an ethnic practice into a co-ethnic one? The answer lies in the shifting neighborhood dynamics and the very material exigencies of pigeon-keeping. The Brooklyn neighborhood Jerolmack studied has been changing from a white ethnic enclave to a majority black and Latino neighborhood. The children of the former residents moved away, and the population gradually went through an ethnic transition. In this context:

> Italians could no longer rely on their sons to help them clean the coops or train the birds while they were at work. As many of their neighbors left, it became increasingly difficult for white ethnics to rely on their peers for assistance. I found that some of them started to recruit incoming Puerto Rican and black boys to help them. (Jerolmack 2009, 447)

Here, then, are the origins of an interactional mechanism: faced with the hard work of pigeon-keeping, and without the help of their children, the older white ethnics open their hobby to black and Latino kids. But this moment of action does not constitute the ethnographic mechanism by itself. In order to get the neighborhood kids to work with pigeons, the men allow them to keep and fly pigeons on their own roofs, turning them from workers to semi-equal members of their pastime. The white old-timers transform a previously homogeneous world of pigeon-keeping into a more ethnically heterogeneous social world through a shared involvement in checking pigeons out in pet stores, nursing sick pigeons, making competitive attempts to outfly each other from different rooftops, and joining resources to fly races.

The mechanism at work in Jerolmack's ethnography contains a two-stage process. First is the transformation of the helper–employee relations to a shared avocation. Here, we already need to think interactionally. If we think about this stage simply through the lenses of the pressing problems older white ethnics face, we cannot account for the transformation of "help" into "junior pigeon-flyer." It is the specific ways in which older white ethnics and young blacks and Latinos negotiated these relationships as apprenticeships (rather than, for example, as cheap labor) that set up the process Jerolmack describes.

At the second stage, the dyadic relationship between older white and younger non-white pigeon flyers is replaced with the way in which the shared exigencies and "goods" in the social world of pigeon-flyers induct younger Latino and black flyers into a wider social world. Here, too, a different outcome could have been possible—a segregation of flyers to white and non-white groups may have been conceivable.[5] But, since black and Latino flyers were inducted into the social world of pigeon-flying through white ethnics, the social world becomes ethnically heterogeneous. The "white versus non-white" distinction overlaps with the distinction between old-timers and the younger generation of flyers. Once again, the social pattern cannot be disaggregated into individual actions, but only into highly patterned interactions shaped by similar practical exigencies.

Throughout these ethnographies, both Stuart and Jerolmack balance their focus on interactional explanations with the attempt to do justice to the complexities of biographies and narratives. But finally, focusing on a mechanism-based analytic story means looking at patterns rather than at specific people. Protagonists may exist, but they are grouped into a set based on the causal pathway. To paraphrase Erving Goffman, processes and their people, not people and their processes, structure action.

Focusing on "processes and their people" also facilitates our attempts to think across cases. Although the mechanism's form and its content can never be completely severed, mechanisms allow us to see how other cases fit a similar mold. Thus, Jerolmack's case can be used to think about how small-group interests can not only create boundaries but also create bridges to others. The pragmatics of needing a number of people for a basketball or soccer game, to take a different set of examples, may come to mean that others

---

5. We note here that this argument has traces of counterfactual thinking. For the relationship between mechanism-based explanations and counterfactual accounts, see Woodward (2002).

who are usually excluded are brought in, sometimes deeply changing local social dynamics. Similarly, Stuart's ethnographic case gives us a way to think about how power refracts the way actors live their lives by shaping the way they literally see the world around them—something that could prove useful both in the kinds of urban settings Stuart studies as well as in an array of other cases, from parent–child relationships to the way that people hospitalized for mental illness learn to interpret their own experiences, and others' behavior, as symptoms.

Misalignments

These two examples focused on interactional mechanisms by which people align their positions and negotiate a shared definition of the situation. But misalignments are often just as instructive as interactional successes. The effect of remaining at odds about what is going on may be substantial and follow specific interactional sequences.

A brilliant example of a mechanism-based explanation that relies on the co-construction of misalignment—and one in which protagonists are even more abstracted than in the examples above—can be seen in Diane Vaughan's (1986) *Uncoupling*. The book deals with the patterned ways in which people disengage from a romantic relationship, resulting in a breakup. Vaughan finds that couples do not arrive at the breakup juncture at the same time and in the same way. The typical sequencing of uncoupling involves an initiator and an unsuspecting partner. The initiators of the uncoupling process begin to realign their lives before the other person realizes that there even is a problem. The actual breakup is often extremely disorienting for the partner and quite obvious to the initiator of the separation. The reason is simply that one member of the dyad has constructed an alternative life—both in terms of how they learn to conceive their relationship and personal happiness and in terms of the networks they slowly forge—from which the other person is *already* excluded.

In short, "the typical situation is asymmetrical: the initiator is prepared and the partner is not" (Vaughan 1986: 132).

In terms of interactional mechanisms, Vaughan observes that during the time leading to the breakup, *both* partners typically sustain the situation—"separated in many ways, the partners remain full-fledged partners in one endeavor: suppressing information about the status of the relationship" (76). They do this, however, for different reasons. For the initiators, there is a stretch of time when they reevaluate the relationship, or simply aren't yet ready to break the bond. For them, it is a game of secrecy, cover-up, and preparing as well as possible for the exit. For the partner, however, the reason for going along is different. Faced with a larger number of anomalous situations, they try to smooth these out as part of the regular maintenance of the ups and downs of any partnership. As Vaughan notes, the partners act on the most mundane of interactional pressures: to keep the relationship going and avoid embarrassing the other. Paradoxically, they end up aiding the breakup by following the normal pressures of the interaction order (Goffman 1983).

Vaughan's example thus shows how relationships fall apart (or at least how people end up with very different accounts of breakups). Misalignment can also be productive as much as it can lead to a breakdown of sense-making and relationships. A good example of such a mechanism can be found in Jooyoung Lee's (2016) *Blowin' Up*, an ethnography that describes the world of aspiring rap artists in Los Angeles' South Central neighborhood. One of the core puzzles that Lee addresses is seemingly simple: considering that almost nobody makes a living from Hip Hop, why do these aspiring young artists persist in their rap dreams? They should realize that their chances to make a living as a musician remain miniscule and spend their time instead on acquiring different skills or pursuing alternatives careers. How is it that, despite evidence to the contrary, the men Lee followed see their big chance of success behind every corner?

As Lee shows, an explanation that centers on individuals would emphasize the aspiring artists' moments of choice. It would be noted, perhaps, that there are so few options available anyway, that hoping for a miracle of success—though still a bad choice—is not as irrational as it seems. In an explanation centered on social norms or "ghetto culture," researchers might also note that most of these men come from an environment in which they couldn't effectively plan ahead. Life in the poverty of South Central is simply too uncertain. In such a situation, the way the men approach their action would be qualitatively different from what we would expect of middle-class youth, whose parents steer them from the moment they enter preschool on a course that will secure their entrance into a top college.

These explanations, as Lee notes, capture only part of the truth. While it is true that the lack of opportunities fosters a kind of "existential urgency" that propels these men to rhyme and make music, on their own these explanations are insufficient. The first assumes that the poor are less rational than those who read about them; the second sneaks in a "culture of poverty" argument that implicitly blames the young men's culture for the choices they make.

Moreover, listening to the men Lee worked with quickly dispels such views. As one of his interlocutors notes in a moment of reflection:

> "You go to Myspace right now and there's a million motherfuckers putting they CD out! You think none of them believe? All those motherfuckers believe that they're the next one! . . . If people actually start realizing that only one person out of two billion rappers is going to blow up, who would keep going?" (Lee 2016: 10)

Lee takes seriously the social world in which these dreams take shape—fostering the collective act necessary for these young men to believe they are going to "blow up." He focuses on what he calls "momentous interactions." Living in Los Angeles and surrounded by the entertainment industry, the men Lee follows sometimes rub shoulders with established artists and celebrities or get minor gigs. For men constantly on the lookout for such opportunities, these interactions are momentous—they signify that they are, after all, on the right track. Although there are "a million motherfuckers putting they CD out," the small acts of encouragement suggest that each of Lee's subjects would be the one to make it. For the tastemakers in the music industry, however, these interactions don't carry this kind of significance. Many of the interactions are fleeting: a brief, accidental meeting in an airport or a brush with yet another young man who wants them to listen to his track. Even when the interaction is somewhat more sustained, it does not mean a commitment to career-building. It is simply one out of countless daily interactions that come with the territory of working in the music industry.

Lee's interactional mechanism, then, is one in which the misalignment of actors allows one party (the rappers) to validate their course of action and their artist ambitions (see also Glaeser 2011). Making the "choice" to pursue a Hip Hop career, as he shows, does not occur as a single moment of realization. Rather, it is nurtured over many years through the reverberation of actors' projects, the social world they are enmeshed in, and the social worlds they are so close to. It is through interaction that the social effect Lee is interested in here—deciding to take a chance at "blowing up"—is validated.

Once again, what makes a focus on mechanisms so productive in these cases is the ways it allows us to theoretically transpose the processes we find to other cases. In Vaughan's case, we can think of different moments of decoupling that aren't romantic—from some of the ways in which people quit their jobs to the breakdown of political parties and movements. Lee's example allows us to think productively about a host of situations in which people are intermittently aware of the objective obstacles they face, yet persist in a trajectory that seems set to fail—whether they are athletes who dream of going pro or graduate students in fields where few jobs are available. Or, to turn to his notion of "momentous interactions," we can immediately think of romantic life, where such situations are common. But we can also think, for example, of sites such as the relationships that evolve between NGOs in poverty-stricken countries and the people they work with in one of their many short-lived projects.

Coding-in-Motion

Even with sustained ethnographic research, finding interactional mechanisms is not ensured. Becoming sensitive to mechanisms is part of the craft of ethnography—something researchers learn from experience, their advisers, other works, and their community of inquiry through the years. And as with other approaches, some students never learn to look carefully at unfolding situations and identify mechanisms within them. In some research traditions, ethnographers treat the field as an example rather than as a place where processes are shaped; other ethnographers tend to focus on actors' narratives rather than on ongoing meaning-making in action; still others see interactions as nothing more than puppet play determined by macro-structural forces.

To raise the probability that social mechanisms are identified in the tangle of observations, ethnographers need to attend more to the coding of their observations. Rather than simply perform "open coding"—that is, brainstorming about an excerpt in the data in an open-ended fashion—and hope for inspiration to strike, ethnographers are better off if they explicitly think about the way action unfolds. Instead of taking a single utterance as the relevant unit of analysis, ethnographers can discover interactional sequences if they adopt what we call "coding-in-motion."

In this form of coding, the analyst begins by isolating an observational block that includes interaction among actors (or, in the case of interview data, a reported interaction). Having identified this observational block, we then code for both action and interactional emergence. In other words, we ask, "What are actors doing?" "What are the (intended and unintended) consequences of their actions?" "How do actions shape, and how are they shaped by, others?" It is important to note that we do not presume interaction is simply an arena where action plays out (although this could be the case in some instances), but try to see what happens when we take the back-and-forth of multiple iterations of meaning-making in interaction as our unit of analysis.

A first example of the use-value of coding-in-motion can be gleaned through the work of Iddo Tavory. His book *Summoned* (2016) is an ethnography of a Jewish Orthodox neighborhood in Los Angeles. The book traces the different ways Orthodox residents sustain a religious life in a Los Angeles neighborhood bordering Hollywood, an area better known for vibrant youth culture and creative subcultures than for religious life. Through empirical examples, Tavory outlines the relationship between different situations as they congeal into a recognizable social world and into actors' recurrent identifications. One of the puzzles animating the book is how Orthodox residents managed to sustain a seemingly insular religious social world when most men (and many of the women) worked in non-Orthodox, non-Jewish jobs. How did people balance the non-Jewish world they inhabited daily with the requirements of a religious world that sought to minimize such entanglements?

One way in which Orthodox residents did so was by erasing their participation symbolically. Usually people simply did not talk about their "non-Jewish jobs" when they were in Orthodox settings such as the synagogue or the Sabbath table. This erasure of the secular, however, was not simply an aggregated effect of the decision of individuals to mask the secular lives they took part in. After building relationships over years, some people opened up and talked about how passionate they actually were about their jobs. But more significantly, Tavory shows the collective correction and post factum erasure that occurs when, for example, a man talked about his job around the Sabbath table:

> At the Alstein family dinner attended by Mr. and Mrs. Alstein, their teenage daughter and a male guest from the synagogue, Mr. Alstein—an engineer—talks about a conversation he had with a non-Jewish colleague. The guy was an Egyptian-born engineer that works in his department. They started talking about religion, and his co-worker reminisced about his childhood in Egypt, and about the Jewish friends he used to have. . . .
>
> As he is talking about his conversation, his daughter asks, aghast, "you were talking to this Arab?!"
>
> Performing a double-take, Mr. Alstein quickly says something like "Yeah, I was talking to him, and then I got into my car, and sped out of there as fast as I could." Everybody laughs, and the conversation turns to another topic. (Tavory 2016: 119)

How does one go about analyzing this interaction? Following actors' iterations of meaning-making, we can divide the event into three sections (depicted by the three segments above). In the first iteration, Mr. Alstein tells of his work and of his conversation with his Egyptian colleague. Here, it seems, he tries to position himself both as a professional and as a man who brings his Judaism into the workplace. It is both a professional and a religious performance. In the second, his daughter challenges his story by casting moral doubt on the entire episode—how could he have a nonantagonistic relationship with a non-Jew (and worse, an Arab)? In the third, Mr. Alstein slyly retracts his own story by adding a face-saving but obviously invented humorous ending.

There is much of interest in each iteration of meaning-making. We can focus on Alstein and see how a religious-professional narrative is constructed, or focus on his daughter's reaction as the analytical point of the story. For example, we could construct a sociological narrative about how other actors guard the symbolic boundaries of the community from inadvertent ruptures of their imagined insularity. As with any fieldwork excerpt, the question of where to begin and end the interaction is always fraught.

While this is definitely analytically fruitful, following the interactional chain of meaning-making allows us to make a different point. Rather than an arbitrary decision (White 1987), we follow the way that actors themselves parsed out the flow of interaction. The story began, was challenged and retracted, and then the interactants turned to a different topic of conversation (see also Tavory and Timmermans 2009). Thus, by taking the *inter*action as his primary unit of analysis, Tavory shows how social worlds cohere rather than simply how pressure is exerted. In retracting his own story, we can see how Mr. Alstein himself solidifies the moral force of the boundaries between Jews and non-Jews in this case. In interactionally yielding to his daughter's demands, Mr. Alstein, and others around the table who pivoted away from the story, reaffirmed that raising the specter of non-Jewish selves in this context was a wrong move. It is precisely by knowing how to retract his story and how to reconstruct his image (even if humorously) that the Orthodox social world is maintained. In Tavory's terms, it is about knowing how to be correctly summoned into interaction where both identifications and social worlds are kept intact—a point that would be completely lost if we didn't take the interaction as a whole.

A second example of coding-in-motion comes from Stefan Timmermans's (2013) work on the interpretation of genetic testing results to find a cause of serious disabilities. To illustrate how coding interactional units provides clues for mechanisms beyond an elementary three-step process, we provide an example of a family of a child with global developmental delay and seizures. The eight-year-old boy, Michael, is unable to feed himself and requires around-the-clock care, provided to large extent by his single mother. The genetic test locates a variant in the *WDR45* gene, which is associated with iron accumulation in the brain and may be a cause of developmental delay. However, the variant is often lethal in boys, and the inheritance pattern does not seem to fit the situation. The geneticists decide to classify the gene as a "variant of uncertain significance" because clinicians can check for iron accumulation in the brain with a series of MRIs. If there is indeed iron accumulation, it will confirm that the variant is (at least partly) responsible for the disabilities. Still, this is not a clear genetic cause, and the geneticist has to convey the uncertainty to the mother during the clinic visit. When the geneticist explains the possibility that the *WDR45* variant may be responsible for the issues Michael faces, the mother tries to get a better handle on the uncertainty. The geneticist and genetic counselor explain the nuance between having a variant associated with and having a variant causing symptoms. The ensuing conversation carefully parses genetic causality in which the presence of a genetic variant does not necessarily imply a symptomatic effect.

Since we use a longer excerpt in this example, we present an abbreviated coding next to the text of the interaction. The coding centers on how the certainty about genetic causality shifts over the course of the conversation.

Mother: So this is saying that, I mean, that gene is related to this, or this is the condition he has?	*The mother offers two scenarios of varying levels of certainty, giving the geneticist an opportunity to causally upgrade or downgrade the variant.*
Geneticist: Well, I mean, this is the condition that he has, and this is that this gene causes a clinical presentation very similar to those types of conditions . . . Does that make sense?	*The geneticist presents the variant as likely causal. He responds that they already know what disease Michael has from clinical observations. The gene they found is closely associated with these symptoms. Ergo, it is a likely suspect.*

Mother: Yeah, and then this gene, though, that causes this, you're saying also has never been seen or has never been found. I don't know the word for it.

The mother adds more uncertainty: she wonders about the fact that little is known about this gene.

Geneticist: The gene is **associated with** the condition. We know that the gene **causes it**, but how the change that he specifically has . . . How, whether that actually caused this disease or not, right? Because, there are many changes that we carry in genes that could cause disease, right, but the change itself doesn't affect the function of the gene. Right? We don't know if this one has been associated with the disease because we haven't seen it before in another person that has the same condition. These are very rare conditions, so the number of individuals that are available with changes in the gene are very limited. So it's difficult to say if you had a change exactly like him that this is what you would expect because we haven't seen that specific change that he has in other people. Because it could be a change that doesn't have an effect on the gene. Makes sense?

The geneticist reiterates a position of certainty but then backs down. He clarifies that the gene is suspected of causing symptoms and although Michael has some of those symptoms, he is not sure that in this specific case, the variant causes his symptoms. He explains the uncertainty with the lack of familiarity with the gene.

Here, the geneticist adds more uncertainty about causality. He raises the possibility that even if Michael has this variant, it would not necessarily need to have a pathological effect.

Mother: Okay. Yeah. I know, and it's kind of, I guess I'm trying to figure out how I can ask the question. Umm, but because it is associated with this condition, does that mean for sure he's gonna end up with iron deposits or . . .	*The mother now asks a direct certainty question about the variant causing Michael's symptoms.*
Geneticist: We don't know that. Exactly. And that's the variant of uncertain significance, and that's why it's uncertain what the clinical relevance is of this change because even though it is associated with a condition that presents similar to this, right, and he may or may not have the changes in the brain, we'll see when the authorization for the MRI gets done. It may still be the case that even though that's normal, the brain MRI, he may still have the condition, or this change does not predispose him to have this condition at all.	*The geneticist again backs down, directly admitting that the exact causality is unknown. He reinforces the uncertainty through a reference to the classification of the variant.* *He renders the variant conditionally certain, conditional on MRI findings.*

Coding-in-motion shows here how the interaction as it develops in the clinic works toward a shared understanding of conditional genetic causality. In light of our previous discussion of interactional mechanisms, what we have here is an attempt at alignment centered upon uncertainty. The subject of contention—whether *WDR45* causes Michael's symptoms—is unknowable given current medical technologies. During the conversation, the mother pushes to understand what the genetic variant explains. Even though the geneticist initially presented the variant as potentially causal, the mother's clarification questions require him to delineate what is known and remains uncertain about the role of the variant. Over the course of this conversation, the variant shifts from a likely cause to a variant burdened by uncertainties and ends up, at best, a conditional cause. At every turn of the conversation, the mother and clinician then render uncertainty meaningful while at the same time remaining unable to come to a definitive understanding of what the variant does. Coding-in-motion allows us to map how the genetic variant's causal certainty shifts over the course of this exchange. The interactional mechanism at work here is the collective working out of uncertainty. This is interesting because we would expect the physician, an expert in genetics, to define causality, but the mother's questions actively influence the variant's role in the patient differently than initially presented.

Discussion

As they observe interactions over time, ethnographers are in a unique position to make claims regarding the unfolding of action and interaction, laying out the components of the social processes they try to explain. Although the humanistic urge to give voice to people's biographies and narratives is surely part of the seduction of ethnography, its most powerful draw lies in part in the ability to trace the processes through which social life unfolds. Such a mechanism-based approach, we argue, is best grounded in an account of meaning-making that treats interaction as an irreducible aspect of the social world. To locate interactional mechanisms it is useful to conduct "coding-in-motion"—to look at field note and interview excerpts and try to see the back-and-forth of action and interaction as a primary unit of analysis rather than as an aggregation of actors' discrete actions.

A mechanism-based approach to ethnography largely transcends specific levels of analysis. As some of the examples presented in this chapter clearly show, the processes the ethnographer traces may be at a macro, meso, or micro level. Zero-tolerance policing, for example, is far from being a "micro" phenomenon.[6]

Here, however, the reader may have noted a disjuncture in the text. The examples make it seem as if ethnographers implicitly work through mechanisms whether or not they think in those terms. In our own work, we have been thinking explicitly about mechanisms, but this is not the case for Jerolmack or Lee, for example. And yet if we accept that, as Molière put it, we are "speaking prose without knowing it," why do we even need to think in terms of mechanisms? Couldn't we just continue doing good, careful ethnographic work and trust that the mechanisms would already be there?

There are, we think, at least two reasons for ethnographers to be explicit about the mechanisms they identify. The first has to do with the clarity of our claims. Ethnographers often obscure the actual causal processes they describe. Requiring ethnographers to think and write explicitly about the identified causal pathways, and the evidence they have for them, is one way of holding them responsible for their claims (Tavory and Timmermans, 2014).

A second reason, however, is more practical. Ethnographers are notoriously bad at figuring out "what is this a case of?" This is, quite often, the charge leveled against ethnography—that the scope validity of the work is too narrow and that the case ends up being only "an N of 1." And while it is true that some ethnographers

---

6. Of course, unless the analysis is extremely situated, ethnographic work will not explain it all. If we are interested in zero-tolerance policing, we would do well to attend to large-scale institutional and economic shifts. But as long as ethnographers remember that their analyses provide only part of what is usually a multi-sited, multilevel set of processes, we thus hope that a mechanism-based approach transcends some of the quibbles over micro vs. macro that ethnographers are plagued with.

don't *want* to think in terms of cases, most ethnographers and outsiders see the lack of transposable findings as one of the thorniest issues of the method (see, e.g., Becker and Ragin 1992; Tavory and Timmermans 2009).

By attending to mechanism-based explanations, ethnographers make explicit the logic of their causal claims. This allows them to see more clearly what other cases might be part of the same set. In each of the cases we outlined, the process the ethnographer depicted is potentially transposable to other cases, some of which may at first seem completely different. Thinking about Vaughan's notion of uncoupling in intimate relations, we can find connections to the rise and fall of careers and social movements; thinking about genetic testing may lead us to better understand far-flung cases in which people are still struggling to frame new forms of knowledge; thinking of Orthodox Jews in Los Angeles may lead us to imagine all the cases in which people have to carefully monitor what they reveal about the web of relationships they are tied to when an institution makes powerful demands upon their identities.

It is here, finally, that the tension between processes and protagonists emerges most clearly. Mechanism-based explanations are not blind to people—ethnographers such as Lee, Jerolmack, and Stuart pay careful attention to the people they describe. And yet by attending to the structure of processes in the field, the true protagonists of the work are always the processes themselves. It is precisely because the process is central that ethnographers can begin to chart a terrain they may not have even been aware of. By accounting for the logic of the process they describe, they avoid being bogged down by questions about the representativeness of their sample and can leverage the structure of their mechanism-based explanations to show the surprising connections among different situations in social life. Thinking in mechanisms, then, is a helpful way for ethnographers not only to be explicit about their claims but also to better theorize what they find.

References

Abend, Gabriel, Caitlin Petre, and Michael Sauder. 2013. "Styles of Causal Thought: An Empirical Investigation." *American Journal of Sociology* 119(3): 602–654.

Becker, Howard S. and Charles C. Ragin. 1992. *What Is a Case? Exploring the Foundations of Social Inquiry.* Cambridge: Cambridge University Press.

Blumer, Herbert. 1969. *Symbolic Interactionism: Perspective and Method.* Englewood Cliffs, NJ: Prentice Hall.

Elster, Jon. 1989. *Nuts and Bolts for the Social Sciences.* Cambridge: Cambridge University Press.

Geertz, Clifford. 1973. *The Interpretation of Cultures.* New York: Basic Books.

Glaeser, Andreas. 2011. *Political Epistemics: The Secret Police, the Opposition and the End of East German Socialism.* Chicago: University of Chicago Press.

Goffman, Erving. 1983. "The Interaction Order." *American Sociological Review* 48: 1–17.

Gross, Neil. 2009. "A Pragmatist Theory of Social Mechanisms." *American Sociological Review* 74(3): 358–379.

Hedström, Peter. 2005. *Dissecting the Social: On the Principles of Analytical Sociology.* Cambridge: Cambridge University Press.

Hedström, Peter and Richard Swedberg (eds.). 1998. *Social Mechanisms: An Analytical Approach to Social Theory.* Cambridge: Cambridge University Press.

Hedström, Peter, and Petri Ylikoski. 2010. "Causal Mechanisms in the Social Sciences." *Annual Review of Sociology* 36: 49–67.

Jerolmack, Colin. 2009. "Primary Groups and Cosmopolitan Ties: The Rooftop Pigeon Flyers of New York." *Ethnography* 10(2/3): 211–233.

Jerolmack, Colin. 2013. *The Global Pigeon.* Chicago: University of Chicago Press.

Lee, Jooyoung. 2016. *Blowin' Up: Rap Dreams in South Central.* Chicago: University of Chicago Press.

Machamer, Peter, Lindley Darden, and Carl F. Craver. 2000. "Thinking about Mechanisms." *Philosophy of Science* 67(1): 1–25.

Reed, Isaac. 2011. *Interpretation and Social Knowledge: On the Use of Theory in the Human Sciences.* Chicago: University of Chicago Press.

Reiss, Julian. 2009. "Causation in the Social Sciences: Evidence, Inference, and Purpose." *Philosophy of the Social Sciences* 39(1): 20–40.
Stuart, Forrest. 2016. *Down, Out, and Under Arrest: Policing and Everyday Life in Skid Row.* Chicago: University of Chicago Press.
Tavory, Iddo. 2016. *Summoned: Identification and Religious Life in a Jewish Neighborhood.* Chicago: University of Chicago Press.
Tavory, Iddo and Stefan Timmermans. 2009. "Two Cases of Ethnography: Grounded Theory and the Extended Case Method." *Ethnography* 10(3): 243–263.
Tavory, Iddo and Stefan Timmermans. 2103. "A Pragmatist Approach to Causality." *American Journal of Sociology* 119(3): 682–714.
Tavory, Iddo and Stefan Timmermans. 2014. *Abductive Analysis: Theorizing Qualitative Research.* Chicago: University of Chicago Press.
Timmermans, Stefan. 2013. *Saving Babies? The Consequences of Newborn Genetic Screening.* Chicago: University of Chicago Press.
Vaidyanathan, Brandon, Michael Strand, Austin Choi-Fitzpatrick, Thomas Buschman, Megan Davis, and Amanda Varela. 2015. "Causality in Contemporary American Sociology: An Empirical Assessment and Critique." *Journal for the Theory of Social Behavior* 45(1): 3–26.
Vaughan, Diane. 1986. *Uncoupling: Turning Points in Intimate Relationships.* Oxford: Oxford University Press.
Vaughan, Diane. 2009. "Analytic Ethnography." In *The Oxford Handbook of Analytical Sociology*, edited by Peter Hedström and Peter Bearman, 688–711. Oxford: Oxford University Press.
White, Hayden. 1987. *The Content of the Form: Narrative Discourse and Historical Representation.* Baltimore: Johns Hopkins University Press.
Woodward, Jim. 2002. "What Is a Mechanism? A Counterfactual Account." *Philosophy of Science* 69(23): S366–S377.

Chapter 6

Embodiment

A Dispositional Approach to Racial and Cultural Analysis

BLACK HAWK HANCOCK

Perhaps we are able to see only that which we are prepared to see, and in our culture, the cost of insight is an uncertainty that threatens our already unstable sense of order and requires a constant questioning of accepted assumptions. (Ralph Ellison 1995: 31)

My book *American Allegory: Lindy Hop and the Racial Imagination* (Hancock 2013) examines the revival within white America of the Lindy Hop, the original Swing dance that emerged out of the ballrooms of Harlem in the late 1920s. It addresses the contradiction between the centrality of African American culture in American society and the simultaneous marginality of African American people. This essay reflects on my own ethnographic experience in order to explicate the relationship between the racial imagination and an embodied approach to ethnography. I reflect back on two key themes—minstrelsy and whitewashing—that emerged out of my commitment to doing embodied ethnography. Drawing on these themes, I demonstrate how using the body as a phenomenological tool opens up new ways to think about both racial classification and cultural practices. I conclude with a discussion of three other examples of embodied ethnography, as well as some generative remarks on what embodied ethnography offers us as a methodological approach to the study of social life.

Embodied Ethnography and the Racial Imagination

Embodied ethnography requires that we develop practical knowledge to understand our world. Because practical knowledge can be acquired only by putting oneself in the line of fire and subjecting oneself to the social forces under analysis, it cannot come from a detached perspective. Embodied ethnography demands not only a new methodological entry into the world one is studying, but also a new mode of theorizing the body as both a tool of inquiry and a vector of knowledge.[1] This approach requires one to be both a practitioner of a particular art (trade, craft, occupation) and a sociologist, without necessarily being able to remove the one from the other (Hancock 2009).

Embodied ethnography differs from autoethnography in that the latter focuses exclusively on the researcher's personal experience in the field. Autoethnography focuses on the self, knowledge of the self, the dynamics of personal interest, and the investment of one's personal experience. Embodied ethnography, by contrast, is not about the meaning of personal participation. Rather, it uses full immersion into a particular world of study in order to fully understand the phenomena under investigation from the inside out, a vantage point that is inaccessible through observation alone (Fine and Hancock 2016). In this way, embodied ethnography also differs from traditional participant observation, as the processes

---

1. This approach follows Wacquant's reworking of Bourdieu. For an explanation of how Wacquant explicates his own radicalization of Bourdieu's "habitus" see my article "Taking Loïc Wacquant into the Field" (Hancock 2009). See also Wacquant 2015.

of immersion and conversion that the embodied approach affords enable us to unearth the practical knowledge—that is, the skill set, or *disposition*, of knowing how to do something—of the phenomenon in question, which often remains unspoken. In this way embodied ethnography resonates with what Pierre Bourdieu defines as "participant objectivation"—a methodological approach to comprehending a social world through its practices, while simultaneously maintaining one's reflexive knowledge and commitment to seeing the world as a sociologist (Bourdieu and Wacquant 1992: 68).

Embodied ethnography also differs from Paul Stoller's (1997) "sensuous scholarship," despite their surface similarities. Sensuous scholarship shares one of the aims of carnal sociology in that they both seek to move beyond treating the body as a text to be deciphered and instead incorporate the sensing body—the smells, tastes, textures, and sensations of the agent—into scholarly practices, representations, and descriptions. However, sensuous scholarship retains an outsider perspective on the issue of embodiment. The methodological approach of sensuous scholarship offers no understanding of how people feel, no account of how emotions and senses shape everyday embodiment and comportment in relation to their existing conditions, and no descriptive resources to provide an explanation of how embodiment animates social conduct and structures social relations.

The case in question here, dance, is an embodied, nonlinguistic cultural form that cannot be fully understood from the outside. Dance is an art that is learned, understood, and expressed through the body. In order to acquire this dispositional knowledge, I could not simply watch and ask questions about the Lindy Hop. I had to reach a point where I could perform the art as a dancer. Therefore, I had to come to understand the dance practically, through my own body. Learning to dance is the process of acquiring the competences of choreography, leading and following, improvising to music, and expressing oneself aesthetically, all simultaneously in time and space. This retooling of the body was a demanding process of inculcation and training whereby my awkward pre-dance body had to be re-formed and cultivated into an educated fluid dancing body. As with riding a bike, conceptual mastery of dance is of limited use; it is only after the dance has been assimilated into the body through endless drills and repetitions that it becomes fully understood. Only by embodying the dance could I become a dancer, but also, and more important, could I see and comprehend the details and subtleties that remain invisible to those who have not acquired that practical knowledge. Only through an embodied ethnographic approach could I have come to understand the anxiety and tension that Lindy Hop dancers undertake consciously or unconsciously and the ways that race gets refracted through culture in learning how to dance. Focusing on the embodiment of dance allowed me to see the ways embodiment becomes a tool for interpreting and understanding the world.

In order to address the issues of race, culture, and embodiment within the world of the Lindy Hop, this project draws inspiration from the work of Ralph Ellison and poses a series of Ellisonian questions: How does the simultaneous embrace of African American culture and the marginalization of African American people serve to secure and perpetuate white racial domination? How do cultural forms become both expressions of racial groups and mechanisms of social closure that separate and strengthen those very racial classifications to which those forms are ascribed? Finally, and most important, how does the world of Lindy Hop allegorically characterize the way that race is played out in American society?

As Ralph Ellison drew our attention to the question of American identity, he captured the historical complexities of the white engagement with African American culture, which has never been straightforward; in fact, this interaction has been a complex, contradictory, anxiety-riddled process of negotiation by which whites have simultaneously embraced and rejected, desired and disdained, African American culture within the constraints of the dominant racial order (Lott 1995; Rogin 1996; Toll 1974). This anxiety is not always based on conscious awareness; rather, it mostly exists below the level of consciousness without direct comprehension of how people come to embody cultural forms and perform cultural practices (Bourdieu 2000). This enduring anxiety is at the very basis of racial formations, racial conflicts, and the history of black and white relations in American society.

The racial imagination, the dominant racial categories through which we understand the world, illuminates how cultural practices such as music and dance are understood only after being refracted through the racial categories that come to define them. Filtering our appreciation and interpretation through the racial imagination forces us to think through essentializing categories that conflate competence, culture, and race. An analysis of the racial imagination enables us to understand the underlying unquestioned racialized commonsense through which whiteness and blackness are interpreted (white men can't jump, blacks are naturally rhythmic, etc.). This orientation shapes not only the expectations and assumptions about people's competences and abilities based on race, but also the very ways that people are disposed to act based on those racial differences. As a result, the racial imagination becomes embodied and enacted through cultural practices and unreflexive dispositions, as is the case with dance and the Lindy Hop.

An exploration of the racial imagination reveals two dominant modes of embodiment—minstrelsy and whitewashing—in which culture, bodies, and race all intersect. Minstrelsy can be defined as white people intentionally performing the role of black people, drawing on historical stereotypes and mythologies of the black body as innately and essentially exotic, sexual, expressive, and rhythmic. This sense of blackness is constructed as exterior to whiteness, whereas the white body is marked by its rationality, restraint, and rigidity. By contrast, whitewashing, whether intentional or unintentional, is the erasure or omission of the racial identity associated with the history of a particular cultural practice or cultural form. By illuminating these particular modes of engagement as modes of embodiment, we can come to see how racial domination is produced and operates not only through conscious intentions and actions, but also through the enactment of embodied cultural forms in everyday life, as black and white bodies perform, consciously and unconsciously, notions of blackness and whiteness.

Even in today's "multicultural" and "colorblind" society, this racial logic continues to define the interactions and cultural-racial politics of white society. As a result, white interaction with African American culture must be situated against the larger sociohistorical context of racial domination in order to break from the liberal myth that cultural appreciation serves to generate social equality. White attraction to, identification with, and enactment of African American cultural forms are often undertaken either in an explicit resistance to white societal norms and aesthetics (e.g., gangsta rap) or implicitly as a symbol of multicultural unity (e.g., the Lindy Hop). In either case, cross-cultural embodiment, in the extremes of minstrelsy and whitewashing, ultimately works to affirm and perpetuate racial domination, despite conscious intentions, through the simultaneous marginalization and domination of African American people. As a result, this cultural engagement and cultural embodiment not only oppresses African Americans, but also simultaneously (and ironically) dominates whites themselves as they remain trapped in their own essentialized whiteness. Had I relied on discursive narratives or on larger structural/cultural explanations, I would have missed the ways that race becomes embedded and embodied within us, defining the very racial logic, practices, and social relations that generate and reproduce racial domination in twenty-first-century American society.

Minstrelsy

Despite their billings as images of reality, these Negroes of fiction are counterfeits. They are projected aspects of an internal symbolic process through which, like a primitive tribesman dancing himself into the group frenzy necessary for battle, the White American prepares himself emotionally to perform a social role. (Ellison 1995: 27–28)

White engagement with African American culture generates minstrelsy, by which the desire to perform African American culture "authentically," or correctly, leads to a caricature of African Americans in style, mannerisms, or motion. While this new incarnation of minstrelsy has shed its blackface paint, it continues to be a racial ventriloquism that is at once a racial embrace and a racial distancing, enabling whites to work out their attraction to African American culture while simultaneously distancing themselves from blackness through an implicit degradation. This new form of minstrelsy, or what we may call "neo-minstrelsy," works through the racial imagination that has normalized meanings of blackness and whiteness, enabling whites to enact their understandings of African American dancing without self-conscious reflection on the symbolic meanings generated by their performances. As a result, neo-minstrelsy is able to continue its historical function of maintaining racial essentialism and racial domination not only in the staged performance of the dance, but in everyday social dancing, in the cultivation of the dance through teaching, and in the more general ways that whites conceptualize how African Americans act. The embodied ethnographic approach provided a visceral awareness of the ways that aesthetic/cultural practices mask the social and political mechanisms that structure racial dominance. In addition, through an embodied ethnographic account, I was able to bring to light the modalities of social interaction, often existing below the level of consciousness, that reveal the arbitrary and conventional nature of all social relations.

As a mode of engagement, minstrelsy is not something over and above the dance or something added to it; rather, it is constitutive of the dance's embodiment and enactment. By excavating the implicit understandings of blackness and whiteness that come through in the performance of the dance, we are able to examine these embodiments in action. The following vignette is reconstructed from my field notes:

"Sing, Sing, Sing," the signature Benny Goodman dance number, came booming over the PA system, and almost instinctively all the dancers flocked to the center of the dance floor. They congregated in a "jam" circle, a ring of people forming a showcase space where dancers strut and perform their flashiest and most complicated tricks for the audience. One after another, couples burst into the center of the circle and tried to outduel each other for the status of best dancers. As the song is lightning fast, the couples had only a short time to dazzle and impress the onlookers. As I stood amid the crowd, taking in the spectacle of twists and turns, one particularly admired couple leaped into the circle and captured everyone's attention. They immediately began to execute extremely complicated moves. After a few partnered moves, the couple broke apart and performed individualized steps; the male dancer paraded around the female by strutting and waving his hands, while the female dancer started into the "crazy legs," where the woman wobbles her legs as if to appear out of control. The crowd went wild over this display, and instantly another couple jumped into the circle to outdo them and earn the applause for themselves. One after another, couples entered this self-constructed fishbowl of performance, seeking the attention and acclaim of the dance community; as couples attempted bolder and more ostentatious moves, the dance became more and more theatrical. The crowd's expectations rose with each improvisation. Yet the more ostentatious and burlesque the Lindy Hop becomes in these "jams," it only seems to garner more mutual enthusiasm, respect, and applause among the dancers.

Removing the burnt-cork greasepaint, which defined the black mask of minstrelsy, makes it harder to document these caricatured performances of what whites imagine African Americans to be like; minstrelsy is no longer so explicit. As a result, I was able to understand, as an embodied ethnographer, that we must be hypersensitive to the mode of engagement that defines this new minstrelsy and to understand how it may go unnoticed by others. Whereas the stereotyped language and racialized speech of the minstrel stage shows, such as racialized songs and poems, provided easy access to documenting the minstrel performance, today's minstrelsy continues to signify racial difference without those explicit forms. While these cross-cultural engagements can appear merely literal, we can also read the visual vocabulary of these performances as enactments of stereotypes of African Americans as wild, primitive, and out of control. As these notions of blackness are worked out as vehicles for personal and group expression, they become over-the-top spectacles of racial performance undertaken within the controlled and localized community of the Lindy Hop scene, serving to reinscribe racial essentialism.

While this minstrelsy is enacted through imitation, it is also cultivated through teaching the dance. This was apparent to me many times when I was working as a performer.

When I worked for a Lindy Hop performance company, we were often hired to give performances and teach dance lessons to middle and high school students. One engagement took us to a wealthy all-white high school in the north suburbs of Chicago. The owner of the company had hired me to assist her in two short dance workshops for the school drama class. We first did a demonstration of the Lindy Hop, and then we were to teach the students a short lesson in partner moves and a few individual jazz steps. After showing them the basic step and a couple of turns, the company's owner moved on to the individual steps. She said to the class, "I want all the guys to pay attention to me. Girls, you can relax for a moment. Okay, now I want the guys to do a 'pimp walk.' Do you guys know what a pimp is? And do you know how a pimp walks? I'll show you." (The owner, who was a slender white female, hunched over and started to swing her right arm from side to side as she lazily strutted across the room, leaning to one side in a mimic of the "pimp" stereotype.) "Now guys, I want you to do it like this; make sure that the girls see you strutting your stuff, so they check you out. Show them how cool you are. So try it, just pretend you're a pimp." She turned to the girls. "Now girls, when the guys do their thing, I want you to do what's called a fishtail." (She bent over and started to swivel her hips, walking backward in lunging steps.) "And girls, when you do this, I want you to really stick it out and give them something to look at. While the girls do that, I want the guys to pimp walk around them and check them out—really show your stuff, guys, and girls, I want you to check them out . . . get ready, I'll count you in with the music." The students were thrilled and took to the steps without missing a beat, as if they were veteran dancers.

As they acted out these parodies, the visual image of the hypersexualized pimp and the fishtailing of the women's posteriors served as titillating entertainment for the high school students. I had to wonder what myths of blackness were being reinscribed within the safe confines of this elite high school auditorium. As this dance workshop was unfolding before me—and I watched these youngsters enact the steps according to the visuals we had provided them—I wondered if they were making a connection in their minds to a racial other, absent from the room but implicitly there as they enacted these movements with gleeful abandon. Since the students so easily grasped the movements, I had to wonder if this visual imagery was already socialized into them, already buried in their subconscious as a perception of how black folks are supposed to move. The minstrelsy that circulates throughout the Lindy Hop was not just occurring in the elite spaces of the jam session. It was finding its way through all modes of enactment, even in the teaching of the dance. While these exaggerated and overdone stereotypes were being offered up by the instructor, their easy embrace suggested that these myths of blackness were already somewhat in circulation, merely needing someone to activate them.

When considering minstrelsy in relation to the Lindy Hop, we must examine the ways that the dance is inculcated with a series of racial mythologies implicit in its movements. The "twist-twist," the defining female movement of the Lindy Hop, is an all-encompassing bodily rotation that emphasizes the hips, thighs, pelvis, and feet. The female dancer rotates her hips back and forth in a twisting motion, which serves as both a dance step and a ready position for the next move. This twisting motion emanates a particular stylized and sexual dynamic by emphasizing the buttocks and hips in its gyrating display. Mastering the twist-twist is essential in order to develop a feeling for the dance and to capture its aesthetic. The twist-twist movement also allows individualization and stylization; no two women will twist exactly alike, as each tries to stamp her signature or personality on the defining movement. Yet, as with all art forms, the fundamentals are always the most elusive and difficult things to master, requiring constant practice and revision.

Late one afternoon in July, at the Herräng dance camp in Herräng, Sweden, I was taking an advanced Lindy Hop class from Angela Andrews, a black British woman who is one of the leaders and revivalists of the dance in England. We were working on the basics of Lindy Hop, including the twist-twist, when suddenly Angela started yelling, bringing the class to an abrupt halt: "Stop! Stop! Stop! Okay, all right. I didn't want to have to say this, but I have to. Ladies, what is this?" She demonstrated the follower's basic step in an overly dramatic motion, with her buttocks way out behind her as if she were about to fall over. "All right, I'll tell you. It's ugly. In your face, it's ugly! Be ladies! This is not ladylike. Okay, now I didn't want to say this, but look, I know a lot of you are trying to copy me and stick your bums out when you dance, but it's ugly; don't do it. Look, this is God-given. I am not trying to stick it out. Dance with your bum under you; don't stick it out! Be a lady when you dance. Don't try and make your body do something it can't do."

The class stood there stunned, uncertain what to make of this. What did she mean? "What is she saying?" one woman whispered to me, as I stood there, speechless. Had she just said what I thought she said? I was shocked; the women were embarrassed and confused. Wasn't this what they had been taught as long as they'd been doing the dance? Wasn't this how the step looked in the old black-and-white movies? Didn't this step require them to extend their buttocks out in a twisting motion? How or why would the women do anything else if this was what they were taught? Here we were in the backwoods of Sweden, learning Lindy Hop in a class with some of the best dancers from around the world, and everyone looked around at each other like they had never heard or even thought of this before. What exactly was the problem? Was it simply that they were sticking their butts out too far, or was there something more?

Angela was pointing out something so subtle, so implicit and unspoken, that they could not see it. Yet it was so offensive and significant to her that she had reached her boiling point. Ostensibly this was about mere body movements, not the movements' literal meaning. But what was really happening was that Angela was treading on taboo ground, articulating the unspoken racial tension of the Lindy Hop—the minstrelsy that pervades and dominates its revival. The ugliness that she pointed out came not just in body positioning, but in the minstrelsy that posture signified. It was the representation that had angered Angela, the imitation of black physiology according to how whites envision it. Its ugliness came not in white bodies dancing a black dance, but in the grotesque exaggeration of the body in motion. This was not about the superiority or the aesthetic of the white versus the black body; it was about dancing within the limits of your own body, not in an imitation of what the white racializing imagination perceives that a black female body must look like.

Later that week when I interviewed Angela, asking her if she saw this as a problem, she replied:

> Oh, I do think it's a problem. Nobody wants to talk about it; no one ever does, because when you do . . . But I had to say something. I mean, it really is offensive in this white perception of black physiology that they are trying to do but won't acknowledge. Look at the girls, they're trying to dance with their asses way out, in what they think is the way black people dance! But look, I don't stick it out. I've got a big bum, but I don't stick it out; it does that on its own. But for some of these girls, it looks so outrageous, so I had to confront them on that. I don't even think they realize on a conscious level how offensive that really is.

Here was the underlying problem of the Lindy Hop revival that was never articulated, never confronted, never even spoken, yet constantly present: this white obsession with black physiology, an unspoken and maybe even an unconscious mimesis in whites' performance of the dance that is illuminated here in Angela's words. It is here in this confrontation that the white racializing imagination is made visible, as it produces and cultivates minstrel performances that are symbolically racist—even if unknowingly. The performance of the dance, the way it was done, represents something that whites have normalized and accepted. Minstrelsy is subtly at work, and yet it more often than not escapes whites' consciousness, since that is not their intention. This contradiction was made apparent when I followed up with one of the women from Angela's class later that day. When I inquired about how she felt about what happened when Angela interrupted class, she responded:

> I really don't understand what she was so mad about. I don't think anybody meant anything by it. We were just trying to

dance like her. I wasn't trying to stick my butt out. I mean, how are you supposed to learn how to dance with style if you don't model the teachers you are taking the classes from? They are the experts, right?

The minstrelsy being illuminated here is a performance that is socialized, not just last week, but from the very beginning, as it is woven into the fabric of our racial imagination and the culture we inherit. This was not a class of beginners; these were advanced dancers from around the world who had danced for years and traveled all the way to Sweden to attend one of the world's best Lindy Hop camps.

Even when whites weren't dancing, the racial engagement with African American culture was present. It was not just the dance alone that reproduced notions of racial essentialism; it was circulating through everyday culture and affected all the African American cultural forms that whites engaged in. The following anecdote reconstructed from my field notes proved useful to the extent that it was not just the Lindy Hop that was at issue here, but rather all forms of African American culture that whites engage:

Outside the building where the workshop was being held, I leaned against the wall and watched the dancers return from their lunch break. I was talking to Steven, an African American instructor, when two white dancers in their early twenties walked by. When they saw Steven, they greeted him with a dramatic "Whasssssup," the colloquial greeting recently made popular in a national Budweiser advertisement featuring several twenty-something African Americans. Steven laughed and greeted the two men as they passed him. Then he turned to me and said, "I understand it—and it's cool that they want to be a part of it—but it's just so much sometimes." These two young men were prime examples of neo-minstrelsy, staring us in the face. I asked Steven if the exchange had bothered him. He replied,

"This is my job. This is their party; this is not my party. But I do what I have to do because I'm a professional, and this is my job." I asked, "Is everything okay? You look a little shaken all of a sudden." He looked at me and said, "They kill it for me. No, I don't even want to go there, I don't even want to go there, I can't."

This sense that all African American cultural forms are enacted without people recognizing the significance of their actions was something brought to light in my interviews. A Lindy Hop master who had been one of the principal revivalists described his feelings about the sometimes awkward outcomes when whites participated in the dance:

> For most people it becomes artificial. You don't believe it at all, really. It's the same sometimes when you see people that dress up in their zoot suits and things; most people can't wear them, it just hurts when they come into the room—they can't even walk in them. I think you need a certain attitude to carry such a thing, and it's the same with the dance: you need a little bit of an attitude to carry off such a thing, to bring it to a certain level, and most people, they don't have that attitude or that inside feeling for it. It's only when you have that attitude that it can become part of you. If you look at it critically, at least to me, it's a little bit pathetic. It can be like a big masquerade, something like that—something artificial, I can't touch it—it's something false—it's a bit off, but I don't know if you can put your finger on it. It's a lot of big hats and costumes walking around, and there's no one inside them, really. But then you see that some people are able to do it, and it's normally the black people. It seems to be their thing, because for them it's so natural.

This sense of something happening in the dance, something that cannot be articulated, seemed to me to be the very issue of the way the racial imagination generated these distorting modes of embodiment. While it exists, most often below the level of consciousness, it continues to shape and inform the ways that whites embody the dance.

As Ellison's remarks echo through the cross-cultural embrace of the Lindy Hop, the minstrel, the mask, the imitation, and the question of what identity is continue to confound our understandings and enactments of what race is. Only by embodying the dance myself and exploring the ways that race became internalized through cultural practices could I have come to focus on how whites embodied the dance in particular ways. This was not something that could be revealed through interviews; rather, it was by understanding the production of culture in action that I came to realize how and why race matters the way it does, in the "two-fold naturalization" of both racial categories and the racializing logic of the world around us. Race resides within our dispositions and orientations as well as in the world so as to appear transparent and natural (Bourdieu 2000: 187).

Whitewashing

Being "highly pigmented" as the sociologists say, it was our Negro "misfortune" to be caught up associatively in the negative side of this basic dualism of the white folk mind, and to be shackled to almost everything it would repress from conscience and consciousness. (Ellison 1995: 213–214)

As Ellison remarks, it is the symbolism of blackness and whiteness that shapes and influences the ways we interpret race, whether consciously or unconsciously. The conflation of blackness with negative traits and whiteness with positive traits leads to an either conscious or unconscious repression. One way this repression of blackness can occur is through the process of whitewashing. Whitewashing, whereby black cultural forms are severed from their origins, is another mode of engagement that defines the white embrace of African American culture (Lott 1995). Whereas minstrelsy is a caricatured performance of an allegedly black cultural disposition, whitewashing is its antithesis, defined by its underexpression and inhibition by which whites maintain their distance from blackness (Gabriel 1998). While these poles of engagement have nothing in common in terms of their presentation, their effects are the same, in that they serve as mechanisms to reinscribe racial essentialism and racial domination. Through whitewashing, white society is able to indulge in its desire for and attraction to African American culture, while at the same time, through assimilation, it does not have to confront blackness and the consequences of its embrace.

As a way of embodying the Lindy Hop, whitewashing occurs through two forms of distancing: first, through the failure to actively acknowledge the historical origins of the dance in context and, second, through the inhibition of expression that characterizes the cultural logic of the dance. This dual process of whitewashing (historical-emotional) has nothing to do with the capacity of white people to perform or excel at the Lindy Hop. It has everything to do, rather, with the consequences of white engagement with African American cultural forms and with how this embodiment changes the cultural logic and aesthetic to fit the needs and tastes of white society. This assimilation, when taken to its fullest extent, removes all signs, traces, and articulations of blackness, resulting in a complete racial and cultural erasure of African Americans, as these cultural forms become normalized and canonized within white society. This whitewashing can be seen in the following description reconstructed from my field notes of the "Khakis Swing" ad by the Gap clothing company that ran during the spring and summer of 1998:

As horns began blowing the tune "Jump Jive and Wail," the Brian Setzer Orchestra's cover of the classic Louis Prima song, around ten couples of white twenty-something dancers, all clad in khaki pants, began dancing in front of a stark, empty white background. As the music played, they jumped, twisted, spun, and performed acrobatic lifts and tricks, all caught up in the movement and pleasure of swing dancing. This flurry of passion lasted a brief fifteen seconds, and the Gap commercial ended with the lone words "Khakis Swing."

This group of attractive, fashionable people provoked a feeling of viewer participation—as if the audience could be there, too, dancing away with their friends. Yet nearly all Lindy Hoppers I spoke with who had seen the ad were disappointed and outraged that it didn't feature "real" Lindy Hoppers like themselves who could really dance, not just "models." Most dancers felt that the commercial distorted the dance for the public because it didn't portray the dancing "like we do it," or "authentically."

What none of the Lindy Hoppers called into question in their critique was the racial politics of the images presented; all the dancers were white, set against a white background, with white musicians performing the music. The "distortion" for them had nothing to do with race; it was not that this was the complete erasure of any connection with African American culture but that it did not portray "the dancing" properly. While missing the racial dynamic at play, these dancers could discern what the "proper" movements were as opposed to the choreography the ad showcased. These layers of whiteness (the dancers, the music, the setting itself—an empty space with whiteness as the background) overdetermined the image as a complete absence of context, which inadvertently mirrored the relationship between white society and African American culture. This stark acontextual representation becomes the epitome of the whitewashing of African American culture; without acknowledgment or recognition, African American cultural forms like the Lindy Hop have become the ahistorical backdrop for white pleasure and white consumption.

Embodiment: A Dispositional Approach

I interviewed Ryan Francois (a black British Lindy Hop master instructor, dancer, and choreographer who is considered one of the three best male Lindy Hop dancers in the world) on what he thought of the Gap ad. Ryan spoke candidly:

> What was the catalyst that actually made this a worldwide phenomenon? It was a commercial, a Gap commercial. The thing that is so powerful about that commercial is the fact that we got young, wholesome-looking, lily-white Americans, clean-cut right down to their haircuts, clean image, sweet and wholesome, acceptable to the white community. Slap! Bam! Instantly the white world is happy, we have a craze on our hands. Louis Prima and "Jump Jive and Wail" and this white guy pulls it out, Brian Setzer . . . It was so clean I thought of that ad as almost being Nazi; it was not seeing it in its approach, it was so "white people are beautiful and this is a clean thing that they do" that it was scary. If that made Swing extremely successful on a world scale—I mean, they show this in London, across the world—what does that say about them and what they consider an acceptable image about what they enjoy about the planet? It says to me that in an era where we're supposed to have dealt with these problems, we are still in a period where we're more comfortable with seeing this white Nazi image of white Gap commercial dancers. If you look at the top three teachers of this dance, they're black: me, Steven [Mitchell], and Frankie [Manning].

Ryan's comments were not the only ones I encountered that made race and representation the central issue. Another African American dancer and professional dance choreographer I interviewed expressed her concern over media representation and the Lindy Hop accordingly:

> It is hard not to be disheartened; you don't want to be paranoid and think, "Oh, God, white people are taking over

everything." But it seems so systematic with everything going on. You look at the Gap ad, and the movies, and the ways that black dancers don't get any publicity or airtime. I choreographed this commercial for Eddie Bauer that was all Lindy Hop, and I insisted that I wanted at least some black dancers in it. We put so much time in on that and it was barely ever shown. It had more black dancers than any other commercial out there that had Swing going on. I didn't think about it, really, until you asked, but I mean it makes more sense to me now.

It is these dominant representations of Lindy Hop that highlight the tension between the origins of the dance and its current representation circulating in a global context. With little or no visibility, the African American influences and historical connections with the dance become obscured. Whether intentional or not, this lack of representation leads to a sense that the Lindy Hop is exclusively a white cultural form.

It is not simply the media that whitewash African American culture through their representations. The Lindy Hop is also whitewashed in its enactment by Lindy Hop dancers themselves. The following anecdote taken from my field notes represents the performance of the dance at its height of popularity in Chicago. This was a rare performance for the Jazz Rhythms night at Dance Chicago, a five-week-long dance festival featuring a panorama of jazz dance styles and showcasing some of its best talent.

As the lights faded and the audience clamor tapered off into silence, I could feel my heart beat in my chest. My stomach churned with nausea as I waited for the music to begin and the curtain to rise. I heard the cheers of the swing kids in the balcony above us as they anticipated our friend's performance. Here in the crowd of the Athenaeum Theater at the Dance Chicago festival, I was waiting for Big City Swing, one of Chicago's Lindy Hop performance groups, to perform a Big Apple (various jazz steps taken from the Lindy Hop, danced in a circle with a finale culminating in Lindy Hop partner dancing that is often undertaken at a breathtaking pace). Big Time Swing Time is a commercial dance troupe that sold Lindy Hop performances as entertainment to weddings, corporate parties, and social events. The troupe was performing tonight amid some of the best jazz dancers in the city. Expectations were high for all the Lindy Hop dancers, because while most dancers would have loved to be part of this troupe, it was by invitation and audition only, with only a handful of dancers asked to participate. Here was a prime opportunity for a group of white dancers to show that their engagement with the dance was not some act of minstrelsy, but rather its finest contemporary cultivation of the dance. I opened my program to the description of their performance:

> Big Time Swing Time "Saturday Night Fish Fry" by L. Jordan
>
> With the rediscovery of swing music and social dancing, Lindy Hoppers around the world have maintained strong ties to the dance. It was in the Savoy Ballroom in the '30s and '40s where African American dancers combined traditional African dancing and the Cake Walk of the slave era with the popular dances Ragtime and Charleston. To strut their stuff, the original Lindy Hop troupes would circle up to show off their best jazz steps in a dance called the Big Apple. This is our tribute to those great entertainers.

As Louis Jordan's "Saturday Night Fish Fry" started to play over the speakers, I watched the performance unfold in front of me. The dancers emerged in their bright candy-colored costumes and began to circle around the center of the stage, proceeding to run through a litany of dance steps from the '30s and '40s. Rather than overwhelming the crowd with dynamism and enthusiasm, their lifeless interpretation fell flat, as their tricks failed to muster any spectacle. While the choreography included many of the classic steps, their performance was sluggish and hesitant as if running at half speed. The frenetic and reckless abandon that marks the Big Apple as a dance was missing. The dancers' steps and figures were recognizable, but their movements were staid, almost a clinical reproduction. My friend, seated next to me, turned to me and laughed, "What's next?" with an eye-rolling look of disappointment. I looked back at him, stunned. This was not a tribute that captured the spirit of the dance. Instead, it was something we wanted to forget. What made this performance any different from the mass-media treatments of the Lindy Hop, as seen in the Gap ad?

The underperformed and inhibited style often displayed in performance was not limited to the subculture of the Lindy Hop; it influenced national productions and live presentations of the dance itself. At its zenith, the Lindy Hop revival became such a popular dance craze that it made it onto the Broadway stage for *Swing! The Musical*. After its run on Broadway, which included Ryan Francois and his partner Jenny Thomas, the show toured without them in the cast. I reconstructed that evening from my field notes:

Tonight we went to see the musical *Swing!* downtown at the Oriental Theater in Chicago. The show is now touring after the craze has faded and the dance has receded back to a small subculture. While this felt like the endnote of the dance, many of us in the Lindy Hop community hoped that as the Broadway show made its way across the country enthusiasm for the Lindy Hop could be drummed up again. The show was so bad I couldn't imagine anyone being interested by it. Unfortunately for the dance, all the dancers on stage, including the two African Americans in the show, were trained ballet dancers. Classically trained dancers move like classically trained dancers, with their stiff upright posturing trying to do a street dance like the Lindy Hop. It was so stiff, so uninspired, so wrong; none of them looked like they were doing anything that closely resembled Lindy Hop. I can't believe that with all the labor the Lindy Hoppers have put into reviving the dance and cultivating it, this is the product that comes out. This is worse than what the very beginning Lindy Hopper could do. I wonder deep down how the audience would've reacted if they'd seen real Lindy Hoppers up there, who could dance the dance with the right movement and enthusiasm—I wonder what a traveling show like that, of this magnitude, could do for the dance?

Afterward I called Ryan Francois to discuss how the show turned out the way it did and what happened to the role he played in it. As he commented:

Both the choreographer and the director wouldn't have known what a Big Apple is unless we told [them]—however, [the choreographer] represents the establishment of the Broadway community and of course she became the choreographer. This concern with making Lindy Hop palatable for white audiences not only shapes the way it's presented to audiences, but it also reflects the audiences who come to see those performances. And then you remove the one swing couple . . . and there you have it.

In another interview, Ryan commented on how this process of embodiment affected the whole of society:

Whites come in and assimilate these cultures, break them down so they're much more presentable to white audiences. And pretty soon what you have is a version of the original style which is simplified to meet the needs of white audiences, who have money and culturally still go back to the idea that Glenn Miller is the King of Swing. It maintains the status quo that you don't have to be truly educated as to the reality of what that is—because the reality is that you have to move over to somebody else's culture to understand it.

Assimilating African American cultural forms into white communities by altering their aesthetic and style leads to a whitewashing of the dance from its original context.

This process of whitewashing goes on not only in the performance of the dance, but in everyday social dancing as well. In an interview, Steven Mitchell commented:

> People are not dancing together. They're going through the steps and motions but they are not dancing together. You can't find the pocket by yourself. Together you must find that pocket, that groove—just right in there. Dancing together—trying to do this so people dance together, that's what it's all about. That's why black people don't like it, because there is no connection in it—there's no spirit in it—there's nothing in it now. Mind you, it's better now than it was before. But what's missing in the dance is the love, the love and—I don't know—if love is enough, it's just because love means different things to different people. What's missing is the sensuality. There's no sex in the dance—I think we are afraid of using those kinds of metaphors. There's no passion; it's just been sucked out of it.

This notion of the sexuality of the dance, the blackness of the dance that has been removed is a result of the white mode of engagement that simultaneously desires the dance and yet holds back from its execution. Just as the racial imagination conceptualizes blackness as more sexual, it negotiates that boundary by denying the sexuality of the dance in whites' enactment of it. When asked if this could change, Steven replied:

> If you never felt the blues then it is hard to get people to feel the blues, it is hard to mime something you never felt. Part of the problem is that if you have never felt these things before, it is hard for me to convey to you and have you move to it. I'm not saying it's impossible. Why would I teach if I thought

it was pointless? It just takes a long time to get people to get into expressing themselves in ways they are not used to at all. It is one of the biggest challenges, to open up. People are just so constrained and tight. It's like people are scared to express themselves. Once you start hesitating and being self-conscious, then you lose the feeling.

This sense of "feeling" linked to notions of expression is a key element in the way that the dance becomes underexpressed. As indicated earlier, it is not impossible for whites to feel the dance, but unfamiliarity with this type of dance leads to a hesitancy and self-consciousness that prevents dancers from fully engaging the dance.

Since so few images of African American culture or identity accompanied the contemporary formation of the Lindy Hop, I decided to ask the few African American Lindy Hop dancers how they thought this identity shaped the ways that people engaged in the dance. Two close friends and former students of mine, David Stevens and Michelle Boyd, sensed this feeling of racial erasure. One evening after dance class they told me that sometimes they made an effort to go out and dance, less for the pure enjoyment than for the political aspect of representation: "We feel like we need to go out and dance sometimes if for no other reason than just to remind people that there are black people who dance, who do it, so they don't forget that black people do it too, or that it was a black dance. I mean, if we didn't, there wouldn't be any black people out there."

The more the Lindy Hop is whitewashed, the more complete the racial erasure becomes. This ends in a perverse irony: the few African American Lindy Hop dancers learn from white instructors, who are teaching them an African American social dance. When I shared this thought with an African American dancer I met at the Herräng dance camp in Sweden, she agreed that it was one of the dangerous outcomes of white engagement with African American culture. But she offered a way out: "Man, if Puff Daddy made a video and put a bunch of black dancers in it doing Lindy Hop, and he did it, too—if they saw Puff Daddy doing the Lindy Hop—this place would be overrun with black people. There would be so many of us here that you wouldn't know where to put us." If there were a visible or articulated link to African American culture, this could help prevent the dance from becoming erased from African American consciousness.

By examining the way that whitewashing underexpresses the dance, I saw how we can come to understand both the erasure of the African American cultural influence and history, and the mode of white engagement it fosters. As a result, I realized how notions of race create ambivalence and hesitation, whether subconsciously or consciously, about the ways that race operates within the world of the Lindy Hop. Through an embodied ethnographic approach I not only realized the ways that race informs how people perceive and understand each other culturally; I also came to see how race informs how dancers perceive and understand themselves and others as they dance the Lindy Hop.

Conclusion

By conceptualizing the emptiness of their own whiteness in relation to the natural richness of blackness, whites reinscribe racial essentialism in society, dehistoricize the dance as a cultural formation of a particular era, and conflate race and cultural competence. Thus, it is not only African Americans who are dominated through white cross-cultural engagement; whites themselves are dominated by these racial cosmologies as they are locked within their own essentialized racial identity that prevents them from fully understanding and embodying the dance. Exposing these mechanisms enables us to understand that these are not natural or inherent outcomes, but rather contingent social constructions, opening up possibilities for alternative modes of embodiment.

Without an embodied ethnographic approach, the Lindy Hop may have appeared as just another subculture of people blowing off steam in nightclubs and not as a microcosm of how race operates in contemporary American society. By crossing back and forth from theory to fieldwork, I slowly came to see that what seems innocuous or neutral on the surface has enormous symbolic power when the real effects of racial mythologies continue to go misrecognized. While one can try to understand the racial dynamics of the Lindy Hop cognitively, my own lived experience of these dynamics opened up new insight into the intersections of the body, culture, and race. Learning to dance enabled me to read the body symbolically, and to comprehend what the development of this bodily disposition means within the wider historical context of the white embodiment of African American cultural forms. The result was a novel understanding of how the perpetuation of racial mythology and racial essentialism occurred *without conscious awareness*.

An embodied approach to ethnography allows us to unpack the ways that larger social forces and cultural discourses inscribe themselves on the body, engendering durable habits of thought and action—*dispositions*—that can be so taken for granted that actors may not even be aware of them. In order to reveal these dispositions and understand how they guide social behavior, we must go beyond interviews or situational observations—we must acquire these dispositions ourselves, as I did by learning the Lindy Hop. While I have focused on race and dance in this chapter, the dispositional approach to ethnography has been used to generate new insights across a variety of domains.

For instance, it was only by becoming a forest firefighter that Desmond (2007) was able to debunk his fellow firefighters' claim that they had chosen the job because of its thrills. Rather, Desmond shows that the job chose them—their rural, working-class background conditioned their bodies and minds to be ready and willing to perform gritty, backbreaking labor. Putting one's body on the fire line also requires self-restraint rather than rash action. Wacquant

(2004) seeks to show how one becomes a boxer, or specifically how one comes to embody the "pugilistic habitus," which goes into forging not only the body but also the character of the boxer. His work offers a window onto the ways that the embodiment of boxing, as an activity of ongoing training, cultivates a work ethic that structures the regimes and routines of daily life for men living in the deindustrialized ghetto of South Side Chicago. Mears's (2011) work explores the world of modeling, focusing on the ways that fashion insiders create aesthetic value. It was only by drawing on her own experiences as a model that Mears was able to draw out how the cultural production of racial and gender inequalities occurs in practice. Mears exposes how "the look" that talent scouts desire is *not* a physical quality of models waiting to be "discovered" but rather a social classification that tastemakers can arbitrarily bestow on models they may have decided to promote for other reasons (e.g., their social connections).

The dispositional approach can give the ethnographer a powerful tool for linking micro and macro. It enjoins us to take seriously the participant dimension of participant observation, and it provides a way of conceptualizing and mapping precisely how social structure gets "inside" actors, which is arguably the central task of sociology.

References

Bourdieu, Pierre. 2000. *Pascalian Meditations*. Stanford, CA: Stanford University Press.

Bourdieu, Pierre and Loïc Wacquant. 1992. *An Invitation to Reflexive Sociology*. Chicago: University of Chicago Press.

Desmond, Matthew. 2007. *On the Fireline*. Chicago: University of Chicago Press.

Ellison, Ralph. 1995. *Going to the Territory*. New York: Vintage Books.

Fine, Gary Alan and Black Hawk Hancock. 2016. "The New Ethnographer at Work." *Qualitative Research* 17(2): 260-268.

Gabriel, John. 1998. *Whitewash: Racialized Politics and the Media*. London: Routledge.

Hancock, Black Hawk. 2009. "Taking Loïc Wacquant into the Field." *Qualitative Sociology* 32(1): 93–100.

Hancock, Black Hawk. 2013. *American Allegory: Lindy Hop and the Racial Imagination*. Chicago: University of Chicago Press.

Lott, Eric. 1995. *Love and Theft: Blackface Minstrelsy and the American Working Class*. Oxford: Oxford University Press.

Mears, Ashley. 2011. *Pricing Beauty: The Making of a Fashion Model*. Berkeley: University of California Press.

Rogin, Michael. 1996. *Blackface, White Noise: Jewish Immigrants in the Hollywood Melting Pot*. Berkeley: University of California Press.

Stoller, Paul. 1997. *Sensuous Scholarship*. Philadelphia: University of Pennsylvania Press.

Toll, Robert. 1974. *Blacking Up: The Minstrel Show in Nineteenth Century America*. New York: Oxford University Press.

Wacquant, Loïc. 2004. Body and Soul: Notebooks of an Apprentice Boxer. New York: Oxford University Press.

Wacquant, Loïc. 2015. "For a Sociology of Flesh and Blood." *Qualitative Sociology* 38: 1–11.

Chapter 7

Situations

MONICA MCDERMOTT

Ethnographers are masters at describing the "real-life situation." In fact, it can be considered the very definition of what ethnographers do. But what in fact is meant by "situation"? Everyday phrases such as "We have a situation here," "Don't turn this into a situation," or "hostage situation" indicate a clear break with the regular flow of events. What demarcates the beginning of a situation and the end of inchoate social life? Why is it significant?

The answers to these questions are of considerable importance for the practice of ethnographic research. While an ethnographer's unique ability to capture social processes and interactions emphasizes fluidity, these processes are often given a temporality and boundedness by virtue of their location within a particular situation. Hence, the way that the situation is understood can form the basis of the analyses of data that follow and can frame the theory that emerges from a series of observations. The nature of the situation is of obvious, special importance to ethnographers who explicitly make comparisons of phenomena across types of situations or micro-level contexts, but it is also an implicitly essential component of any ethnography. With the possible exception of composite descriptions of behaviors or interactions, ethnographic accounts describe the particulars of time, space, actors, and objects that make up a situation. These situations are then linked together in particular ways—in some cases as separate units, in other cases as indistinguishable, continuous manifestations of real life—to produce the narrative arc explaining the important phenomena of a social world.

Situations are thus the often invisible building blocks of ethnographic data. As such, it is important to be clear about how they are defined and the ways in which they are used in analyses. Using particular characteristics or dimensions of situations as the bases for comparisons between contexts to gain theoretical insight can be an especially powerful means of conducting an ethnographic study. Before one even heads into the field, planning to focus on specific types of situations and/or targeting particular characteristics of interactants can provide analytical leverage that may result in powerful new theoretical insights.

Before situations are used as the primary units of analyses, the constituents of the situation must be made clear. The boundaries of a situation need to be determined in some explicit fashion; depending on the aims of the project, these boundaries can be determined before, during, or after the project has commenced—or, as is most typical, during some combination of the three. Each strategy presents its own benefits and pitfalls. But in every case, social life is, to a certain extent, broken up into discrete units. The processual nature of interactions, reactions, gestures, behaviors, emotions are still of primary focus, but they are contained within a particular arena—the arena of the situation. By thinking about ethnography as a number of situated observations, the key factors generating patterns of behavior can be more readily identified. While multi-sited ethnography is often trumpeted as a means of gaining analytical leverage, comparisons of the important characteristics of a situation, or "situational context," within a single physical site or case study enable one to do the same.

In addition to determining just what a situation is, one must also determine what it is about a situation that is important to observe and consider for analysis. Characteristics of interactants in a situation are often an important dimension—how might a situation in which non-whites are present shape white behavior, for instance? How does the introduction of certain conversation topics into a situation shape interactions and/or behaviors? To pay attention to the situational element of observational findings is to progressively narrow the boundary conditions around an ethnographic finding. Rather than view the utterance of particular types of speech or the expression of particular gestures as ebbing and flowing over time, a particular array of factors determining a situational context can be mined to discover patterns of occurrence. In order to demonstrate what a situational approach to ethnography looks like in practice, I will provide examples from my ethnographic research on immigrant/native-born relations in a new immigrant destination as well on research I conducted in Atlanta and Boston on interracial interactions.

Defining Boundaries

Before comparing actions, words, or outcomes across different situational contexts, it is important to define just what is meant by "situation." At first glance, the term seems to reflect common sense—a situation is simply what is happening in the environment. But how do we know something is "happening" or what separates one situation from another? Rather than being a mere exercise in semantics, such questions have important implications. If an analysis of ethnographic data hinges upon the influence of the context of a situation, then the determinants of that context must be made explicit and they must be relatively consistent across comparisons.

There is no single concrete variable that is a necessary or sufficient determinant of a situation. Rather, it is important for the researcher to think clearly about the ways that situations are distinguished from each other if they are to be treated as discrete units in any analyses. Although often unacknowledged (however, see Tavory and Timmermans, chapter 5, this volume), this is precisely what ethnographers do when making micro-level comparisons across time and space in their work. A common bound of a situation is *a set of interactions in a particular space over a continuous, finite period of time*. For example, one situation at a doctor's office might be the space in which a physician has an interaction about a treatment protocol with a patient, which could then be compared with the space of the dining room of the house of a friend of the patient in which an interaction occurs between the friend and the patient's spouse about a treatment protocol, which could then be compared with the space of the meeting room at a hospital in which an interaction occurs between a physician and his colleagues about the treatment protocol suggested for the patient. The situational contexts are obviously very different, and one would expect each to yield conversations of differing content and emotional valences. Decisions about which dimensions of the situations to compare (such as the relative status of interactants) can then form the basis of an analysis that might yield insights about the relationship between elements of contexts and an outcome of interest (such as emotional valence of speech).

For a detailed example of the comparison of two tightly bounded situational contexts from practice, I provide instances from my own ethnographic research on immigrant/native born relations in a new immigrant destination (McDermott 2011). Between August 2005 and September 2006, I conducted ethnographic fieldwork in and around Greenville, South Carolina, in order to understand the impact that the "new" Latino immigration was having on the native-born population. My particular focus was on the poor and working-class population, as they were the most likely to have contact with the new immigrant population as well as the most likely to experience economic threat.

I lived and worked alongside both black and white southerners in order to capture the extent to which the Hispanic presence had an impact on their lives—if at all. My primary means of participating in the community was by holding a job as a sales vendor for a company that stocked DVDs and CDs in discount stores and drugstores throughout the southeastern United States. My job consisted of spending several hours each week in stores filing accounts with the store manager, cleaning and stocking the product racks, and removing outdated merchandise. The entire process provided ample time to observe what was occurring in the stores, and the clipboard that I carried to keep track of the accounts provided cover for the field notes I collected. After the job itself was completed, I made a point of hanging out with the cashiers and, on occasion, the manager.

In addition, I rented a home in a working-class neighborhood in Greenville County that was approximately 50 percent Hispanic, 30 percent white, and 20 percent black. The subdivision was located in one of three sections of Greenville that had a heavy concentration of Latinos; in this case, the homes were all quite new, with the oldest having been built in 2002. In some cases, Latino construction workers moved into the houses they had just finished building as part of their jobs. Perhaps because the neighborhood was less established than others and the surrounding area was racially mixed, the subdivision was, after Latinos, roughly evenly divided between blacks and whites.

My time living and working in the community was augmented by observations of public spaces such as stores, restaurants, churches, parks, hair salons, and government offices. One of the government offices I occasionally observed was the Department of Motor Vehicles (DMV). Since public transportation in the Greenville area was limited and inconvenient, a relatively large proportion of residents drove a car. As a result, there was a cross section of community residents at the DMV, with those in the waiting room at the office located in my neighborhood seemingly representative of the native-born population in terms of race, class, and gender.

For the purposes of comparing the effects of the racial and ethnic identities[1] of interactants on the tenor of the interactions, I defined

---

1. As identified by the author.

a situation as verbal and nonverbal exchanges between people in the impersonal, public, physical space of the DMV. No two situations are identical, by definition, but bounding situations in this admittedly somewhat broad way means that *substantial differences in an outcome of interest—in this case, the tenor of interactions—is a result of factors that vary across situations within the shared context of the public and impersonal interactional site.*

To illustrate the importance of clarifying the boundaries of a situation for the purposes of comparison, I will provide descriptions of two sets of interactions that occur in comparable situational contexts that differ according to a key dimension. Both situations occur in the public space in a DMV in Greenville, and both are bounded by the start and finish of the interactions between a particular set of observed strangers. The situations can then be compared on the basis of specific factors that differentiate them from each other; in this case, one primary factor is the race/ethnicity of the interactants.

While I was conducting research with the native-born community in Greenville, Laura Lopez-Sanders, at the time a graduate student, was studying the experiences of the local Latina/o immigrant community. A native Spanish speaker herself, Laura and I would sometimes travel to the same locations, where she would act as if she did not know how to speak English and I would linger in the background observing the reactions of those in the situation. Since the use of Spanish in public and the perceived inability of immigrants to communicate in English were issues motivating some of the negative attitudes of white and black residents of Greenville toward immigrants, the use of a confederate Spanish speaker enabled me to observe the nature of the reactions and dialogue that the native-born had with each other in the wake of this "immigrant" act.

Laura walked up to a white female clerk sitting at a reception desk just inside the front door of the building. The desk was positioned at the edge of a waiting area for customers waiting to be seen at a bank of windows on the far side of the room. Three white people, a woman and two men, were sitting in the waiting room just behind the reception desk. The receptionist appeared to be in her forties, while the whites in the waiting room were seemingly in their twenties and working class. As Laura began to speak, asking the receptionist for help in Spanish and looking quizzically in response to the clerk's statements, the three whites in the waiting room began to pay attention to the interaction. The clerk was quite polite and patient, firmly insisting that she did not speak Spanish and could not understand the student.

After about two minutes of communication between the clerk and Laura, the young white woman jumped up from the seat in the waiting room and said, "I can help. I speak Spanish." The two white men sitting with her looked at each other with apparent incredulity; one of the men's eyes grew wide, and the other man began to gently shake his head. The woman quickly walked over to Laura and looked at her expectantly. Laura repeated the request she made to the clerk; the young white woman seemed to have difficulty understanding her and asked her to repeat herself (in Spanish). At this point, the white woman translated Laura's question for the clerk—this interaction continued for about two minutes (according to Laura in a conversation I later had with her, the white woman's Spanish was not very good). The two white men who had been sitting with the young woman were closely watching the scene unfold. After Laura smiled, nodded, and thanked the white woman for her help, the woman returned to her seat. As she walked back, both of the white men were laughing at her; one of them was shaking his head. Their expressions seemed to reflect a sense of discomfort or embarrassment about their friend's actions.

A few months earlier, a similar set of clearly bounded interactions—with a clearly noted start and stop point—were held in the same physical space of the DMV. Yet the characteristics of the participants in, and the contents of, the interactions were very different. The situations were different yet readily comparable given their similarly bounded nature.

In the earlier situation, a white middle-aged man sat next to two young African Americans one afternoon, one a man and one a woman, and loudly stated that "you could lose your license for things that had nothing to do with driving." The couple laughed and said something I could not hear in response. A middle-aged black man standing nearby then joined the conversation and began complaining about a form he had to fill out. At this point the topic of high school emerged; the white man asked the man where he went to school. When he responded with the name of a school in Greenville, the white man shot back, "Rich school!" The black man was taken aback, and asked, "Rich?!" The white man said that it was rich compared with the high school he had attended. The black man defused the situation by responding, "Rich in spirit!" and both men laughed. After the white man left the DMV, the young African American couple sitting together looked at each other, one of them smirking, and they both shook their heads. While the young people may have been shaking their heads at the forwardness of the white man, their response came so quickly on the heels of his assertion of lower-class status that it was likely related to this component of the conversation.

In both cases, there is a member of a dominant race who is being laughed at or disapproved of for trying to connect with someone from a lower status group. In one case, a white woman attempts to connect with a Latina on the basis of a shared language (and, as a result, is judged by her fellow whites); in the other, a white man attempts to connect with blacks on the basis of shared class background (and, as a result, is judged by blacks). Within the boundaries of the same space that brings together strangers from disparate racial backgrounds, similar dynamics can play out in unexpected ways. The attempt at connection can in some cases bring about disapproval from one's own group and in other cases bring about disapproval from the group with whom the individual is trying to connect. The next step would be to identify the reasons for these different reactions—are they related to the fact that the interactant was Latina in one case and black in the other? Are the differences a matter of the number of non-white interactants in the situation? These dynamics would be missed if situations were not linked as the units of analysis.

Determining Categories

Once the boundaries of the situation are clearly defined, the next analytical determination to make is the dimension(s) that will be compared across situations. For example, the characteristics of the interactants might be one dimension that is compared across situations. Do women speak the same way about politics when in the presence of men as they do when in the presence of women only? Or, as in the previous example, do whites interacting with Latinas exhibit styles similar to whites interacting with blacks? Comparing the content or patterns of discourse in situations with, in the former example, mixed-gender interactants with discourse in situations with only female interactants can provide an answer to this question.

Characteristics of interactants need not be the only dimension upon which situations are compared. The content of their conversations is another potentially important dimension. The conversational contexts of situations can strongly shape behaviors as well as elicit the expression of attitudes that might ordinarily be held in reserve. If one notices a pattern across situations that discussions of church attendance lead to a condemnation of a particular political policy, then one can reasonably draw the conclusion that the expression of policy opposition is situationally dependent. Similarly, in an environment in which status is understood to be anchored in race, situations in which the status of whites was challenged could bring forth an assertion of white privilege or even supremacy.

In research that I conducted in Atlanta and Boston for my book *Working Class White* (2006), I found that the situational contexts of racial prejudice involved many such conversational subjects and cues. The participant observation research involved my working as a convenience store clerk for six months in Atlanta and six months in Boston, in order to surreptitiously study interracial interactions in a public setting. The two sites were selected as nearly identical demographically; both were in majority white working-class neighborhoods that bordered majority black working-class neighborhoods. As with the study in South Carolina discussed earlier, I lived in the neighborhood and frequented local stores, restaurants, bars, and so forth.

The neighborhoods were chosen so as to maximize the opportunities to witness interracial interactions and to observe the words and actions of working-class whites for whom matters of race were likely to be relatively salient. By working as a clerk in the stores, I was able to form deep relationships with my fellow cashiers and with regular customers and, at the same time, witness a large number of bounded interactions—or situations—within the same space. In a number of these cases the interactants were complete strangers to me, as in one of the examples from the DMV discussed earlier. In other cases the interactions took place between people I knew well and strangers, and in others still I knew all of the interactants well and had an opportunity to witness their interactions in response to different situational cues. It was important for my study that the race and, to a lesser extent, class of the interactants varied across situations. In this way, I had the opportunity to witness the content of whites' speech about social issues while in the presence of blacks as well as in mono-racial settings.

There are, of course, an enormous range of conversational topics that emerge over the course of a year's worth of participant observation research. In thinking about expressions of racial prejudice as emerging within particular situational contexts, one can then identify some of the key features of those contexts that influence such expressions. For example, I found in a number of situations during my fieldwork in Atlanta that racially prejudiced comments followed shortly after the individual uttering them had been embarrassed or humiliated in some way. Even though the original source of the embarrassment had ostensibly nothing to do with race, the response of the white interactant would be to reclaim his or her standing in the interaction by invoking a stereotype or casting a racial aspersion.

This type of reaction was illustrated the first day that I moved to the white working-class neighborhood in Atlanta when my elderly white landlord introduced me to one of my neighbors. The landlord was a well-known and respected real estate agent in the community. My new neighbor, a middle-aged, grizzled white man, was covered in engine grease, as he had been in the midst of repairing a pickup truck parked on blocks in the driveway. The landlord stared at my neighbor's hands and commented that he "usually didn't look quite so greasy." My neighbor immediately shot back, "No, I usually look like a white man," then shook my hand and introduced himself. Equating dirtiness with blackness, my neighbor reacted to the disrespect he received from the more affluent and respected landlord by asserting his own privileged racial status and, implicitly, denigrating his racial counterpart.

Another categorical dimension to compare across situations is the characteristics of the people present. These characteristics could apply not just to the interactants themselves but to anyone in the situation. Demographic characteristics are one basis for comparison, as understanding the content of interactions that occur in situations with people with certain demographic characteristics (male, young) but not others (white, gay) can provide considerable analytical leverage when constructing theoretical explanations about micro-level phenomena that connect with larger structural forces.

In one example from the ethnographic research I conducted in Atlanta, I had the experience of observing the behavior of a middle-aged white man when he was in the presence of African Americans and when he was only around whites. While it is unlikely to be much of a surprise that his behavior regarding discussions of race was not identical in the two settings, it is nonetheless important to understand the ways that this man thinks about the role that race plays in terms of behavior, cognition, and identity, and how his assumptions influence his own behavior.

"Hank," the owner of General Fuel, told me that he anticipated charges of racism from his black employees. One week, he went over every timecard with a blue highlighter if it showed a time that was later than the time we were expected to be at work; in the case of my shift, this time had recently been changed from 6 AM to 5:45 AM. I had clocked in between 5:46 and 5:49 AM each day, and had a timecard filled with blue ink. I complained loudly about this to the white assistant manager, "Stephanie," who was on duty with me at the time. I had forgotten that everything I said and did was being recorded by the store's surveillance system that was focused on the area near the cash registers. Hank watched and heard the entire exchange between me and Stephanie on the video screen in the back office; he stepped out into the store and called me into the office. He asked, "What was the reaction to the timecards?" "Negative," I replied. He said that he did it only to get everyone's attention. "But *one* minute late?" I complained. He smiled and said, somewhat paternalistically, I thought, that it wasn't directed at me. He said that he had to color the times on my timecard because he would be accused of favoritism if he didn't and that this accusation would be made because I was white.

He went on to say that the ink on timecards worked better than warning letters, which he claimed didn't work at all. I replied that such a strategy "would sure work for me." His response: "But you aren't like them." The "them" in this case clearly referred to blacks, as he had just made a point of noting that I was white. He went on to say that jobs are important to whites, but that an entire generation of blacks has been ruined by the welfare system. Hank clearly has strong opinions about the superior work ethic of whites as well as of the importance of jobs to whites—in his mind, whites are not willing to live off of government support as are blacks. Not only do his actions suggest that he is well aware that such attitudes should not be voiced in mixed-race company, they also hint at a greater irony. Hank, who openly voices racist stereotypes to other whites, is worried about being accused of racism by blacks; he thus concocts a plan that will jolt the black employees he deems to have little concern about gainful employment while also angering white employees who are thought of as collateral damage. Ultimately Hank believes that he is, in fact, not guilty of racial discrimination but that he must go through the motions of fairness to prove it.

If one were to observe Hank's friendly, jocular manner and generosity with his black employees, one would likely assume that he was at least without conscious racial animus. Yet these interactions belie Hank's assumptions about fundamental moral differences between blacks and whites, assumptions that may potentially underlie many of his actions but are only situationally evident.

Similarly, the degree to which the threat of crime—especially violent crime—was associated with blacks in the working-class community in Atlanta was especially discernible when situations with interactants of different racial backgrounds were compared. Once again, my own white racial identity led me to be privy to the extent to which both blacks and whites, men and women, felt the need to steer white women away from black men and black neighborhoods. On the other hand, the very real threat of violence from white men went unnoticed or ignored.

For example, in one predominantly black neighborhood in Atlanta, I drove slowly down a side street with a number of duplexes in various states of disrepair. A group of about five black men were sitting outside one of the partially boarded-up buildings. As one of the men made eye contact with me, he leapt up from where he was sitting and began walking toward my pickup truck, waving a packet of drugs back and forth. It was 2:30 in the afternoon. When I expressed my surprise at the brazenness of the man to Jan, a black cashier who had grown up in the neighborhood, she said he thought I wanted drugs because I was white. Doug, a middle-aged white man who was a regular customer, shared Jan's opinion and castigated me for being in the neighborhood in the first place. He said he didn't ever want to hear of me driving in that part of town again, not even in the middle of the afternoon.

A few weeks later, an entirely different situation unfolded, in this case seemingly without any racial elements. Doug invited me to a small party with some of his friends that was being held in a house not far from where I was living. Since he was a regular at the store, we had gotten to know each other fairly well, and he was excited to introduce me to people he knew. When I arrived at the house I was stunned. The rundown condition of the exterior of the home was not unlike that of others in the neighborhood, but the interior was chaos. Drug paraphernalia were in the living room, and kitchen items were spread in disarray throughout the living space. The people Doug introduced me to, all of them white, middle-aged, and seemingly working-class or poor, were not unfriendly yet in various states of intoxication. As everyone coalesced in the living room, a group conversation began, led by a large man with a large beard wearing a baseball cap. The exchange between him and Doug grew progressively more heated until the man ended up pulling out a knife and holding it to Doug's throat. Doug laughed and talked the man down, completely defusing the situation. When I expressed my concern about this to Doug, he told me not to worry; he "had it all under control."

When treated as separate situations to be compared, Doug's approach to the party and its aftermath stands in sharp contrast to his attitudes toward my traveling in a black neighborhood. His association between blackness, violence, and threat is so great that my merely viewing poor African American men from a vehicle is tantamount to putting myself in danger. Yet his lack of association between whiteness and threat means that he has no concern about my direct physical proximity to a potentially imminent violent assault, neither before nor after its occurrence. In contrast to Hank's conscious unwillingness to express negative racial stereotypes in front of African Americans, Doug is quite willing to acknowledge that he associates black neighborhoods with risks to whites. When comparing his expression of concern in the face of no observable threat (my driving through a black neighborhood) in one situation with his complete lack of concern in the face of demonstrable threats in a situation with only whites present, one can appreciate the depth of the association between race and violence (and, by extension, crime).

Another especially striking case of whites expressing anti-black prejudice only in the presence of other whites occurred in a store I was working in during my participant observation research in Greenville on the impact of immigration in a new destination. In the discount store located in a rural area in the Greenville region, there was a backlog of people demanding the manager's attention, so I stood off to the side and awaited the time when I might be able to speak with her and get the signature I needed for the paperwork I had to file for the job. I looked over and smiled at a man sitting in one of the display recliners at the front of the store. He responded by saying he was sitting down because he had "the asbestos in the lungs" as well as a history of five heart attacks. He then asked me where I was from; after I replied "Greenville," he responded that "they've been having a lot of trouble over there, robbing from the Hardees and McDonalds" (there had recently been a string of robberies of fast-food restaurants in Greenville). I said I heard they had some leads in the case; he said, "Yeah, they hit another one this morning. The guy ripped them off, pulled a knife, and walked right out of there." He then looked around, leaned in close to me, and said very quietly, "He was black. It's those blacks." I initially didn't respond, but I then asked, "It must be pretty quiet up here." He responded, "Yeah, but when it breaks it breaks real hard. A fellow was shot eight times the other day and lived." I said, "That must be some kind of record; what did he do, shoot him in the arms?" He said, "No, all over. Now if he shot him with a .357 Magnum he'd be dead." We then had a brief discussion about different caliber weapons.

He said he didn't know what was wrong with this country, that things were much worse now than they used to be. I gamely responded that I thought drugs were often involved. He replied, "Yes, ma'am. They are ruining this country." Again, he looked carefully around and said, "It's the blacks. They get them when they are teenagers." After complaining for a while about insufficiently long prison sentences, he stated, "This is a good country except for the people in it." At this point, a black cashier walked over to me to hand me the paperwork that the manager had finally signed. The man I had been speaking with abruptly got up from his chair, said it had been good speaking with me, and walked away. As the situation changed to include a non-white participant, the white man quickly exited. This fit with his earlier behavior of carefully surveying the store to make certain no one was within earshot before discussing blacks with me.

Important dimensions upon which to compare situations include not only the characteristics of the interactants but also the relationship of the situations to each other across time. While situations themselves constitute contexts, they exist within a larger span of time that itself shapes the broader context within which one considers the meaning of what occurs during a situation. Such is the logic, after all, behind the standard practice of repeated observations—the regularity of a category of actions suggests its lack of dependence upon a larger chronological context. But the irregularity of situational interactions can also be of great analytical utility if couched within a broader comparison of situations across time. In the starkest case, if interactions within situations are characterized by a certain valence for one period of observation and then shift to become quite different during a second period of observation, a change in the extra-situational context has taken place that is shaping the words and behaviors of actors.

For example, I noticed while coding my field notes from the research I conducted on immigration to South Carolina that there was a shift in the ways that the native-born interacted with Latinos. Despite key features of situations being the same, interactions that had once been constituted of friendly smiles and nods now involved the offer of a cold shoulder. While I hadn't been aware of the extent of its effect at the time, the nationally coordinated immigrant rights' marches had occurred eight months after the start of my field work in South Carolina. The presence of a largely Latino and immigrant contingent of thousands taking to the normally quiescent streets of Greenville had a profound effect on the ways people interacted with each other on a daily basis. In essence, a macro-level event changed the context in which micro-level contexts operated.

This finding raises an important question about the connection between micro-level contexts and macro-level contexts: How does one specify the linkage between the two? If I had begun my fieldwork after the marches, I would very likely not have noticed its impact on interactions. Yet the opportunities to notice such effects of larger context over time were maximized by the selection of a site that was poised to undergo change—a substantial demographic shock had occurred (the rapid influx of immigrants) that was likely to result in a period of unsettled social relations. Similar site selection criteria cannot guarantee the observation of direct linkages between interactions and broader contexts, but it can make such opportunities more likely.

One of the many examples of these linkages in the Greenville case occurred in one of the largely white, rural communities that I studied. A discount store that I regularly worked at was located next door to a trailer park that was inhabited by a largely male, Latino population. There would routinely be loud Spanish-language music playing from the trailers, and a number of the men would frequent the store and hang out nearby. Typically, the men were ignored by the native-born population, although both black and white cashiers would sometimes make friendly conversation with them.

However, a number of the situations involving the men and their music were quite different in the time period after the marches. In one case that potentially could have led to significant hostilities, a black man came running out of a store yelling at three Latino men to "cut down on that racket!" as he stood and stared them down. The three men turned away, laughing, and left the parking lot. I had been sitting in my car in the parking lot and had heard the three men talking loudly, but I did not find their behavior out of the ordinary or especially disruptive. In fact, it was nearly identical to behavior that was typical of the pre-march era.

Another example of a subtle but noticeable shift in the ways in which whites interacted with Latinos was through the withholding of friendly greetings and small talk between strangers, a common part of the social fabric in southern communities like Greenville. In one case, an older white male greeter at a discount store acknowledged customers entering the store with a nod, smile, and greeting; before the marches, I noted that this included *all* customers, including Spanish-speaking ones. After the marches, however, the greetings became more selective—the native-born (both blacks and whites) received a nod and a smile, while Latino men were ignored (I did not see any Latinas enter the store during my observations of the greeter). While this behavior may have gone completely unnoticed by the Latinos entering the store, it nonetheless is one small illustration of the widening gulf between whites and Latino immigrants in the wake of the marches.

In both of these examples—the case of the music blaring from the trailer park and the case of the store greeter—the differences in situational context were not along the dimension of categories of participants or of the content of the interactions. Instead, they differed in terms of the larger context in which the situations themselves were embedded. By using situations as the unit of analysis and comparing them with each other, the clear influence of time and the probable occurrence of a key event on the contours of interactions become evident. Since multiple factors such as demographic categories and content of interactions *are* held constant across situations, one is better positioned to make arguments about the influence of macro-level factors with only micro-level data as empirical evidence.

Emergent Issues

While there are multiple advantages to considering situations as the unit of analysis in ethnographic research, there are nonetheless two sets of issues that pose potential problems to the analyst privileging the role of situational context. The first set of issues are tautological—if any element of real-world social life is situational, then isn't any aspect of it arbitrarily and necessarily a situation? The second set of issues are teleological—aren't situations defined according to the degree to which they make sense of actions and processes that have already been interpreted?

When focusing an ethnographic analysis upon processes that reflect the dynamics or characteristics of particular situations—the "context" of the situation—it obviously is important to know what one means by the term "situation." Yet rigidly defining a term such as "situation" that inherently captures the fluidity and unpredictability of social life can be seen as sacrificing insight for the sake of precision. The key components of a situation are to be understood as any other aspect of ethnographic work—through the careful interpretive lens of the researcher. This is certainly true. However, when situational contexts are under consideration—which necessitates some degree of comparison between situations—the determination of what a situational context is can be overdetermined by the outcome being explained. The situation in this case will be what encapsulates the empirical findings that support the narrative the ethnographer has already crafted.

This would be perfectly acceptable if "situation" were being used as a heuristic device, but to think about situational contingencies and contexts in any kind of systematic way, "situation" must be less predefined. If the determinant of a situation is that something substantively noteworthy has occurred within its bounds, then the utility of the concept for analytical purposes is muted. To really capture the importance of situational contexts, one must be certain not to define situations solely on the basis of the generation of a particular outcome. Rather, there must be some general definite properties that distinguish one situation from another that are independent of any correlation drawn between context and outcome.

Another potential issue with the use of situations as the unit of analysis in ethnographic research is the tendency to impose the boundaries around situations after looking back upon one's time in the field. What feels like one uninterrupted series of intertwined events can be divided into discrete units post hoc, but this would very likely place a framework upon the data that would reify the moments surrounding a key event or an interaction as constituting the situational context. In this way, a predetermined narrative would lead to the demarcation of situational boundaries and, by extension, contexts that would be based upon a known outcome. If, for example, one believes that the presence of police officers will always lead to a reduction in the number of shoplifters in a retail location, then a situation might be determined as a set of interactions during which a police officer was present. This would miss any orthogonal dynamics between shoplifters and cashiers that transcend police presence in the store and reflect an important influence of situational context on observed behavior.

It is important to note that a situational approach need not conflict with more dispositional or character-driven ethnographic methods. Classic ethnographies such as William Foote Whyte's *Street Corner Society* (1943) revolve around and gain much of their power from central figures such as Doc. Willis's *Learning to Labor* (1977) traces the cognitive frameworks of working-class boys through their daily lives with a focus on the dispositions of the young men. Works such as these bring us within the worlds of particular individuals in a way that is seemingly distant from a more deliberate situational approach. However, a situational approach combined with a more character-driven approach can highlight the structural constraints and external influences that shape the actions and beliefs of richly drawn individual lives. A compelling ethnography will demonstrate a connection between the researcher and the researched, a connection that can sometimes be so strong as to miss the role of immediate external influences on behavior (much as we typically miss such influences in our own lives).

Benefits and Insights

A focus on situational contexts can benefit from the strengths of the ethnographer's ability to capture key processes and important contours of interactions that would be left uncovered by any other ethnographic approach. At the same time, thinking about ethnographic research as a comparison of these interpreted dynamics over bounded settings facilitates insights about important mechanisms—even potential causal mechanisms—that might be left unrecognized with a focus solely on unbounded process. While there are many excellent counterpoints to the critiques of ethnographic research for being hampered in its ability to contribute to social science research as a result of its lack of generalizability, analyses of qualitative data that focus on the importance of situational contingencies add another arrow to the ethnographer's quiver. If each situation is thought of as a discrete case, then the sample of cases upon which a narrative is based is huge (albeit nonrandom). This is by no means to suggest that situations should be counted, coded, and forced into a regression model—the nonrandomness of the sample is one issue, but the other more important consideration is the interpretive nuance of the ethnographer's judgment that is guiding the conclusions drawn about the key elements of interactions within situations. Especially if there is resonance between the differences in the content of discourse and the variance on a key dimension of the situation such as the race of the interactants, the dismissal of conclusions drawn from observational research will be less convincing.

One of the thorniest issues in the study of race relations is that of perceptions of prejudice. We know that non-whites are more likely to perceive racial prejudice the greater their exposure to whites, that interpersonal rather than structural forms of racism are subject to greater awareness. But little else about the extent to which racist actions occur in everyday life is known. Simply looking at survey data and comparing white attitudes with non-white rates of reporting experiences of prejudice suggests an underreporting of incidents, yet no such underreporting has been documented. To the contrary, many whites assert that non-whites *over*report incidences of racial prejudice. They believe that blacks and other racial minority groups are hypersensitive about perceived acts of racism, attributing prejudicial intent to mere acts of rudeness or surveillance that all individuals are subject to. It is almost certainly the case that whites engage in acts of prejudice that blacks aren't even aware of, while there may be times that blacks misperceive acts of rudeness as racially discriminatory. And there are of course many, many cases of accurate perceptions of prejudice.

How might one begin to address the conundrum of perceptions versus misperceptions of prejudice? The ethnography of situational contexts is uniquely suited to do so, as observations of interracial interactions in similar situations with notable variations in context can help to distinguish rudeness from racism. Several examples of situational ethnography from my research in Atlanta highlight the ways in which this clarification is possible.

One of my fellow cashiers at the convenience store in Atlanta was Molina, a black woman in her late thirties with braided hair, a large scar on her forehead, and a gold-capped tooth. She encountered numerous customers who treated her with disrespect. In one such instance, she shoved an American Express card at me (I was working at the other register) and snapped at the customer, "She'll take you over here." The customer was in her thirties, well dressed, with blonde hair and sunglasses; she appeared to be white and middle-class. I rang the woman up for her gas purchase with no problems. When the white woman left the store, Molina said, "You know why I let you ring her up? She threw her credit card at me. Now I didn't see her throw nothin' at you now, did she?" I replied that she did not. "Now what is the only difference between me and you?" At this point she came up next to me, pulled our arms together, and said, "All right then!" When I asked her if this sort of thing happened a lot, she said, "Yeah! Don't you see it? They look at me, look at you and then dip over into your line." I asked her what kinds of people did it; she replied, "Every kind."

Clearly there was no way to discern the racist intent of the white customer. Even had she no idea what was motivating her behavior, however, her rudeness was clearly distinguished by the race of her target: she interacted quite differently with two strangers with precisely the same visible gender, class status, and occupational function who differed only in terms of race. The perception of the African American woman that the rude treatment she received from the white woman was racially motivated occurred in one situation; it was given considerable support in her mind when she compared the treatment I received in another situation. At the same time, the white customer presumably had no idea that she had just played a part in the perpetuation of racial prejudice and its resulting injury in the course of paying for her tank of gas. Yet such is the way that mutual suspicion and anger continue to characterize black/white interactions, and such is the role of ethnography in uncovering how it does so.

Molina's interpretation of the line-switching customers' actions as expressions of prejudice was even more interesting. While I very likely missed the extent to which this occurred, I certainly had noticed the phenomenon—there was a clear preference for my line among white, but not black, customers. However, I also noticed that the only customers who switched into my line were those dressed in business suits and highly unlikely to have been from the neighborhood. None of the customers I knew to be locals switched lines. I was trying to sense whether or not Molina had picked up on this apparent class difference with my "what kinds of people switch lines" question, but she apparently did not make the connection that I did.

On a separate occasion, Molina was watching closely as a white middle-aged man claimed to have given me a twenty-dollar bill, although he actually gave me a ten-dollar bill (this happened with some regularity). I eventually convinced the customer that he had, in fact, given me just ten dollars, and he eventually stopped complaining and left. After he exited from the store, Molina said, "You know that he would have been cursing me out for it. And you know why too, don't you?" I took her to clearly mean that the man left quietly only because I was white. I thought she was right in her suspicions; however, Molina did not witness the occasions when black customers gave me a ten-dollar bill and claimed to have paid with a twenty-dollar bill and did not walk away calmly but created a commotion and demanded to see the manager. Similarly, Telika, a black cashier in her early twenties, had long thought that customers threw their money down on the counter rather than place it in her hand because she was black. After watching situations in which a customer threw his money at me, she marveled at the fact that a white man would throw money at a white woman—that customers were simply rude. No doubt, there were occasions when people *did* throw money at Telika because she was black, or at me for any number of idiosyncratic reasons. But the interesting element of a situational comparison, both for researchers and for participants, is the opportunity to gain a multifaceted perspective on components of interactions that might otherwise seem straightforward. That the racial dynamics across situations are more complicated than individuals have the opportunity to know or appreciate is yet another warrant for the practice of participant observation research. By considering the racial dynamics particular to each situation, the effect that the race of interactants has not only on the behaviors within exchanges but also on perceptions about general patterns of race-based interactions, the ethnographer attentive to the influence of situational context can unearth some of the confusions and contradictions that perpetuate social conflict.

The advantages of an ethnographic approach and analysis that is sensitive to the importance of situational context extend far beyond its ability to disentangle some of the factors influencing perceptions (and misperceptions) of individual mistreatment. While the focus in this chapter has been primarily on race relations, ethnographic research that seriously engages with situational context is of value in a wide range of substantive fields. For example, a variety of situational contexts could be identified in an organizational ethnography of a corporate setting (e.g., team meetings, client interactions, informal conversations). In her ethnography of masculinity in a public high school, Pascoe (2012) explicitly compares discourses and behaviors around issues of sexuality in distinct situations. For example, the performance of gender in traditionally masculine settings and male-dominated situations is compared with its performance in situations with multiple genders to yield new insights about the varied discourses of sexuality among adolescent boys.

Combining the true gift of ethnography—the ability to capture and interpret the everyday processes that structure social life—with the advantages of being able to systematically compare discrete units of bounded interactions to each other can result in a study that simultaneously captures structure and process. To appreciate the importance of the situational context is to gain insight into some of the central patterns governing social interaction in a particular site. An account of structured contingencies is at the heart of what an ethnographic narrative can provide.

References

McDermott, Monica. 2006. *Working Class White: The Making and Unmaking of Race Relations*. Berkeley: University of California Press.

McDermott, Monica. 2011. "Black Attitudes towards Hispanic Immigrants in South Carolina." In *Just Neighbors? Research on African American and Latino Relations in the United States*, edited by Edward Telles, Mark Sawyer, and Gaspar Rivera-Salgado, 242–266. New York: Russell Sage Foundation.

Pascoe, C. J. 2012. *Dude, You're a Fag: Masculinity and Sexuality in High School*. Berkeley: University of California Press.

Whyte, William Foote. 1943. *Street Corner Society*. Chicago: University of Chicago Press.

Willis, Paul. 1977. Learning to Labour: How Working Class Kids Get Working Class Jobs. Farnborough: Saxon House.

Chapter 8

Reflexivity

Introspection, Positionality, and the Self as Research Instrument—Toward a Model of Abductive Reflexivity

FORREST STUART

Introduction

Like all other social scientists, ethnographers ask questions, formulate hypotheses, gather evidence, conduct analyses, and make arguments about the way the social world works. Yet ethnography is different in a number of critical and, at times, potentially problematic ways. First and foremost, the ethnographer—a living, breathing, feeling individual—is the primary instrument of data collection and interpretation. Whether ethnographers intend it or not, we invariably become part of the social settings and interactions that we aim to witness, measure, and analyze. Our presence represents an intrusion into the local social world, whether we are an active participant in a conversation or merely a passive audience to mundane behaviors or events. This practical reality has produced an active debate about the subjective and often contingent nature of ethnographic findings. One result, which is the focus of this chapter, has been a sustained conversation about how to be more *reflexive* in our work. Stated simply, *reflexivity* refers to the practice of consistently and candidly examining how we, as fieldworkers, constantly impinge on, and even transform, the phenomena we aim to study. Reflexivity demands that ethnographers critically interrogate how their particular point of access, personal identity, social position, and subjective perspective are all inextricably tied to the kinds of data they are bound to encounter.

Pick up an ethnographic book written in the past three decades and you are increasingly likely to find a lengthy discussion about the dilemmas the researcher faced while entering the field, establishing rapport, and navigating the inquiries and requests posed by ethnographic subjects. These are typically found in an introductory methods section or, if the author is particularly introspective, in a methodological appendix strapped to the end of the text. Here we find subsections with titles like "Getting Access," "Dealing with Difference," and "The Researcher Role." In these pages, readers are often treated to reflexive confessionals about how the author's particular traits and characteristics affected the kinds of entrée and relationships that were possible. If these appendixes seem defensive, it is because they are. For at least a century, ethnographers have been asked to convince fellow sociologists that our in-depth, "small-*n*" studies live up to conventional standards of validity and generalizability. As a result, our discussions of reflexivity often resemble the limitations sections found at the end of quantitative studies, full of caveats and disclaimers. This, I believe, has been a step in the wrong direction. But rather than offer yet more arguments about ethnography's myriad warrants—enough volumes have already been dedicated to this well-worn debate—I hope to steer our discussions of reflexivity onto a different and, I think, more encouraging path.

The point of this chapter is straightforward. I suggest that rather than *apologizing* for the fact that we are participants in the scenes and interactions we aim to research, ethnographers are better served by more fully *embracing* our unique position and its capacity to generate novel analyses. While reflexivity is often relegated to the realm of methodological limitations, it constitutes a powerful analytical tool that has been responsible for some of our most important insights. Finding ways to articulate this process in our work helps us to improve our arguments, silence critics, and provide valuable lessons for students and novice ethnographers. To be clear, many ethnographers already leverage reflexivity as a strategic analytical tool (for an outstanding recent example, see Orrico 2015). Unfortunately, given the conventions of academic publishing, there are few opportunities to formally account for this process within the bounds of our work. While book-length projects certainly provide some space for piecemeal discussions about the relationship between our positionality and our moments of discovery, we seldom detail this process in any organized, structured fashion. This chapter attempts to do just that.

In the following pages, I sketch a systematic outline of how ethnographers typically use reflexivity as a central tool in their analytical toolkit. My goal is to shed light on a process that is often left unspoken and informal. First, I trace how ethnographers build on the insights of ethnomethodology to treat their own presence in the field as a kind of *breaching exercise* that allows them to reveal and make sense of the invisible social orders and norms that guide action and pattern behaviors. Second, ethnographers integrate these breaches, transgressions, and outsider statuses as part of an iterative process of theorizing, hypothesis testing, and subsequent theorizing. We can refer to this process as *abductive reflexivity*. Despite its complex name, abductive reflexivity is actually quite straightforward and can be utilized by *all* ethnographers, regardless of their field site, topic, or personal attributes. After detailing the logic of this approach, I offer one of my own reflexively informed analyses to trace how this approach unfolds during the course of research and yields unexpected discoveries.

Fieldworkers and Their Outsider Statuses: More than a Limitation

It seems only fitting to open a discussion of ethnographic introspection by painting the scene in one particular "field site" where this issue is typically encountered: the ethnographic methods seminar. Every year, I teach a course on urban ethnography, and every year the course produces a nearly identical moment, when my students first begin thinking seriously about reflexivity. Unfortunately, these initial thoughts produce a fair amount of angst, insecurity, and self-doubt.

This moment occurs around the fourth class meeting, as we are discussing Elijah Anderson's (1978) classic, *A Place on the Corner*. Over the course of several years, Anderson immersed himself in a group of black "streetcorner men" who congregated in front of a bar and liquor store on Chicago's South Side. In true Chicago school fashion, Anderson reveals the complex social order maintained among this seemingly disordered population. He finds a nuanced hierarchical system by which these men jockey for status and "become somebody." At the end of the book, Anderson treats the reader to a notably robust methodological appendix. Anderson describes how the project began as an assignment for a methods course, why he gravitated toward the setting, and how the men came to consider him a "cousin." He roots much of this explanation in his own background, his racial identity, and important aspects of his childhood. Like those he ultimately ended up studying, Anderson confides that he himself "loved being 'out in the streets,'" that he grew up playing "the dozens," and that he already knew many of the unspoken rules and interactions found among urban black men.

Like clockwork, class discussion quickly finds its way to this particular section of the appendix. No doubt stressing over their own hopes of conducting an impactful ethnography, several students launch into a chorus of doubts, lamenting that even if they wanted to, they would never be able to produce an equally impressive study of streetcorner men. In the most recent version of this scene, one of the white men students in the class leans back in his chair in defeat.

"I could never do a study this good," he complains. "As a white guy, I could never get data that good. I could never 'go for cousins' with these guys."

A woman student chimes in. "Yeah, neither could I." Other women in the class nod in agreement.

A Sikh Indian student joins the chorus. He points to the turban on his head. "Yeah. No matter how hard I tried, they would never see me as one of them. Anderson will always get better data than I will. His research will always be better."

At this point, I ask the entire class to take a deep breath. Having encountered this exact scenario before, I direct them to several dog-eared pages in my copy of the book. I point to key moments of Anderson's entry into the field, data collection, discoveries, and analyses. We review how one of the group's "regulars," a man named Herman, came to "vouch" for Anderson. We discuss how the high-status members of the group steered Anderson away from fraternizing with lowly "wineheads" and "hoodlums." We trace how these acts illuminated the subtle, but central processes of hierarchical sorting. We confirm that these moments turned out to be some of the most illuminating aspects of the study. I ask my students to reflect on some of the common denominators in all of these instances. It does not take them long to realize that, rather than emerge as a result of Anderson's *similarity* to the men, his insights are the result of his *difference*. Anderson's revelations emerge precisely at those moments when he realizes that although he shares a racial identity and background with his subjects, he is also quite distinguished from the group. First and foremost, he is the only one in the group who is currently a doctoral student at an elite university. Ultimately, the social status and sense of decency conveyed by Anderson's affiliation with the University of Chicago led the streetcorner men to treat him in ways that illuminated key group processes.

As my students' shoulders relax a bit and the tension in the room begins to fade, I continue with the lesson. Of course, I tell them, we can move into the neighborhood we are researching, like Sally Merry (1981) in *Urban Danger* or Philippe Bourgois (1996) in *In Search of Respect*. We can take a job at the workplace we hope to study, like William Kornblum (1974) in *Blue Collar Society*. We might enroll in the police academy to study cops like Peter Moskos (2008) in *Cop in the Hood*, or even get a job as an exotic dancer, as Katherine Frank (2002) did in *G-Strings and Sympathy*. Even so, we begin and end the day as outsiders. We often differ along racial, class, gender, or religious lines, but even those of us who are not distinguished by these standard demographic characteristics are nevertheless set apart by an even wider gulf: we come into these spaces primarily as researchers. So even if we don the same uniform or pay rent in the same building as our ethnographic subjects, we inevitably experience these contexts differently than they do. And in turn, those who inhabit these contexts as a matter of everyday life will experience *us* differently than they might others. A few students let out a cathartic chuckle as I remind them that this would still be the case even if they were conducting an ethnography of graduate students with their exact same characteristics. The fact that they will likely be the only one who is "on the clock," so to speak, means that there will always be at least *some* characteristic that will make them an outsider to the social world under study.

Once we concede that we are *always* outsiders in at least some fashion, we can begin to alleviate some of the paralyzing thoughts faced by apprentice and veteran ethnographers alike. Most immediately, this recognition works to dispel the myth that some people, due to their constellation of attributes, are somehow able to encounter and record "better" data than someone else. Simply put, this is a myth. A dangerous one, at that. While some attributes certainly yield particular kinds of fieldwork interactions and observations, these are not necessarily of a higher quality. Different? Yes. Better? Not necessarily. In fact, those very moments when researcher difference becomes palpable—when access feels especially frustrating, rapport seems strained, and fieldwork takes unexpected (and perhaps unwanted) turns—often result in the most innovative and fruitful analyses. But this can happen only if we are prepared to capitalize on these moments. One way to do so is by acknowledging that ethnography is an inherently transgressional practice.

Fieldwork as Breaching Experiment

Let us take a step back and think about the underlying objective of ethnographic research. At its core, ethnographic research endeavors to describe and analyze how members of particular social groups or populations define their own identity and culture, as well as the consequences of these actions. Ethnographers strive to reveal the local conditions in which subjects live and operate, how they experience their lives, interpret and define others, and act upon these subjective meanings. Of particular interest is how individuals and collectives meet the exigencies of life, group themselves socially, and arrive at their shared understandings of the rules of everyday life—what Clifford Geertz (1983) famously calls "local knowledge." Many of these issues cannot be fully revealed using surveys or questionnaires. Nor can we discern them very accurately or robustly by asking informants to explain them for us. So how do we lay bare such information? How do we illuminate the common sense that our subjects take for granted and accept unconsciously?

One possible strategy is to become a full-fledged member of whatever group or culture that we hope to study, to smooth over any and all differences. We could, in a word, "go native." But this is impractical for a number of reasons. To start, most academic researchers simply do not have the time or resources to pull it off. We have classes to take, classes to teach, papers to write, and other commitments and relationships that cannot be placed on hold. What is more, even if we could somehow forgo these professional responsibilities and become wholly enmeshed in a local social world, it is unlikely that we, even then, would be able to translate local knowledge for outsiders, such as our colleagues waiting back at the university for our return. Even if we were able to adopt our subjects' common sense as our own, communicating this now-taken-for-granted perspective is often far more difficult than communicating those of others.

A better strategy is for fieldworkers to instead embrace their differences, to embrace the fact that they are engaged in an act of transgression each and every time they set foot in the field. The idea that transgression can provide methodological and analytical advantages is not new. In the mid-twentieth century, ethnomethodologists, most famously UCLA sociologist Harold Garfinkel (see Garfinkel 1967), set out to devise an approach that would allow them to illuminate and thus study common sense. They sought to reveal the rules, norms, and conventions that allowed for the "normal state of things." What allows interactions to proceed normally? How do groups tacitly agree to view certain behaviors and events as normal? Garfinkel and others came to realize that the key to determining what is considered normal is to find an example of something *ab*normal. It turned out that by studying the periphery—things that are impermissible, out of the ordinary, or out of place—ethnomethodologists came to understand a great deal about the center—things that are considered appropriate, right, and proper. By pinpointing the people, behaviors, and events that upset the balance of common sense, they determined, we can shed light on what, precisely, constitutes common sense.

This all sounds helpful in theory. But what exactly does it look like in practice? As graduate students at UCLA, I and several others were treated by a handful of senior professors to some legendary and often-comical stories about Garfinkel and his ethnomethodological high jinks. As part of his effort to pinpoint the social rules and conventions that allow for normal conversation and interaction, Garfinkel deployed his students to engage in breaching experiments throughout the department's hallways and offices. Sometimes referred to as "Garfinkeling," breaching experiments entail a strategic disruption of conventional ways of behaving and interacting. According to local lore, Garfinkel was particularly fond of sending students off to conduct breaching experiments during other professors' office hours. At the onset of the meeting, these students would begin acting oddly, and then escalate unusual behaviors. They might suddenly delve into non sequiturs and unrelated topics of conversation. They might have sudden verbal outbursts. They might remain standing rather than take a seat, or perhaps stand in the corner of the office, facing the wall. In short, they broke the rules taken for granted at professor-student meetings.

Much to the frustration (and occasional panic) of his colleagues, Garfinkel's breaching experiments quickly revealed the glue of social interactions. By violating the norms of office hours, Garfinkel was able to make visible the otherwise invisible social rules and conventions that were most important for holding the situation together. By paying attention to the precise moment that an interaction broke down, Garfinkel knew that he had pinpointed yet another one of the necessary pieces of the normal state of affairs. Through this process, ethnomethodologists came to realize that although the abnormal is logically secondary to the normal, it often comes first in practice and discovery. In other words, we often have to witness some transgression before we even realize that a norm or boundary existed in the first place. Furthermore, in addition to revealing the norms at work, transgression can key us in to the origins, sources, and guardians of these norms. At very least, transgression casts light on the processes, people, and events which ensure that these norms persist. These are the authors and guardians of "the way things ought to be."

Theoretical Sampling and Abductive Logic

After we acknowledge the insights made possible by paying attention to transgression and deviance, we can begin to integrate this sensitivity into the formal research process. One of the most fruitful moments to do so is during early stages of what ethnography textbooks broadly refer to as *theoretical sampling* (Charmaz 2006). Stated simply, theoretical sampling refers to a particular strategy of data collection and analysis. Theoretical sampling entails collecting data, constructing tentative ideas and hypotheses about that data, and then examining (or "testing") these initial theories through further rounds of data collection and theorizing. As the researcher moves back and forth between data collection and data analysis, she constantly tries to predict where and how she might find the data necessary to evaluate emerging hypotheses. She seeks statements, events, or cases that force her to either dismiss or refine the working theory.

A brief, concrete example of theoretical sampling is helpful here. Imagine that you are in the early stages of data collection of an ethnographic study of urban violence. After several weeks of collecting field notes, you review your notes and suddenly realize that some people perpetrate physical assaults upon others in the hours (or even minutes) after they themselves were victims of a physical assault. On the basis of this preliminary data, and after consulting the prevailing theories of urban violence, you develop a tentative hypothesis that individuals engage in violent behavior in order to "take back" the respect, dignity, or reputational standing they lost during their own victimization. As you head back into your field site the next day, you give yourself marching orders to test your new idea. In particular, you stay on the lookout for situations that might *disprove* your hypothesis. You might look for instances where victims did not engage in future assaults. You might also look for assaults that were not preceded by victimization. By discovering these "negative cases"—times when your hypothesis failed to unfold precisely as you expected—you can now add mediating factors, contingencies, and mechanisms that refine and improve your initial theory, which you will test again the next time you head back to your field site. At any given time, researchers carry multiple hypotheses, about multiple phenomena, into the field each day. Over time, researchers typically choose or are steered toward one among these multiple avenues of inquiry.

Given this iterative process, theoretical sampling relies on a model of abductive reasoning, most commonly associated with the work of Charles Peirce and the pragmatist tradition of social science (for a recent formulation, see Tavory and Timmermans 2014). At its core, abductive logic starts with experience, considers all possible explanations to make theoretical conjectures about that experience, and then checks those conjectures through further experience. As a result, this form of reasoning simultaneously employs both inductive and deductive models of inference. In other words, it is both "bottom-up" (data-driven) and "top-down" (theory-driven).

We integrate reflexivity into this process by collecting data and forming hypotheses about how our *own* presence alters or transforms the normal state of things in our field sites. We obviously begin by making a conscious effort to detail our own role in the scenes we document—we actively avoid the temptation to omit ourselves from our field notes; we write as active participants, not flies on the wall. Second, we consult these notes to ask a series of reflexive questions: How has our presence been perceived? Why do some people encourage our presence while others do not? Who is most obstructive to our access? What particular attributes might be deeming us out of place? Who holds the ultimate authority to deem us deviant, and why? How are these norms transmitted and enforced? Third, we make informed conjectures about the answers to these questions. Fourth, we constantly return to the field to test these hypotheses.

In many instances, researchers engaged in this form of abductive reflexivity can exert significant direction and control over hypothesis testing. Because the ethnographer is simultaneously a participant *and* the data collection instrument, we can actively contribute to negative cases ourselves rather than wait for them to occur. This might entail wearing different clothes, engaging in different activities, associating with different individuals, or generally altering our usual orientation to the field site. These questions, conjectures, and moments of theorizing while we are in the field are not just about blending in. Rather, by asking how our presence does or does not upset the routine state of affairs, we inevitably shed light on key, usually invisible dynamics of local cultures, knowledge, and processes that *all* ethnographic analyses seek to illuminate.

Abductive Reflexivity in Action: Uncovering the Social Order of Skid Row

While I have come to view and promote abductive reflexivity as a crucial part of the craft of ethnography, this process occurred to me only after having wrestled with the iterative process in my own work. Almost a decade ago, as a first-year graduate student, I began conducting fieldwork for a project that would eventually become my book, *Down, Out, and Under Arrest* (2016). The book draws on five years of fieldwork on the streets of Los Angeles' Skid Row to provide an in-depth look at the new role that policing and criminalization play in the lives of America's most truly disadvantaged. Although the study eventually came to center on the tenuous relationship between the police and Skid Row residents, it certainly did not begin this way. Rather, taking a cue from classic urban ethnographies I was reading in my courses at the time, I initially set out to understand how those operating in Skid Row's informal (and often illicit) sectors maintain social order. How do Skid Row residents regulate the informal market, deal with competition, negotiate supply and demand, and settle disputes without recourse to conventional laws and formal adjudication?

As one of the most impoverished and distressed neighborhoods in the country, Skid Row is an ideal site for asking such questions. Home to somewhere between twelve thousand and fifteen thousand residents, this fifty-block area is predominantly black (roughly 75 percent), with a per capita income of roughly $4,000 per year (Blasi 2007; Deener et al. 2013). Given these demographics, I originally anticipated that research in the area could shed important light on how those at the bottom of our social hierarchy do or do not pull themselves up by their proverbial bootstraps. While doing background research on neighborhood demographics, I had also become aware that the Los Angeles Police Department (LAPD) had recently launched an aggressive zero-tolerance policing campaign—called the Safer Cities Initiative—that had already resulted in historic numbers of citations and arrests for behaviors as minor as sitting on the sidewalk and jaywalking (Blasi and Stuart 2008; Stuart 2011). Looking back, I realize that I was so fixated on the theme of economic mobility (or lack thereof) that I naively anticipated that I would be able to keep the topic of law enforcement tucked neatly at the margins of what I saw as my real focus of research. The research questions were clear—or so I thought. As I began reckoning with my own transgressive presence in the field, however, I serendipitously unearthed new, unexpected questions (and answers) about Skid Row's social order. I would learn, largely through my own reflexive practice, that it is a social order overwhelmed by residents' fear of police. The project quickly changed directions as I concentrated my focus on the causes, contours, and consequences of policing on the lives of the urban poor. My own winding path, ending in a largely unanticipated study, provides a useful example of abductive reflexivity in action.

The Advantages of Poor Rapport

Following the advice of my professors, I began spending a significant amount of time in Skid Row in order to meet and shadow those working in the underground economy. It was a difficult process, to say the least. To help provide a justification for idly standing around on street corners, I began emulating the business practices of those I hoped to meet: I began selling individual cigarettes ("loosies"). In a couple of months, I had gained access to a group of a dozen or so street vendors who set up small sidewalk shops on one of Skid Row's busiest intersections. In addition to cigarettes, they hawked a host of other items, including canned food, clothing, bootleg DVDs, small electronics, incense, and cosmetics.

Although I had become friendly with a handful of the men rather quickly, several others on the corner seemed annoyed, if not angry, with my sudden arrival and constant lingering. Their looks of scorn were undeniable. I also noticed that at least three of these men always seemed to pack up and abandon the corner within minutes of my arrival. I remember arriving one afternoon to an especially cold reception. One of the noticeably unwelcoming vendors, a middle-aged black man named Troy, shot me angry looks as I set down my backpack and exchanged greetings with the others. As he loaded his wares into his own backpack and began to walk away, he muttered under his breath. From ten yards away I could only make out a few words. He complained that the corner was "too hot." While I was not sure what Troy meant by this, I somehow knew his complaint about "heat" had something to do with me. Although the neighborhood sometimes reached temperatures above 100 degrees during the summer, the day was actually quite mild. As an additional vendor packed and departed in a huff, I began to feel uncomfortable. Doubts about my abilities as a fieldworker crept into my mind. This was not the rapport and ease of access I had been reading about in many of the classic ethnographies I admired and dreamed of emulating. This project was not unfolding like *A Place on the Corner*.

The day's events swirled in my head for the rest of the afternoon and evening as I tried to put my finger on where I was going wrong. It felt personal. Yet my sense of inadequacy fueled one of the first of many abductive analyses I would carry out over the following years. Wanting desperately to develop a relationship with Troy and the other disgruntled vendors, I began asking myself a number of questions. Why were these men so averse to me in particular? What was it about me that had generated this kind of response? Which rules of the space had I potentially violated by showing up and being present?

The list of my potential transgressions seemed endless, and I found myself playing the scene from the corner again and again in my mind. Here I was, a young, clean-cut graduate student selling loose cigarettes alongside a group of weathered, middle-aged men who, from even a casual glance, clearly needed these profits to make ends meet. Holding tight to my initial visions of the project as primarily a study of unconventional markets, I gravitated toward an economic explanation of the men's reactions. I consulted the qualitative literature on arguably the most studied informal economics: drug dealing. Researchers like Bruce Jacobs (1999) and Philippe Bourgois (1996) have shown that competition within a market cascades outward in ways that can create a lack of trust, hostility, and even violence among fellow dealers and their customers. I imagined that street vending worked similarly. From here, I formulated my first working hypothesis. I theorized that the vendors' bitterness was due to the additional market competition that my presence and activity brought to the corner. Indeed, I sold the same brand of cigarettes—Marlboro Reds—as some of the other men. I was potentially flooding the market, increasing the available supply, and driving prices down for everyone. I speculated that, by doing so, I had violated key, unspoken norms of the social order and disrupted the market equilibrium that allowed these men to service a shared consumer base.

As should be clear from the earlier discussion of theoretical sampling, as an ethnographer I recognized that I possessed unique tools to begin testing this early theory. Over the next two weeks, I devoted much of my energy to observing and talking to the vendors about their inventories. I soon realized that my theory was well off the mark. One afternoon, Warren, a charismatic vendor in his mid-thirties, showed up with five cartons of Newport menthol cigarettes, which were by far the most prevalent of all brands sold on the corner. It was rare to see the vendors with more than a few packs, much less a carton, so I closely watched the others' reactions. Much to my confusion, they did not appear to take any issue with Warren's actions. They seemed to pay no mind to the sudden increase in the supply of menthols. Prices stayed the same and conversations between the men unfolded as usual. There seemed to be no repercussions or negative effects on Warren whatsoever. If anything, the vendors seemed to be gravitating *toward* Warren, even putting away their own supply of menthols and providing Warren sole control over sales for the day. I left the corner confused, with more questions than answers.

I quickly struck my early hypothesis from my list and went back to the drawing board. But if it was not increased market competition, what else was driving my cold reception? What else might I be doing that was disrupting the social order and angering (or at least irritating) a portion of the vendors? Holding tight to the hopes of an economic explanation, I speculated that perhaps I was interfering with sales in a different way. I took a hard look at my own actions while on the corner. Perhaps my conspicuous style of participant observation was putting customers, and thus the vendors, on edge. Following the orders of my professors, I had been keeping a meticulous log of observations, which I constantly jotted down in a small spiral-bound notebook. Once I returned home, I would type up these handwritten notes in longer, narrative format. Back on campus, in my ethnographic methods seminar, fellow students and I shared our notes with the class for critique and commentary.

Anticipating these sessions, I had become a bit obsessed with recording the minute details of conversations, behaviors, and interactions in the field. Over time, as my relationship deepened with the vendors, I found myself pulling my notebook out of my backpack ever more frequently. In fact, I sometimes simply kept it in my hand as I sold cigarettes or assisted the friendlier vendors with their customers. After each sale, I liked to take a step back, lean against a nearby fence, and update my log.

Thinking through possible reasons for my lack of rapport, I came to the conclusion that it might be helpful to find a more inconspicuous method for recording my observations. The vendors and their customers were a generally paranoid bunch, and for good reason. Most of the activity on the corner was illegal, or at least operated in the gray area of the law. I imagined how I might appear to unfamiliar customers, taking copious notes on their transactions. I knew from several of my initial interactions with the vendors that some in the area had suspicions that I was an undercover police officer. While I had eventually convinced most of the men of my real identity and intentions, I speculated that perhaps I was still giving off this impression to wary customers and, as a result, interfering with profits.

After some thought, I devised a strategy that would test my newest hypothesis while hopefully putting customers and vendors at ease. I decided to swap my suspicious spiral-bound notebook for a newspaper, folded to the crossword and Sudoku puzzles. This particular page provided ample blank space for me to write notes, which I did at far more infrequent intervals. I used a green pen to help my jottings stand out from the newsprint. Now, I imagined, wary customers would be put at ease. My constant scribbling would appear to be merely my innocent hobby, unconcerned with recording transactions. While I remained upfront and honest about what I was doing on the corner and explained my intentions to anyone who inquired, I wanted to see what would happen once I stopped advertising my research role so blatantly.

Once again, my hopes and hypothesis failed to pan out. While customers clearly viewed my presence and note-taking with less suspicion than they had before, it did not seem to smooth the antagonisms with vendors like Troy. To make matters worse, jotting notes on the crossword section of the newspaper actually seemed to irritate these men further. Feeling increasingly frustrated, I became obsessed with unearthing the exact source of my transgressions. I was hesitant to ask the men outright, mostly out of fear of aggravating them more than I already had. Instead, I took stock of what I had gathered so far. As maddening as the previous few weeks of poor rapport had been, I had actually discovered a good deal about the social order maintained by the vendors. I now had data to suggest that increased supply, market competition, and customer satisfaction were not necessarily strong factors that shaped sociality among this loose-knit group. Although I had entered the field naively expecting to uncover deterministic, market-related explanations of social relations, my own reflexivity forced me to look elsewhere for answers. Luckily, I did not have to look for very long, even if the answers emerged from a source that I had been reluctant to consider.

Transgressing Race, Class, and Police Assumptions

A third, serendipitous round of theorizing was set in motion one late evening. While monumentally helpful to my ensuing analyses, it unfolded entirely out of my control. At the hands of two LAPD officers, I learned that the vendors' cold reception was directly attributable to the fact that my presence was a severe transgression of the prevailing racial order—a transgression that threatened to land vendors like Troy in handcuffs in the back of squad car.

A quick word about my own background is necessary here. Racially, I am mixed. My father is black and my mother is Mexican. Despite my light brown skin tone and the fact that I inherited my mother's thinner lips and nose, I typically self-identify as black or, depending on the situation, as mixed race. It was likely because of this self-identification that I assumed I was something of a racial "insider" in Skid Row. I also felt that I shared a somewhat similar class background. Like at least one vendor, I grew up sixty miles east of Los Angeles in the city of San Bernardino, which consistently ranks as one of the most impoverished cities in the United States. I spent my childhood among urban poverty, gangs, and violence. I consider myself streetwise and felt comfortable navigating Skid Row's streets.

None of this background information mattered much to the vendors, however. To my disappointment, these men read me in a rather straightforward manner—as a white, privileged man. They saw me this way in large measure because this is how Skid Row police officers—the unofficial, yet dominant arbiters of racial classifications in the neighborhood—read my identity.

At about eleven o'clock one weekday evening, I stood chatting with several vendors and their customers on the usual corner. One of the vendors was previewing an episode of *Gangland* on his portable DVD player. A patrol cruiser, yellow auxiliary light flashing, pulled to the curb in front of us. Without warning, two officers abruptly got out of their car and charged me.

They yelled at me as they approached. "Hands on your head! Hands on your head! Up against the fence!"

Before I had time to react, the first officer was on top of me. He spun me around with a shove. Grabbing hold of my backpack, he pushed my face toward the chain-link fence. In the same motion he pulled my backpack off and threw it to the ground. As his partner finished rifling through the contents, they told me the reason for the sudden detainment. Apparently, I "fit the description" of a "white male with a black book bag." They had received a tip from an anonymous caller, they told me. With some of my shock subsiding and my confidence returning, I politely challenged the officers. For me, as I am sure for readers, it seemed like a rather thin, post hoc justification for stopping, frisking, and interrogating me. I doubted that there was ever a call.

"Someone fitting *my* description?" I asked skeptically. "See," I said, holding my hand out, palm down, motioning for them to look at the shade of my skin, "that can't be me." My skin was noticeably darker than that of the two officers. "I'm not *white*," I stated. The first officer did not hesitate. His response was illuminating. "Down *here* you are," he said flatly. He pointed to the vendors, who were watching eagerly. "Look at these guys. Compared to them, trust me, you're white."

I decided not to push the issue. Over the next few minutes, I managed to prove to the officers that I was a graduate student working on a research project on Skid Row. Their demeanor soon changed. Now they insisted that they were merely doing their best to protect me from the dangers of the neighborhood. After another few minutes of paternalistic lecturing about my safety, the officers ordered me to go home. I followed their orders and left the neighborhood without any further protest.

The insights continued when I returned to the corner. I nervously anticipated that the police interaction was going to ruin any chance of continuing my fieldwork alongside the vendors. Surely the late-night police stop, in which the officers had singled me out among everyone on the corner, would lead the men to view me as a serious liability. If I had not been jeopardizing their profits before, the heightened attention I was drawing from the police surely would. I expected those who had been friendly only days earlier to join ranks with Troy in resenting my presence. However, this was not what happened at all. In fact, I arrived to surprising fanfare. Even Troy expressed enthusiasm about my return. Apparently, the story of the late-night detainment had spread through the group, particularly the fact that I had "showed the cops what's up" and walked away without even a citation. Some of the vendors marveled that I had somehow even gotten the officers to apologize for my detainment.

I took this opportunity to talk about the police interaction with the vendors. To a man, they explained that my detainment had been the result of the physical differences between me and the "typical" people who live in Skid Row and hang out on the corner. They insisted that whether I wanted to admit it or not, I looked, walked, talked, and generally carried myself in ways that officers were likely to view as white, or at least whiter than my surrounding company.

Given that whites make up a small minority of the neighborhood (roughly 10 percent), the vendors reasoned that my relatively whiter appearance had piqued officers' suspicions as they drove by, leading them to investigate my presence. In this case, the officers likely thought that I was using the vendors' activity on the corner as a cover to sell narcotics. One vendor explained the events by putting himself in the officers' shoes: "The cops are like, 'Who's this white boy over here with the hustlers?' They see you and they *gotta* come over and get in your pockets. They think you got no good reason for being down here with guys like us." He chuckled and sung a line from a classic *Sesame Street* song: "One of these things is not like the other."

I bit my tongue as the men took liberties joking about the various attributes that had most likely led the officers to see me as white, and thus out of place among the regulars on the corner. On the list: my "butt-hugger jeans," my vintage Nike shoes, and my tight shirt. Given that these items had attracted the attention of the police, the vendors instructed me to change my appearance if I planned to continue spending time with them. Luckily, they offered tips for "blackening me up," as they jokingly referred to it. They ordered me to start wearing basketball shoes, baggy pants, and a backward hat. In addition, one vendor questioned the way I had been logging my notes. To appear "blacker," he insisted, I would need to ditch the crossword. Given my earlier assumptions about the inconspicuous nature of my innovative note-taking strategy, his reasoning took me by surprise.

"Everybody knows that niggas don't do crosswords," he explained with a smile. "Come on! That's a dead-bang giveaway that you ain't really from around here. How many people around here do you see doing crosswords?" His point was clear. For him, working on a crossword puzzle was likely to draw attention from passing officers because it demands a relatively high level of literacy and subject knowledge. It requires a level of education that officers do not expect from someone who rightly "belongs" in Skid Row. In other words, my crosswords had made me appear too educated, whiter, even more out of place, and, as a result, more suspicious in the eyes of officers.

Once I started following the men's suggestions, their antagonism toward me soon faded. In the coming weeks, I even began receiving phone calls from the vendors asking whether I was planning to "be on the block." In fact, Tony and several others even tried to sync their vending hours with my fieldwork schedule. Once I had sufficiently "blackened" myself and moved closer to the men along the racial spectrum, the vendors sought to capitalize on what they saw as my ability to de-escalate police contact, convince officers of the vendors' decency, and ultimately shield the men from the constant threat of citations and arrests. While I was never as successful as the vendors imagined (I was still subject to police detainments, a few of which resulted in citations and even arrests for the vendors), they nonetheless continued to rely on me as a kind of protector for the duration of my fieldwork.

Over the subsequent months, I was overwhelmed with new realizations about the workings of the social order on the corner, as well as the powerful role that the police played in creating and enforcing this order. Marveling at the time and energy that these men devoted to thinking about the appearances and behaviors that brought unwanted police contact, I began reconsidering my earlier, unsatisfactory explanations for my lackluster reception. I found the answers I was searching for once I considered my questions in the light of the men's justifiably paranoiac attempts to avoid police contact. My disruptions of the economic market—whether flooding the market with Marlboro Reds or interfering with customer satisfaction—paled in comparison with the danger my presence posed in terms of attracting police attention.

I reanalyzed my earlier field notes. I began to wonder: what had I missed, misinterpreted, or unknowingly omitted? While I did not recognize it at the time, I had actually witnessed a number of occasions when one's ability to thwart police contact mediated peer relations and market behavior. I later learned that Warren, the vendor who glutted the corner with Newport menthols, was seen by the men as the most successful among them in de-escalating police contact and potential punishments. Apparently Warren had established a friendly, if instrumental, relationship with one of Skid Row's senior patrol officers. On a number of widely talked about occasions, the officer had provided Warren with information about upcoming police sweeps, which led Warren and his closest associates to stay away from the corner and avoid being caught up in the enforcement operation. On another occasion, the senior officer had arrived on the scene just in time to prevent two unseasoned patrol officers from giving Warren and the other vendors a citation. The vendors' odd deference to Warren—allowing him to sell cartons of menthols at their expense—was a direct result of his relationship with the senior officer. The other vendors were willing to give up some of their daily profits in order to gain from Warren's ability to deflect enforcement. At other times, I even observed Warren use the power conveyed by this relationship to coercively restructure the market behaviors of others. On one occasion, he pressured another vendor to constrict his inventory and jeopardize his profits after Warren deemed the vendor's sidewalk shop overly diverse, spread out, and thus likely to attract police attention that would have ramifications for the rest of the men on the corner. Warren sealed the man's compliance with a thinly veiled threat to withhold future information about pending police sweeps.

This is all to say that market dynamics, which had been my original focus, were generally subsumed under policing dynamics. It is significant that, had I not relied on my own reflexivity to first test and disprove narrow economic explanations, and then pursue the alternative explanations forced by my racial and class transgressions, I might not have come to this conclusion. Indeed, my commitment to abductive reflexivity allowed me to discover a surprising and, ultimately, more accurate depiction of the vendors' social world.

Relying on my own transgressive presence as a key analytical strategy, I began seeking out the dynamics and effects of policing among other neighborhood groups. I met other residents who structured their peer relations, daily movements through the neighborhood, and political activities by constantly anticipating likely police responses to these behaviors. This would eventually go on to form one of the central arguments of my book: In heavily policed urban neighborhoods, residents have been forced to cultivate and act upon a sophisticated cognitive framework—what I have come to refer to as "cop wisdom." Using their own and others' interactions with officers as data, "copwise" residents engage in a kind of folk sociological analysis in which they actively reinterpret their world through the eyes of officers. How might a passing officer view their appearances, behavior, peers, and spatial location? The answers to these questions provide residents with a new guide for understanding and interacting with their immediate social and physical environment. Cop wisdom shapes how Skid Row residents read and treat others, including curious fieldworkers hoping to learn about their world.

Conclusion

As ethnographers, our unique position as the primary research instrument yields an important set of responsibilities and advantages as we attempt to analyze the social world. Yet intense debates regarding ethics and dilemmas of representation have stymied consideration of the analytical benefits that can be obtained when researchers transgress the norms of the local social orders they study. This means that the insights generated through this process—even though they weigh on the minds of ethnographers during fieldwork—seldom show up in their finished books and articles. Instead, readers are treated to impressive ideas that are already worked out and supported by the necessary data, as though they had always existed this way. Indeed, if reflexive concerns show up at all, they are often streamlined to satisfy concerns about ethnographic research more generally, relegated to sections meant to appease readers from outside the ethnographic community. It is hardly surprising that many aspiring ethnographers—like my students—are able to walk away from these texts with the erroneous notion that some people, attributes, and traits naturally elicit "better" data and thus "better" analyses.

Just as certain traits and statuses do not necessarily yield better data, we could hypothetically engage in abductive reflexivity based on virtually *any* of the many differences that we bring with us into the field. Of course, precisely which outsider status becomes most salient and illustrative depends on the normal state of things in whichever local culture we are studying. The point, however, is that rather than enter the field with ready-formed assumptions about which of our statuses this will be, or how it will impact our reception, we must continue to allow this to remain a question that demands answering. If we can do that, we will no doubt discover a whole lot—about the local social order, and about ourselves—along the way.

We might also make a more concerted effort to articulate our moments of abductive reflexivity as we write up our findings into finished products. No doubt, this is easier said than done. It can already be a challenge to communicate our findings to wider audiences that hold competing notions of what exactly counts as data and evidence. Ethnographic work is strenuous enough without formally accounting for our lengthy paths of discovery, which are often filled with false starts and dead ends that we might want to keep to ourselves. What is more, simply remaining a keen observer, typing up page after page of field notes, writing continuous rounds of memos, pinpointing complex processes, and supporting arguments with rich but concise data are tiresome tasks to maintain over the length of a project. Yet instead of imagining that accounting for our abductive reflexivity is one more item to add to this daily checklist, we might see it as something that can actually make that lengthy, sometimes mind-numbing list of tasks more fruitful, enlightening, and, dare I say, easier.

References

Anderson, Elijah. 1978. *A Place on the Corner*. Chicago: University of Chicago Press.

Blasi, Gary. 2007. "Policing Our Way out of Homelessness? The First Year of the Safer Cities Initiative on Skid Row." Inter-University Consortium on Homelessness, Los Angeles.

Blasi, Gary and Forrest Stuart. 2008. "Has the Safer Cities Initiative in Skid Row Reduced Serious Crime?" UCLA School of Law, Los Angeles.

Bourgois, Philippe. 1996. *In Search of Respect: Selling Crack in El Barrio*. Cambridge: Cambridge University Press.

Charmaz, Kathy. 2006. *Constructing Grounded Theory*. Los Angeles: Sage.

Deener, Andrew, Steve Erie, Vlad Kogan, and Forrest Stuart. 2013. "Planning LA: The New Politics of Neighborhood Development and Downtown Revitalization." In *New York and Los Angeles: The Uncertain Future*, edited by D. Halle and A. A. Beveridge, 385–412. New York: Oxford University Press.

Frank, Katherine. 2002. *G-Strings and Sympathy: Strip Club Regulars and Male Desire*. Durham, NC: Duke University Press.

Garfinkel, Harold. 1967. *Studies in Ethnomethodology*. New York: Prentice Hall.

Geertz, Clifford. 1983. *Local Knowledge: Further Essays in Interpretive Anthropology*. New York: Basic Books.

Jacobs, Bruce. 1999. *Dealing Crack: The Social World of Streetcorner Selling*. Boston: Northeastern University Press.

Kornlum, William. 1974. *Blue Collar Community*. Chicago: University of Chicago Press.

Merry, Sally Engle. 1981. *Urban Danger: Life in a Neighborhood of Strangers*. Philadelphia: Temple University Press.

Moskos, Peter. 2008. *Cop in the Hood*. Princeton, NJ: Princeton University Press.

Orrico, Laura A. 2015. "'Doing Intimacy' in a Public Market: How the Gendered Experience of Ethnography Reveals Situated Social Dynamics." *Qualitative Research* 15(4): 473–88.

Stuart, Forrest. 2011. "Race, Space, and the Regulation of Surplus Labor: Policing African-Americans in Skid Row." *Souls* 13: 197–212.

Stuart, Forrest. 2016. *Down, Out, and Under Arrest: Policing and Everyday Life in Skid Row*. Chicago: University of Chicago Press.

Tavory, Iddo and Stefan Timmermans. 2014. *Abductive Analysis: Theorizing Qualitative Research*. Chicago: University of Chicago Press.

INDEX

abductive
  analysis, 220, 221, 225
  reflexivity, 211, 213, 221, 222, 223, 234, 235, 236
acculturation, in Burning Man, 42–43
activities
  mechanism-based explanation with, 136–38
  in organizations, 38–39, 46–47
activity frameworks, 9
addiction
  as homelessness cause, 73, 74–75, 81–82
  identity with, 85–86
  mandatory treatment for, 83–88
  poverty as, 88
  rehabilitation, 83–86
African Americans. *See also* racial essentialism; racial imagination; racial prejudice; racism
  assimilation from, 177–78
  crime association with, 197–99
  culture of, 155, 158
  in fiction, 160–61
  identity of, 179
  marginalization of, 155, 158, 160
  oppression of, 160
  stereotypes of, 163–64, 166–68
  violence association with, 197–99
  white engagement with, 158–59, 160–61, 168, 170–71, 178, 179, 180
alignments, in mechanism-based explanation, 134–39
American Allegory: Lindy Hop and the Racial Imagination (Hancock), 155
analysis
  body as unit of, xxv
  clarity in units of, xxviii
  conversation analysis, 5–8, 6n7, 6n8, 6n9
  interactions as unit of, xx, 130, 143, 144, 146, 150–51
  meaning-making as unit of, 133, 144

analysis (*cont.*)
  organizations as unit of, xx–xxi, 17, 20, 33–34, 37–38, 44, 56
  situation as unit of, 202, 203, 204
  unit of, xiii, xv–xvi, xxvi
  unit of, for Burning Man, xx–xxi
  video, 9, 12, 15, 26, 27
analytic lens, xii, xiii, xviii, xxiv, xxvii, 62–63
Anarchomex, 67, 68, 69
Anderson, Elijah, 3n3, 214, 215
Andromex, 67
anthropology
  contrasting approaches to, xii
  Manchester school of, xvi
Arcadia House, 82–83, 85, 87
archaeological digs, 9
Argentina, 80
The Argonauts of the Western Pacific (Malinowski), 96, 111
assimilation, 177–78
Atlanta, Georgia, 195
attention zone, 13–14
attitude, 169
autoethnography, 156

Bali, 98, 131
Bars, 2n2
Bboy (breakdancer), 2, 8n11
behavior, modification of, 136
Big Apple, 175–76, 177
Big City Swing, 174–75
Big Flossy, 11, 22, 23, *23*, 24, 25, 26
Big Time Swing Time, 175–76

blackface, 161, 162
blackness
  as implicit degradation, 161
  interpretation of, 159
  performing, 160, 161, 163
  repression of, 170–71
  richness of, 180
  as sexuality, 178
  symbolism of, 170
  whitewashing and, 171
BLM. *See* Bureau of Land Management
Blowin' Up (Lee), 140–41
Blue Collar Community (Kornblum), 216
blues, 178–79
Blumer, Herbert, xviii
The BMorg, 45
body. *See also* embodiment
  as memory pad, xxiv
  as phenomenological tool, 155
  sensing, 157
  as unit of analysis, xxv
  as unit of observation, xviii, xxiv
Bologna, Italy, xxiii, 96–97, 109
The Borg, 45
Boston Blackie, 115, 116, 117
boundaries
  language as, 190–91
  of organizations, 53–54
  race as, 190, 192–93
  of religion, 145–46
  of situations, 186, 187–93, 204
  spacial, 188
Bourdieu, Pierre, xxiv, 156n1, 157
Bourgois, Philippe, 216, 225
Boyd, Michelle, 179

breaching exercise, 213, 218–19
breakdancer, 2, 8n11
breakups, 139–40
bricoleur, 120, 122
Brooklyn, New York, 136–37
Burawoy, Michael, xvi–xvii, 70, 89
bureaucracies, xvii–xviii
Bureau of Land Management (BLM), 50–51
Burning Man
  acculturation in, 42–43
  Black Rock Rangers, 42
  Department of Public Works, 49, 56
  explicit decision-making in, 40, 46, 47–48
  fees for, 50n4
  Found, 42–43
  framework for, 55
  government and, 50–52
  Greeters, 42, 45
  hierarchy in, 40–41
  law enforcement at, 52–53
  legal partnership for, 32–33, 33n3
  media and, 50–51, 52, 53
  member interests in, 44–46
  Playa Info, 42
  in San Francisco, 31–32
  training for, 41, 42–43
  unit of analysis for, xx–xxi
  values of, 47–48

CA. *See* conversation analysis
Cake Walk, 175
California
  San Bernardino, 229
  San Francisco, 31–32, 70, 71, 73–74

canned resource, 15, 20
Carl, 100–101, 114–19, 116*f*, 118*f*
causality
  conditional, 147–50
  establishing, 131–32n3
  with genetics, 146–50
  for homelessness, 73, 74–75
  in language, 131
  with mechanism-based explanation, 130–32, 152
  thick description and, 130–31, 131n2
centaur, metaphor of, 48
Challenger, xvii–xviii
Charitable Choice, 83
Chicago, Illinois, xxiv
  Dance Chicago, 174
  South Side, 182, 214
  University of Chicago, 95–96, 215
cigarettes, 225, 226, 227
ciphers, 2, 3
  battles, 20–25
  collaboration in, 27–28
  falling off in, 26
  improvisation in, 15–16, 18–19, 20
  jumping in, 26–27
  transitions in, 10–15, 16, 18, 21, 26–27
  turn-taking in, 10–14
  video from, 12, 15, 26, 27
cockfighting, 98, 131
coding-in-motion, 130
  conditional causality through, 149–50
  interactional mechanisms through, 150–51

coding-in-motion (*cont.*)
  mechanism-based explanation, 143–50
  open coding or, 143
collaboration
  bodily, in microsociology, 8–9
  in ciphers, 27–28
  in interactions, 8–10
  in rap battles, 25
Collier, John, 120
Collins, Randall, 22, 24n18, 24n19
common sense, 218
competition, within market, 225
conversation
  context, of situations, 193
  turn-taking in, 6n7, 11n16
conversation analysis (CA), 5–8, 6n7, 6n8, 6n9
conversation-analytic perspective, xv
cop wisdom, 234
counterfactual accounts, 131–32n3
CP, 16–17, 18–19, 21
crime, 197–99. *See also* law enforcement, policies of
criminal justice, 89
crosswords, 227, 228, 231–32
cultural competence
  race and, 180
  for winking, xv
culture
  acculturation, 38, 42–43
  of African Americans, 155, 158
  context of, in microsociology, 25–26
  cross-cultural embodiment, 160, 163
  of farms, 104
  ghetto, 141
  of organizations, 38, 48
  perception of, through race, 180
  poverty, 141

dance, 157. *See also* Lindy Hop
  dueling, 162
  embodiment of, 158, 181
  as embodiment of race, 158, 159–60, 161, 180
  Herräng dance camp, 165–68, 179–80
  as racial embodiment, 161
  sexuality in, 178
  teaching, 163–64
Darwinism, social, 111
decision-making, explicit, 40, 46, 47–48
deduction, xii, xiii, xvii, xviii, xxvii, xxviii
demographics, 201
  as dimension of situations, 195
  skid row, 223
Department of Motor Vehicles (DMV), 189
Department of Public Works, 49, 56
Desmond, Matthew, xvii, xviii, 82, 181
disability, inheritance of, 146–47
dispositional approach. *See* embodiment
dispositions, 181
Dizaster, 16, 17, 18, 19
DMV. *See* Department of Motor Vehicles

documentation, by organizations, 35–36, 41, 43, 44
Down, Out, and Under Arrest (Stuart), 134–35, 222
drug courts, 83
drugs, 52–53, 197–98, 200. *See also* addiction
dualism, 170
Dubois, Harley, 41, 44, 45, 50, 52
dumpster diving, 71
Duneier, Mitchell, 7

E.Crimsin, 22, 23, *23*, 24, 25
Ellison, Ralph, 158
Elster, Jon, 132, 132n4
embarrassment, 195
embodiment, xv, xxiv–xxv
  alternative modes of, 180
  communication cues through, 14–15
  cross-cultural, 160, 163
  of dance, 158, 181
  distortion of, 169–70
  immersion in, 156–57
  of Lindy Hop, 170
  outsider perspective on, 157
  participant observation in, 182
  racial, 159–60, 161
emotions, 8n10, 9
empathy, 90, 112
employment, 37, 88
English, 78–79, 190
Enloe, Cynthia, 70
epistemology, xvi, xxii, 4
ethics, 125–26
ethnography
  access in, 32n2, 54
  autoethnography, 156
  character-driven, xxii–xxiii, 204–5
  claims in, 150–52
  classic, 204
  deductive approach to, xvi–xvii, xviii
  definition of, xi, 95
  differences in, 215, 216–17, 218
  disclaimers on, 212
  embodied, 156–70, 180, 181
  empathy in, 90, 112
  ethnographer in, 211, 214–18, 221–22
  ethnographic methods seminar, 214
  generalization in, 74, 205
  identity in, 64–65
  inductive approach to, xvi, xviii
  justification for, xi
  macro analytic approach to, xxi–xxii, 48, 61–62, 88–90
  of masculinity, xvii, 209
  mechanism-based explanations, 129–30, 143, 151
  mechanism identification in, 143
  multi-sited, xvi
  nationality in, 80–81
  notes, 227, 228, 231
  objective of, 217
  of organizations, xv, xviii, xx–xxi, 33–44, 46–51, 53–56
  origins of, 95–96
  of place, 96–110, 105*f*, 108*f*
  power in, 62–63, 64, 76
  reflexivity in, 111, 112
  researcher-researched connection in, 205

ethnography (*cont.*)
  separation in, 111
  situations, xxv, 185–88, 203–5, 207–9
  studying up, 63, 64, 76, 90, 91
  subjectification in, xxi, 62, 63–66, 70, 81, 82–83, 91–92
  team approach to, 55
  as thick description, xiv–xv
  as transgression, 217, 218, 234–35
  urban, 213, 222
Ethnography through Thick and Thin (Marcus), 97–98
ethnomethodology, 5–6, 218
ethnonarratives, xiv
existential urgency, 141
expression, 179
extended case method, xiv
  analytic choices with, xvii
  as macro analytic approach, xxi–xxii, 89
  starting point for, xvi

falling off, 15, 26
farms
  culture of, 104
  industrialization of, 105*f*, 107, 108*f*, 109
  place on, 104–10, 105*f*, 108*f*
  pre-industrialization, 104, 106–7, 109
fiction, African Americans in, 160–61
field notes, 11, 27, 62, 110, 162, 168–69, 171–72, 174–75, 176, 220, 221
Flawliss, 11, 12, 14, 16, 18, 21
Francois, Ryan, 173, 175, 176

freestyling, 1–2, 15, 20. *See also* ciphers
freight train, 101

Gap, 171–74
Garfinkel, Harold, 5–6, 218, 219
Garfinkeling, 219
Geertz, Clifford, xiv, xv, 98, 101, 131, 217
gender
  in labor, 65–68, 69
  masculinity, xvii, 209
  performance of, 209
  as situation category, 193
  tropes of, 66–67
generalization, xiv, xix, xxviii, 74, 132, 151–55, 205
genetics, causality with, 146–50
genetic testing, xxiv
global elite, 78–79
Globank, 76
  nationality with, 77–79, 80–81
  New York desk, 78
Goffman, Erving, 5, 26, 138
Good Company (Harper), 115
Goodell, Marian, 32, 45, 47, 51, 52
Good Life Café, 1n1
Goodman, Benny, 162
Gowan, Teresa, xxi, 102n1
Greenville, South Carolina, 188–89
Greenwich Village, New York, 7
grounded theory, xiii–xiv, xv
  micro-level approach as, xxi–xxii
  pure, xvi

habilitation, 85–86
habits, 133

habitus, xviii, xxv, 156n1, 182
Hancock, Black Hawk, xxiv, 155
Hank, 196–97, 198–99
Harlem, New York, 155
Harper, Douglas, xxii–xxiii
 Good Company, 115
 Working Knowledge,
  109–10, 121
Harvey, Larry, 45, 47, 49, 50, 52
helper-employee
 relations, 137–38
Heritage, John, 6n8
Herräng dance camp,
 165–68, 179–80
hierarchy
 in Burning Man, 40–41
 in organizations, 36, 70
 of tramps, 101, 119
high school, public, 209
Hip Hop, 1, 2. *See also* ciphers;
 freestyling; Project Blowed;
 rap battles
 aspiring musicians in, 140–42
 interactional mechanism
  in, 142
Hispanics, 102, 188–89
homelessness, 71. *See also* tramps
 addiction as cause of, 73,
  74–75, 81–82
 causality for, 73, 74–75
 defining, 72, 73–74
 institutionalization of,
  72, 74, 75
 medicalization of, 81–82
 place of, 99–100
 research on, 102
 on skid row, xxvi, 97, 100f
housing, transitional, 81
Humphreys, Laud, 8n13

identity
 with addiction, 85–86
 of African Americans, 179
 in ethnography, 64–65
 of privilege, 229
 religious, 144–46
 of tramps, 119
 whitewashing of, 159, 179, 180
immigrants, 102
 to Greenville, South Carolina,
  188, 200–201
 interactions with, 200–201
 language of, 190
induction, xii, xiv, xv, xxi
inductive-deductive typology,
 xxii, xxvii
In Search of Respect
 (Bourgois), 216
interactionism, 133, 134
interactions
 collaboration in, 8–10
 emergence of, 143–44
 with immigrants, 200–201
 interracial, as
  situations, 193–95
 as irreducible, 150–51
 mechanism-based
  explanation, 136–37
 mechanism of, in Hip Hop, 142
 mechanisms of, through
  coding-in-motion, 150–51
 momentous interactions,
  141–42, 143
 observation of, 10, 10n15
 people's accounts of, 10, 10n15
 with police, 229–31
 study methodology for, 5–6
 as unit of analysis, xx, 130,
  143, 144, 146, 150–51

International Visual Sociology
    Association, 123
interpretation, xv, 130, 133
iron, accumulation of, 146,
    147, 149

Jackson-Jacobs, Curtis, 24
jam circle, 162
Jazz Rhythms night, 174
Jerolmack, Colin, xii, 8n12, 10,
    10n15, 136
Jimbo, 87–88
Juárez, Mexico, 66, 67
"Jump Jive and Wail" (Prima),
    171, 173

KAOS Network, 1n1, 2
Katz, Jack, 8n10, 9
Keleher, Barb, 50, 51
Kelley, Robin, 3n3
"Khakis Swing"
    advertisement, 171–74
Khan, Shamus, xv, 10n15, 37
Kunda, Gideon, 38

labor
    gender in, 65–68, 69
    informalization, 73
    Marxist labor theory, xvii
    play labor, 3n3
    subjectification, processes of,
        in, 65–66, 70, 81
language, 79
    causality in, 131
    of immigrants, 190
    as situation boundary, 190–91
    stereotyped, 163
LAPD. See Los Angeles Police
    Department

Latin America, 78, 79–81
law enforcement, policies of.
    See also police; policing
    at Burning Man, 52–53
    prisons, 83, 89
    privilege with, 229
    zero-tolerance, 135, 151,
        151n6, 223
Lee, Jooyoung, xix–xx, 140–42
Leidner, Robin, 38
Lévi-Strauss, Claude, 120
Lindy Hop, xxiv, 155
    artificiality with, 169
    connection in, 178
    dueling, 162
    embodiment of, 170
    learning, 157–58
    as microcosm, 181
    minstrelsy in, 162–68, 169
    race informed through, 180
    self-consciousness with, 179
    tension in, 158
    twist-twist, 165–66, 167
    whitewashing with, 171–80
local knowledge, xv, 78, 217
Lopez-Sanders, Laura, 190–91
Los Angeles
    Jewish Orthodox neighbor-
        hood in, 144
    skid row, xxvi, 135, 222–23
    South Central, 1, 140, 141
Los Angeles Police Department
    (LAPD), 223, 228, 229–31

macro analytic approach, 61–62
    extended case method as,
        xxi–xxii, 89
    meaning-making with, 48
    power in, 88–90

Malinowski, Bronislaw,
    95–96, 110–12
management, participatory, 69
Manchester school, of
    anthropology, xvi
maquila, industry, 65, 66–67, 76
marches, immigrants
    rights, 201–2
Marcus, George, 97–98
marginalization, of African
    Americans, 155, 158, 160
market
    competition within, 225
    disruption of, 232–33
    dynamics, 233
Marxist labor theory, xvii
masculinity, xvii, 209
May, Reuben, 6–7n9
McDermott, Monica, xxv, 193–94
McDonald's, 38
meaning-making
    chains within, 133–34, 146
    interpretation, 133
    with macro analytic
        approach, 48
    with mechanism-based
        explanation, 132–33,
        150–51
    by organizations, 48
    as unit of analysis, 133, 144
Mears, Ashley, 182
mechanism-based explanation
    alignments in, 134–39
    causality with, 130–32, 152
    chains within, 133–34
    co-construction of
        misalignment, 139
    coding-in-motion, 143–50
    collective acts with, 132
    complexity for, 129
    counterfactual accounts and,
        138, 138n5
    identifying mechanisms
        in, 143
    interactional, 136–37
    with leisure activities, 136–38
    meaning-making with,
        132–33, 150–51
    misalignments in, 139–43
    multilevel processes in, 151n6
    theorizing from, 152
    transposable patterns in,
        134, 151–52
media, 50–51, 52, 53, 142–43
micro-level approaches,
    xxi–xxii
microsociology, xix–xx. *See also*
    conversation analysis
    bodily collaboration in, 8–9
    communication cues in, 14–15
    complexity in, 4 4n4, 5, 25
    cultural context in, 25–26
    definition of, 4
    self-representation in, 20
middle class, 141
Mikel, Michael, 45, 47, 49
Miller, Glenn, 177
Mills, C. Wright, xxi
minstrelsy, 155, 160–70
    definition of, 159
    in Lindy Hop, 162–68, 169
    neo-minstrelsy, 161, 162–64
    socialized, 168
    whitewashing as antithesis
        to, 171
Mitchell, Steven, 178–79
modeling, 182
Molière, 151

momentous interactions, 141–42, 143
musicians, aspiring, 140–42

Nader, Laura, 63
narrative, in ethnography, 96, 130–31, 143, 203, 209, 226
  inductive *versus* deductive, xvii
  as thick description, xiv
NASA, xvii–xviii
nationality
  advantage of, 77–79
  in ethnography, 80–81
  with Globank, 77–79, 80–81
  vulnerability of, 80
negative cases, 220–21, 222
neighborhood. *See also* skid row
  in Greenville, South Carolina, 189
  Jewish Orthodox, in Los Angeles, 144
  racial context in, 197–98
  Tenderloin, 73–74
neo-minstrelsy, 161, 162–63, 168–69
Newman, Katherine S., 37
New York
  Brooklyn, 136–37
  Greenwich Village, 7
  Harlem, 155
  St. Lawrence County, 105*f*
New York desk, Globank, 78
NGOs. *See* non-government organizations
Nocando, 11–12, 13, 14, *14*
non-government organizations (NGOs), 143
norms, 7, 218, 219
notes, 227, 228, 231

observation
  of interactions, 10, 10n15
  participant, 156–57, 182, 193–94, 208–9, 226–27
  repeated, 200
observation, units of
  body as, xviii, xxiv
  discursive organizational culture, xviii
  social mannerisms as, xx
Ogasawara, Yuko, 32n2
open coding, 143
oppression, African Americans, 160
organizational approach, xx, 31–59, 56
organizations. *See also* Burning Man
  acculturation in, 38, 42–43
  activities in, 38–39, 46–47
  boundaries of, 53–54
  as contexts, 36–37
  culture of, 38, 48
  definition of, 34
  documentation by, 35–36, 41, 43, 44
  ethnography of, xv, xviii, xx–xxi, 33–44, 46–51, 53–56
  hierarchy in, 36, 70
  meaning-making by, 48
  member interests in, 44, 55
  milieu of, 48–49
  research questions about, 34–35
  temporality of, 54
  types of, 34
  as unit of analysis, xx–xxi, 17, 20, 33–34, 37–38, 44, 56
Orthodox Jews, xxiv, 144–46
outsider, perspective of, 157

Paak (judge), 84–85, 86
Panoptimex, 66
Particimex, 67, 68, 69, 91
participant objectivation, 157
participant observation. *See* observation
Pascoe, C. J., 209
payment, 79–80
PE. *See* photo elicitation
Peirce, Charles S., 132, 221
people and places approach, xxii, 95–127
phenomenology, 4, 155
photo elicitation (PE), 120–21
photographs, 97. *See also* specific photographs
   actuality of, 123–24
   ethics with, 125–26
   photo elicitation, 120–21
   about place, 99, 110
piazzas, 110
pigeon-keeping, xii, 136–38
pimp walk, 163–64
place
   changes in, 97–98
   of failure, 99, 103
   on farms, 104–10, 105f, 108f
   of homelessness, 99–100
   meaning of, 102–3
   photographs about, 99, 110
   of tramps, 99–104
A Place on the Corner (Anderson), 214
play, sociology of, 8n12
play labor, 3n3
police
   cop wisdom with, 234
   de-escalation of, 232, 233
   interactions with, 229–31
   Los Angeles Police Department, 223, 228, 229–31
   racial profiling by, 228–32
   at skid row, 228–32, 234
policing
   dynamics of, 233–34
   third party, 135–36
Pollner, Melvin, 4n4, 4n6
positionality, xxv, xxvi, 211–13
poverty
   as addiction, 88
   culture, 141
power
   in ethnography, 62–63, 64, 76
   instability of, 91
   in macro analytic approach, 88–90
   symbolic, 181
   types of, 92
   worldview through, 139
practical knowledge, xxv, 156–58
pragmatism, 132
prejudice, xxv. *See also* racial prejudice; racism
pre meds, 15
Prima, Louis, 171, 173
prisons
   increase in population of, 83
   for social control, 89
privilege
   asserting, in race, 195
   in elite schools, xv, 37
   identity of, 229
   with law enforcement, policies of, 229
   making, exercising of, 92
   on skid row, 229
   white, 193

professionalism, 77, 81
Project Blowed, 1, 1n1, 2, 2n2, 3, 13. *See also* ciphers; freestyling; rap battles
protective face work, 26
publishing, academic, 213
Puff Daddy, 179–80

race. *See also* African Americans; blackness; racial essentialism; racial prejudice; racism; whiteness
  ambivalence with, 180
  asserting privilege in, 195
  behavior within context of, 195–97
  cultural competence and, 180
  cultural perception through, 180
  dance as embodiment of, 158, 159–60, 161
  dominance, 161
  dualism with, 170
  internalization of, 170
  profiling by, 228–32
  relevance of, xxv
  as situation boundary, 190, 192–93
  on skid row, 229–31
  status anchored in, 193
racial essentialism, 163, 168, 171, 180, 181
racial imagination, 155–59, 167, 169–70, 178
racial prejudice
  comments on, 194–99
  participant observation research on, 193–94, 208–9
  perception of, 206–8

racism
  anticipation of, 196
  friendliness with, 197
  perception of, 206–8
rap battles, xx. *See also* ciphers; freestyling
  collaboration in, 25
  escalation in, 22–25
  respect in, 20–21
rappers. *See* ciphers; freestyling
reflexivity, xxv–xxvi
  abductive, 213, 221–22, 233–34, 235–36
  definition of, 211–12
  in ethnography, 111, 112
  integration of, 221
  value of, 212–13
regression model, 205
rehabilitation, 83–86
relationships, uncoupling of, 139–40
religion
  boundaries of, 145–46
  identity with, 144–46
religious-professional narrative, 145, 146
respect, 20
  cutting off, 21
  humbling, 21
  subliminals, 21
retraction, 146
rhyming, 10
Rose, Crimson, 47, 48
routinization, 37
rudeness, 206

Sacks, Harvey, 6n7, 11n16
Safer Cities Initiative, 223

sampling
  strategies for, xxvii–xxviii
  theoretical, 220
San Bernardino, California, 229
San Francisco, California, 70
  Burning Man in, 31–32
  dumpster diving in, 71
  Tenderloin
    neighborhood, 73–74
Santa María, Mexico, 67, 69
"Saturday Night Fish Fry"
  (Jordan), 175
Savoy Ballroom, 175
Sayer, Andrew, 88
Schegloff, Emanuel, 6n7, 11n16
Schloss, Joseph, 8n11
schools
  elite, privilege in, xv, 37
  public, 209
self-representation, in
  microsociology, 20
sensitizing concepts, xviii
sensuality, 178
sensuous scholarship, 157
separation, 111
sex
  blackness as sexuality, 178
  casual, 8n13
Simmel, Georg, xxiii
"Sing, Sing, Sing"
  (Goodman), 162
situational approach, xxv, xxviii,
  187, 204–5
situational context, 186,
  187, 203–9
situations
  boundaries of, 186,
    187–93, 204
  categories in, 193–203

character-driven method
  with, 204–5
connection attempts
  in, 192–93
conversational context of, 193
demographics as dimension
  in, 195
determinant of, 203–4
ethnography, xxv, 185–88,
  203–5, 207–9
gender as category, 193
interracial interactions
  as, 193–95
language as boundary
  in, 190–91
larger context of, 202–3
patterns of occurrence in, 187
race/ethnicity as boundary in,
  190, 192–93
in regression model, 205
site selection for, 201
spacial boundaries of, 188
tautological issues with, 203–5
teleological issues with, 203–5
as unit of analysis, 202,
  203, 204
skid row, 97, 100f
  de-escalation of police at,
    232, 233
  demographics, 223
  literacy for, 232
  Los Angeles, xxvi, 135, 222–23
  police at, 228–32, 234
  privilege on, 229
  race on, 229–31
  racial profiling by police
    at, 228–32
  social order in, 223,
    224–25, 232

skid row (cont.)
    third party policing on, 135–36
    tramps in, 101
    underground economy in, 224, 225–26
small-group interests, 138–39
Smith, R. Tyson, 8
sober houses, 83
social forms, xxiii–xxiv
social order, xix, 28, 214, 234–35
    of Skid Row, 222–26, 232
social theory, xvi
social world, 4–6, 27–28, 88
    intrusions into, 211
    Jewish Orthodox, 144, 146
    Lee and, 141–42
    of pigeon flyers, 137–38
sociological imagination, xxi
sociological miniaturism, 4n5
sociology
    carnal, 157
    central task of, 182
    contrasting approaches to, xii
    of play, 8n12
South Central LA, 1, 140, 141
South Side, 182, 214
Spanish, 190–91
Spelletich, Kal, 51
spit, 2, 2n2
Spradley, James, 99
status, 3n3
stereotypes, of African Americans, 163–64, 166–68
stigma, 71
stinking thinking, 86
St. Lawrence County, New York, 105*f*
Stoller, Paul, 157

streetcorner men, 214–15, 224–30
street vending, 224–28
structure, xvi, xxv, 5, 35–37, 61–62, 69–70, 74, 76, 88–90, 124 131 182
Stuart, Forrest, xxvi, 133–35, 222
studying up, 63, 64, 76, 90, 91
subjectification
    agency as, 91
    definition of, 91–92
    processes of, xxi, 62, 63–66, 70, 81
    site for, 82–83
subliminals, 21
Summoned (Tavory), 144
Sweden, 165, 168
Swing! The Musical, 176

talk, as object of inquiry, 6
Tavory, Iddo, xiii, xiv, xxiii–xxiv, 132n4, 144, 146
temporal perspective, 133
Tenderloin neighborhood, 73–74
tension, confrontational, 22, 24n19
testing, genetic, 146–47
theoretical sampling, 220
thick description
    causality and, 130–31, 131n2
    ethnography as, xiv–xv
    Geertz and, 131
Thomas, Dorothy, xiv
Thomas, W. I., xiv
thrill-seeking, xvii
Timmermans, Stefan, xiii, xiv, xxiii, xxiv, 132n4, 146
trading, financial, 76–81

training, for Burning Man, 41, 42–43
tramps, 102f, 118f
  alcohol for, 115, 116, 117, 119
  buddying up with, 114–15, 117–18
  hierarchy of, 101, 119
  identity of, 119
  place of, 99–104
  problem solving with, 113
  in skid row, 101
  work for, 102
transgressions, 217, 218, 228, 234–35
transportation, 189
Trobriand Islanders, 95–96, 110
Troy, 224, 225, 228, 230, 232
turn-taking
  in ciphers, 10–14
  in conversation, 6n7, 11n16
twist-twist, 165–66, 167

uncoupling, 139, 142
University of Chicago, 95–96, 215

Vaughan, Diane, xvii–xviii, 139–40
victimization, 220–21
Victory Ministries, 82–83
video analysis, 9
  of ciphers, 12, 15, 26, 27
  limitations of, 27
violence
  African Americans association with, 197–99
  agreement for, 24
  competence at, 24n18
  confrontational tension, 22, 24n19
  racial perspective on, 197–99
  whiteness association with, 198–99

Wacquant, Loïc, 156n1, 181–82
Warren, 226, 233
WDR45 gene, 146, 147–50
welfare system, 196
Whetstone, Sarah, 82
whiteness, 159, 160
  emptiness of, 180
  symbolism of, 170
  violence association with, 198–99
white privilege, 193
whitewashing, 155, 170
  as antithesis to minstrelsy, 171
  blackness and, 171
  definition of, 159
  of identity, 159, 179, 180
  with Lindy Hop, 171–77, 171–80
Whyte, William Foote, 204
Williams, Hank, 121–22
Willie, 97, 119–23, 122f, 124–25
Willis, Paul, 204
winking, xv
work ethic, 196
Working Class White (McDermott), 193–94
Working Knowledge (Harper), 109–10, 121
wrestlers, 8

YouTube, 12

zero-tolerance, policies of, 135, 151, 151n6, 223
zoot suits, 169